Environmental Law and Policy in the Pacific Basin Area

Environmental Law and Policy in the Pacific Basin Area

Edited by Ichirō Katō, Nobuo Kumamoto, and William H. Matthews

UNIVERSITY OF TOKYO PRESS

Publication assisted by a grant from The Toyota Foundation.

UTP Number 3032-37071-5149
ISBN 0-86008-285-7

Printed in Japan

Contents

Preface

For the past two decades, scientists, economists, lawyers, and citizen groups have been deeply involved in the movement for the protection and improvement of our environments, which have been endangered, damaged, or invaded by the rapid, powerful, and expanding development of the present civilization. The invasion has occurred not only in advanced countries but in growing nations or developing countries as well.

In the advanced countries, however, countermeasures against this type of invasion have been gradually adopted step by step. Through laws and orders of governments, decisions by courts, and strong citizen movements in these countries, sufficient time and technical and budgetary latitude have been allowed for countermeasures against fatal damages to our civilization to be taken. On the other hand, in the developing countries no latitude has been provided for steps against environmental pollution as in the advanced countries. Cars and factories have intruded rapidly and increasingly into these nations without any governmental regulations or preventive equipment against pollution. In addition, demand for development in industry in these less-developed countries has given preference to more rapid and wide adoption of technology and manufacturing to produce, rather than to technique and knowledge for pollution prevention. Thus, the richer and better have become better, while the poorer and worse have become worse, similar to the North-South dilemma in economics.

Anyone who is prudent enough, however, to observe the present situation and the character of pollution itself will be easily aware of the close relationship between the advanced and developing countries. In other words, no country can disregard the serious effect of pollution to another country today. We, the people who live around the Pacific Basin, should recognize this fact. Water is one example. Through rivers it carries hazardous discharged chemical materials to neighboring countries. Or it links one nation to another through ocean water.

These facts, needless to say, require us to adopt international cooperation among the nations in this area. From this point of view, members of the Japan Center for Human Environmental Problems started a survey in 1975 on environmental problems in Southeast Asian countries from the aspect of legal controls. Since then several efforts have been made in this area. The International Conference on Environmental Problems in 1975 (Kyoto, Japan), the Japanese-American Seminar on Land Planning and Regulation of Development in 1977 (Honolulu, Hawaii), and the first Japanese-American Conference on Environmental Protection in 1978 (Yokohama, Japan) are examples of efforts in which the members of the Center have been deeply involved.

In addition, more steady and concrete achievements have also been attained in this area. The effort was mainly directed toward a survey on environmental management and laws in the Southeast Asian countries, such as the Philippines, Thailand, Malaysia, Singapore, and Indonesia between 1977 and 1979. Based on the results of this survey, we organized the first Asian-American Conference on Environmental Protection in Sapporo, Japan, in August 1978. It was, we believe, a step toward ensuring a healthy and hazard-free environment for future generations. On the final day of the conference, two resolutions were proposed and unanimously adopted: to publish the papers presented at the conference as a book, and to organize the second Asian-American Conference on Environmental Protection somewhere in Asia. This book is the achievement of the first resolution, and the second conference was held in Jakarta, Indonesia, in September–October 1980.

It was decided at the Jakarta Conference to organize the third Asian-American Conference on Environmental Protection in Kuala Lumpur in 1982 and the fourth conference in Bangkok in 1984. We strongly believe that these conferences will slowly but steadily attract the attention of all those concerned—governments, organizations, and people alike—with the protection and preservation of the world environment for this and future generations.

We are grateful to the following organizations and persons whose support made those efforts possible: The Commemorative Association for the Japan World Exposition; The Toyota Foundation; Hokkaigakuen University; Institute of Environmental Research of Chulalongkorn University, Bangkok; East-West Environment and Policy Institute of the East-West Center, Hawaii; Mr. Kazuhiko Kurata and Ms. Nina

Raj of the University of Tokyo Press; Mrs. Jane Crane of Honolulu; and President Shin'ichirō Takakura and Professor Masao Morimoto of Hokkaigakuen University.

This publication was subsidized by The Toyota Foundation and greatly assisted by the East-West Center and Hokkaigakuen University.

Introduction
Environmental Laws in Southeast Asia and China: An Overview

Ichirō Katō

In terms of industrial and economic development, East Asia can be divided roughly into three regions: one consisting of Japan and the Republic of Korea, which may be called advanced industrial countries, the second occupied by China, an immense country which is currently in the process of development, and the third made up of the developing countries in Southeast Asia.

Over the past few years, the Japan Center for Human Environmental Problems has carried out research on environmental problems in Southeast Asia and China. The Ford Foundation and The Toyota Foundation, although their parent companies are rival automobile manufacturers, have cooperated with each other and provided us with necessary funds for our research on Southeast Asia. We dispatched researchers to the various countries in Southeast Asia for a period of three years to conduct our studies. In regard to China, fifteen members of our group visited the country in September 1979 and made an inspection tour of the cities of Peking, Shanghai, Nanking, and Wuhan.

Our studies in Southeast Asia have been concentrated on the five ASEAN nations, that is, the Philippines, Indonesia, Singapore, Malaysia, and Thailand. Most of these countries were colonies before World War II, and even today the legal systems of their former colonial masters are either still in existence or have exerted great influence on their systems. For example, the legal system in the Philippines is based on American laws, while Indonesia has Dutch laws, and Singapore and Malaysia British laws as the basis of their legal systems. In the case of Thailand, it has its own original legal system because it has long been an independent country. These countries each have their different histories and their own characteristics; but rather than concentrating on these differences, let us look at what these countries have in common with each other, that is, in terms of environmental laws and the problems of environment.

Environmental problems in developing countries are considerably different from those existing in developed countries. The first environmental problem that cropped up in the countries of Southeast Asia was the urban problem. Overpopulation in large cities in these countries has created slums, poverty, unhygienic conditions, and diseases, which are the major issues in the urban problem. It is very important for these countries to solve these problems, and this is why the environmental problem comes into focus. These problems, however, cannot be completely solved by environmental laws, which have their own limitations. Rather, they could be more successfully solved by policies and countermeasures implemented by the respective governments.

Then, what is the situation in mountain and farming villages? Problems exist in these villages which again are different from those in advanced countries. For instance, there is the problem of overcutting forests, although there also exist problems similar to those witnessed in advanced countries, such as pollution of the air, water, and soil. These problems are aggravated during the process of economic development in Southeast Asian countries and also with the advance of foreign enterprises, including Japanese. A representative case is the deforestation of these countries' woodlands by such foreign enterprises.

Let us see what types of environmental laws are in existence in these countries. The environmental laws in the countries of Southeast Asia are much more effective than might be expected. In some countries, propositions concerning the protection of the environment have been incorporated in their constitutions. There are also countries that have comprehensive laws incorporating provisions against pollution and the protection of nature and the environment. Countries that do not have such provisions at present are currently preparing them, and it will not be long before they will be systemized legally. In my opinion, such legal systems will be thorough because the countries are earnestly studying the laws of such countries as the United States and Japan, where environmental protection laws are developed.

The real problem, however, is whether the laws in these countries are being faithfully carried out or not. The number of government officials in charge of the execution of the laws is extremely small. In Malaysia, for example, there are only about ten people in charge of the enforcement of the environmental laws. Furthermore, these officials are working in the central government, and in many cases there is no one in charge of the environmental laws in local regions. In regard to environmental administration, there is an insufficient supply of instruments and devices required for measuring the degree of environmental pollution. Therefore, even if the control standard of the pollution is specified at a certain ppm, supervising officers, due to the lack of measuring instruments, are unable to detect accurately the degree of pollution that is emitted from a factory or plant. Under these circumstances, there is virtually no way of controlling pollution. We may say that, consequently, the environmental laws exist merely on paper, and that the laws are not being effectively implemented. Regarding this problem, in my opinion developed countries, such as the United States and Japan, can and should help by supplying these countries with necessary measuring instruments and devices or by training the sanitation staffs.

The situation in China is somewhat different. When our delegation visited China, we were at first concerned about the existence of environmental problems in such a vast country. We asked a Chinese official where we should go in order to grasp most accurately the environmental problems of the country. He replied that "there is serious environmental pollution everywhere in China, so you may go anywhere you want to see it for yourself." As a matter of fact, wherever we went we saw voluminous amounts of black smoke being emitted from the smokestacks of plants and factories, while untreated industrial wastes from such installations were being dumped into rivers. Our impression, consequently, was that the environmental pollution problem in China is unexpectedly serious.

One reason why the environmental problem is so serious in China is because, while the country has a vast area, it also has a colossal population. Only several years ago, the population of China was said to be about 800 million, but according to an announcement made in 1979, it was about 975 million at the end of 1978. Actually, it is said that China's population is now one billion and that an increase of another 100 million can be expected in several years. Statistics in China regarding the population are not accurate, and the rapid increase of the figure probably includes the populations that had not been hitherto surveyed. At any rate, China's rate of population increase is extremely high, and this is one factor that has made the country's population unexpectedly large.

Furthermore, the large deserts and high mountains in the western part of China are nearly unpopulated. The inhabitable regions, therefore, are in the eastern part of the country in plains near the sea. The population density in these regions is considerably high. The population density of Japan is also high compared with the United

States, but the population density in China, particularly in the areas surrounding Peking and Shanghai, is higher than that of Japan. For example, one is hardly able to walk straight through the main street of Peking because of the crowds of people flooding the thoroughfare. Under these circumstances, it seems quite natural that the environmental problem should be such a serious issue in China.

Another factor that is contributing to environmental pollution in China is the superannuation of the equipment used in plants and factories. For example, there is a gigantic steel mill in the suburbs of Peking where we found that the equipment was of pre-World War II vintage, and no modern facilities had been installed. The sight that greeted our eyes there was a cloud of black smoke billowing out from the smokestacks. In Japan, when we visit a plant on an inspection tour, the plant authorities usually try to hide the defects of the plant and try not to let out smoke, but in China, when we visited the steel mill, it was almost as though the authorities were trying to welcome us by spewing out a blast of billowing black smoke. In Japan, the people are very sensitive to environmental pollution, and consequently factory authorities also are concerned about controlling pollution, but in China it seemed that the people and the plant authorities do not pay much attention to this problem. This may have been one of the reasons why so much smoke was being spewed out from the steel mill we inspected in the outskirts of Peking. This smoke and the so-called yellow dust transported by the wind from the Gobi Desert in the northwest combine to envelop the city of Peking in a black and yellow haze, particularly on winter days.

In Nanking, there is a huge chemical plant located along the Yangtze River, which we also visited. Industrial wastes from the plant were being poured into the Yangtze too, and the river in Shanghai was also considerably polluted. Since the Yangtze is a large river, it would seem that it could swallow large amounts of industrial waste without being seriously polluted. However, from what we saw, it seemed that solutions to the environmental pollution problem have only recently begun to be found in China. The Chinese government, however, is tackling the problem seriously. Even as far back as more than ten years ago, the then Prime Minister Chou En-lai had stressed the importance of the problem and urged measures for its solution. Chou En-lai, who seems to be the most respected man in China today, had already been aware of the importance of the problem ten years ago.

In September 1979 when we visited China, a new Environmental Protection Law was legislated and promulgated. Why was it that this environmental law was promulgated despite the fact that other laws were still incomplete? I believe that it is because of the government's policy to control environmental pollution first of all before launching its four modernizations program. What then are the contents of the new Environmental Protection Law? The law involves an extremely wide scope of prevention and elimination of environmental pollution and the conservation of nature. It also includes provisions for punishing violators of the law as well as compensation for victims of pollution. This, however, is a basic law, and in the future more detailed laws and regulations concerning the pollution of the air, water, etc., must be enacted under this comprehensive basic law.

Following is a summary of our impressions when we read the law and what we felt when we talked to the Chinese authorities. The authorities are rather optimistic about environmental protection. For example, they believe that prevention of pollution can be realized in parallel with the development of the economy—in other words, that the prevention of pollution itself will favorably affect the expansion of the nation's economy. Generally speaking, environmental pollution goes hand in hand with industrial and economic development, but according to the Chinese authorities, such development can be carried out by preventing pollution. The Chinese authorities say that by preventing pollution from the start, they will not have to spend colossal amounts of money later after the pollution has intensified during the process of industrial and economic development. They add that by preventing pollution in parallel with the development of their economy, it will be more effective from a long-range point of view and also abet the development of the economy. This may be an ideal way of thinking and an excellent one, but since China is still a developing nation, if it starts out rapidly to modernize its industries, a contradiction may ultimately be created between the two.

The second factor that has led the Chinese to take an optimistic view of the environmental problem is that a provision in the new Environmental Protection Law has been incorporated by which waste material could be recycled and turned into usable commodities. For example, after processing, the industrial wastes from factories and plants could be used as fertilizer. It is a constructive idea to utilize wastes, but on the other hand, how much will it cost? For example, in the case of Japan, the only profitable recycling business today is limited to that of used newspapers and magazines. It seems that China, which is a socialist country, is not making realistic calculations regarding the cost of recycling. We witnessed numerous ineffective phases in the production sectors of the Chinese economy. It goes without saying that reprocessing various kinds of wastes into usable products is indeed a good idea, but the fact still remains that the recycling costs would be tremendous.

Another thing that we found characteristic of China is the people's way of thinking concerning laws, which is considerably different from that of the Japanese. Take, for instance, the new Environmental Protection Law. The provisions in the law are not written in strict legal terms but are rather descriptive terms in declaration of the government's policy. Therefore, this law, or, rather, the government's policy, is said to have penetrated deeply into local provinces, and the people of the provinces are said to be respecting the law faithfully. Unlike in the United States or Japan, lawsuits rarely occur in China because the enterprises that are subjected to legal restrictions are all government-operated and the restrictions themselves have been enforced by the government. In Japan, however, the common practice is to solve a problem through negotiations rather than lawsuits, and in this regard the Japanese approach is similar to that in China.

The Chinese bureaucracy is very effective in seeing to the implementation of government policies. For example, when a law is legislated by the central government, the local governments are informed of it very quickly. Unlike the countries of Southeast Asia, there are numerous officials in the local governments of China who are in charge of environmental problems. When we visited the cities of Wuhan, Nanking, and Shanghai, we found that the municipal government officials were studying the new Environmental Protection Law very earnestly. In our discussions with them, we found that they knew precisely how to implement the law. They told us that before a law is legislated, the central government calls in people from the local provinces and hears their experience and opinions. After the law is legislated, the government quickly informs the people in the provinces of the new law. What can be perhaps said is that although the articles and paragraphs of a law may not be precise and complete, the policies of the government are being endorsed by the people. On this point, China is more advanced than the countries of Southeast Asia.

Now to turn to the Republic of Korea, or South Korea. South Korea witnessed tremendous economic expansion during the 1970s, similar to the expansion of the Japanese economy in the 1960s, which also created a serious problem of environmental pollution. It was during the 1970s that the same problem occurred in South Korea, and laws to control pollution were legislated. These laws are generally patterned after those of Japan and are very precise and complete. However, it must be admitted that economic growth in South Korea has stagnated in recent years and the environmental problems have subsided.

In conclusion, by comparing these three regions, we can contribute to the enactment of environmental laws in the developing countries of these areas. Our research has forced us to engage in some self-reflection regarding pollution and pollution prevention laws.

Southeast Asia

The Environmental Law in Malaysia
A Survey

Nik Abdul Rashid

"Why must there be law to regulate and control our environment?" asked a naive first-year law student. "It reflects man's dissatisfaction with what he is doing to exploit the natural resources to such an extent that it endangers his own environment," came a prompt reply. "It reflects an increasing awareness that the quality of life is deteriorating as a result of lack of planning in regulating our day-to-day affairs and in the exploitation of our natural resources," came another reply. The answers to this simple question are endless. Hundreds of books have been written on the topic. Conferences, seminars, workshops, and symposia have been organized on the topic from time to time, yet there is no simple answer to the simple question.

The next question to be asked is, "Is the law adequate to protect ourselves and to ensure that our children will have a place under the sun?" Again, there is no simple answer to this simple question.

Robert Arvill, in *Man and Environment,* summarizes the reasons for our inquiry in the following terms:

> From primitive times man has been making an assault on his environment with fire, water and tools. Until a century or so ago, this attack took place over limited areas and in most cases at a relatively slow pace. Today there is a danger that man may use up the habitable and cultivable land. His activities increasingly outstrip the capacity of natural processes to restore the fertility of the land and water which has taken thousands of years to create. And through errors and misuse of his powers he is ruining or degrading vast areas of the globe.
>
> The great driving force behind this new fierce assault is the population explosion.[1]

This paper does not seek to discuss environmental issues *in toto*, for environmental problems know no frontiers. It will, however, attempt to focus on the legal aspect of environmental protection in Malaysia and to assess whether adequate measures are being taken by the government in overcoming environmental problems.

I. The Law

Law must be viewed as an instrument in preserving society, in resolving acute social conflict, in promoting social order, in promoting nation building and preserving our national heritage, and in regulating and controlling our destiny. Viewed as such, the law on environmental protection must provide some form of guarantee to ensure that we have the right to live and the future of our generation will be safeguarded.

At present there are various sets of laws governing environmental quality in Malaysia, some dating back to colonial days. For purposes of this paper, we may divide them into two categories: (1) laws directly controlling the exploitation of natural resources, thereby indirectly controlling environmental quality, and (2) laws directly and specifically controlling environmental quality.

It is to be noted that most of the pre-*merdeka* ("independence") legislation concerning the exploitation and utilization of natural resources has been production- and revenue-oriented. It is to be understood that the British colonial government was not interested in the development of natural resources in the colonies, but in getting all the natural resources out of the colony as quickly as possible and at minimum cost.

1. Legislation Governing the Exploitation of Natural Resources

a. Mining Enactment

The Mining Enactment provides for licensing requirements, control over use of land and machinery, payment of royalties, fees, premiums and rents, and other administrative provisions. There is no provision concerning wastage, depletion, or resource conservation, although there are some provisions on environmental quality.

The law deals specifically with mining operations, and since mining operations inevitably affect the environment, particularly rivers, streams, and adjoining lands, provisions are made to safeguard the environment against mismanagement and uses detrimental to the economy of the nation. In relation to mining operations, it deals specifically with the use of waters. It prohibits the unauthorized use of river waters for mining purposes, the alteration of river banks, and the use and employment of certain water-based mining techniques. The most important provision relating to environment is the obligation on the part of mining operators to keep the water pure.

b. Waters Enactment

This enactment deals exclusively with matters relating to rivers and streams. It regulates and controls the use of rivers and streams and imposes rigid prohibitions against the unauthorized use of rivers and streams and the alteration and diversion of river banks and river courses. Felling of trees into rivers is prohibited. This is done with the objective of preventing the blockage of river waters and possible pollution of these waters.

c. Forests Enactment

At present each state pursues its own policy in forestry. There are nine different sets of forest laws in Malaysia which have undergone a combined total of forty amendments since their introduction. This confusion is largely a historical legacy. The British were interested in mining products but not in timber products; presumably logs from African colonies were of better quality, cheaper, and easier to transport to Great Britain. Therefore, there was no attempt to rationalize forestry laws.

Environment-wise, the Forests Enactment deals in matters relating to the preservation of forests, logging, and licensing of operations connected with the forest industry. The enactment contains several provisions relating to environment and pollution, which prohibit the use of poison or dynamite for purposes of hunting and fishing in forest reserves.

d. Land Conservation Act, 1960

This act attempts to conserve lands on the hills and to protect them from soil erosion and inroads of silt. It prohibits the earth, mud, silt, or stone from a piece of land from causing damage to other land. It also prohibits interference with any watercourse, whether natural or artificial through cultivation. For purposes of preventing silting and erosion, the owner is required to build dams, retaining walls, drains, and watercourses.

e. Street, Drainage and Building Act, 1974

The main object of this act is to empower local authorities to regulate and control the development, construction, and proper maintenance of streets, drainage systems, and buildings. There are specific provisions on environmental and pollution control; some of the provisions are incidental to that objective, through rigid control and proper maintenance, while others are specific. For example, it imposes an obligation on the owner or occupier of houses abutting private streets to clear away rubbish, dust, ash, and filth of any sort. No industrial effluents should be discharged or allowed to communicate with any river, canal, stream, lake, or sea.

f. Town and Country Planning Act, 1976

The act imposes a statutory obligation on the local planning authority to ensure that the physical and environmental characteristics of that area are complied with. The act also requires the local authority to adhere to the "current policies in respect of the social and economic planning and development and the environmental protection of the state and the nation." (Sec. 8 (4)).

2. The Environmental Quality Act, 1974

The most recent piece of legislation concerning the environment which attempts to regulate resource conversion so as to minimize damage to the environment is the Environmental Quality Act, 1974.

Recognition for environmental preservation and the need to maintain an acceptable quality of life has been given official status in the Third Malaysian Plan. The plan envisages and recommends, "Environmental improvements and protection will receive the full attention of the government in planning and implementation of programmes in the Third Malaysian Plan. It is vital that the objectives of development and environmental conservation be kept in balance, so that the benefits of development are not negated by the costs of environmental damage."[2]

The plan therefore envisages a national environmental policy which will take into account the following factors:

(1) the impact of population growth, man's activities in resource development, industrialization, and urbanization on the environment;

(2) the critical importance of maintaining the quality of the environment relative to the needs of the population, particularly in regard to the productive capacity of the country's land resources in agriculture, forestry, fishing, and water;

(3) the need to maintain a healthy environment for human habitation;

(4) the need to preserve the country's unique and diverse natural heritage, all of which contributes to the quality of life; and
(5) the interdependence of social, cultural, economic, biological, and physical factors in determining the ecology of man.

The Environmental Quality Act, 1974, will therefore be instrumental in bringing about a concerted and gradual progression toward achieving this objective. This act contains six parts:

Part I deals with definitions, followed by Part II which deals with administrative provisions. Parts III and IV provide for licensing and general prohibitory clauses. Part V deals with provisions for appeal against the decision of the authority set up under Part II, and Part VI deals with penalties and prosecution.

a. Part I: Definitions and Interpretations

The most important terms that must be understood are the following:

1. "Beneficial use" means a use of the environment or any element or segment of the environment that is conducive to public health, welfare, or safety, which requires protection from the effects of wastes, discharges, emissions, and deposits.

2. "Environment" means the physical factor of the surroundings of the human beings, including land, water, atmosphere, climate, sound, odor, taste, and the biological factor of aesthetics.

3. "Pollutant" means any substance, whether liquid, solid, or gas which directly or indirectly

(a) alters the quality of any segment or element of the receiving environment so as to affect any beneficial use adversely, or
(b) is hazardous or potentially hazardous to health.

4. "Pollution" means any direct or indirect alterations of the physical, thermal, chemical, biological, or radioactive properties of any part of the environment by discharging, emitting, or depositing wastes so as to adversely affect any beneficial use; to cause a condition which is hazardous to public health, safety, or welfare, or to animals, birds, wildlife, fish, aquatic life, or plants; or to cause a contravention of any condition, limitation, or restriction to which a license under this act is subject.

5. "Wastes" include any matter prescribed to be waste and any matter, whether liquid, solid, gaseous, or radioactive, which is discharged, emitted, or deposited in the environment in such volume, composition, or in such manner as to alter the environment.

b. Part II: Administration

Section 3 provides for the appointment of a director-general of environmental quality. The duties of the director-general are exhaustively enumerated in this section. These duties cover a wide range of activities.

The director-general is responsible for the administration of the act and regulations; he is to coordinate all efforts to prevent pollution; he is to recommend to the minister the environmental protection policy and other measures, and to be responsible for the control of issuing licenses. He must also coordinate research works and surveys, collect and disseminate information to the public in order to educate them, and recommend to the minister amendments to the law. The minister may also appoint deputy directors-general in such number as necessary to implement the act.

Section 4 provides for the establishment of the Environmental Quality Council whose duties are advisory only. The composition of the council is quite representative of all relevant bodies concerned with environmental protection. Several ministers are represented. Other representatives include one each from the manufacturing industry, the petroleum industry and the academic circle. The director-general of environmental quality is not represented.

It would be more desirable to achieve uniformity and coordination that the director-general be given an ex-officio status or made a permanent member of the council.

c. Part III: Licensing

The licensing procedure has been and still is the most popular device for controlling and regulating industrial and economic activities. The various enactments have placed great reliance on this device.

The act provides that the director-general will be the licensing authority and that the license will generally last for one calendar year, after which it is renewable. The issuing of licenses will be subject to the director-general's discretion as to conditions to be attached to the license.

The director-general has also the power to vary conditions in a license. Before doing so he must have regard to the practicability of the existing equipment being adapted to conform to the new varied conditions; the life expectancy of the existing equipment; the quality or degree of cutback of emission, waste, or desposit to be achieved by the varied conditions; the cost of meeting this varied condition; and the size of the trade or industry concerned.

Section 17 (2) provides that fees may be prescribed, according to any one or more of the following factors:

(1) the class of premises

(2) the location of such premises,
(3) the quality of wastes discharged,
(4) the pollutants or class of pollutants discharged,
(5) the existing level of pollution.

This provides for discriminatory fees to be charged with due consideration of the relevant factors. For instance, an industrial activity which is known to pose an environmental threat and which is located in the vicinity of an agricultural area would be charged a high fee, taking into consideration the regularity of emissions of effluents into the rivers and streams, thus rendering them less valuable for agricultural purposes. The fees will be made high enough, and the level of permissible pollution would be very low indeed. These two factors will encourage the operators of such an activity to install waste-treatment equipment.

d. Part IV: Prohibitions Against Pollution

This point seems to introduce the concept of permissible level of pollution.

Section 21 of the act provides that the minister may, after consultation with the council, specify the acceptable conditions for the emission of noise into any area, segment, or element of the environment within which the emission, discharge, or deposit is prohibited or restricted.

This section actually contains two points. The first point deals with the prescription of minimum ecostandards—the level of permissible pollution, beyond which pollution becomes an offense.

The second point deals with absolute and conditional restrictions in relation to certain areas. One such example would be the rise of industries (particularly, palm oil mills) in the vicinity of catchment areas.[3] These areas will be described as absolutely free from any activities that may pollute, or the industries in these areas will be subject to stringent conditions and very high fees.

Where industries do not have the capability or the technology to meet the standards prescribed by the minister under Section 21, then they will have to be licensed to emit or discharge a greater volume of wastes or noise (Sections 23, 24, and 25). This method adopted by the act to bring all economic activities that affect the environment within its orbit is by the device of "prescribed premises."

Section 18 provides that the minister, after consultation with the council, may by order prescribe the premises, the occupation or use of which by any person shall, unless he is the holder of a license issued in respect to the premises, be an offense under this act.

The object of this section is to encompass each industry stage by stage. For instance, if it is established by facts and evidence that most of them damage riverine resources, then the minister may prescribe that all premises carrying out palm oil milling will be considered prescribed premises. This automatically brings the licensing requirement into play. Through the license, relevant controls are exercised. The only defect in this section, it would appear, is in the drafting. The section envisaged the licensing of prescribed premises, non-compliance of which would be an offense, but the clause "unless he is a holder of a license issued in respect of those premises," appears to give the impression that it could be a license under any other law, probably a license by other authority pertaining to the occupation, use, or control of these premises, whereas what is contemplated and intended is a license under the provisions of the Environmental Quality Act.

Sections 26, 27, and 28 deal with the discharge and spillage of oil into Malaysian waters, or into areas outside the Malaysian territorial waters if such discharge results in the oil being washed into Malaysian waters. Section 28 provides for several defenses to a charge of an offense under Sections 26 and 27.

Finally, Section 33 provides for the prohibition of mass pollution, where several persons are licensed to emit or discharge wastes into the same segment of environment, each complying with the condition, but nevertheless the collective effect of the aggregate of such waste is likely to cause pollution. In such a case, the director-general may require each licensee to abate such emission or discharge. This section envisages collective responsibility on the part of licensees. It is innovative and farsighted, for each industry should be blamed for contributing in a small way to the pollution.

II. A Commentary on the Present Legislation

1. Constitutional Problem

Being a federal state, Malaysia is faced with a constitutional problem: Is environmental control a federal or a state matter? The United Nations Task Force on Human Environment recognized three distinct views on the problem.

1. The vesting in the state governments of substantial authority over land, water, forests, and mines presented an insuperable obstacle to making real progress on the environmental front. Thus the federal government has no real power to control the enforcement of soil

conservation measures, water quality restrictions in respect of mining operators, and other activities significant to environment.

2. Since cooperation between the federal government and state government has been extremely good, the legal distinction between federal and state powers does not accurately reflect political reality. This is more so because both federal and state governments are controlled by the same political party.

3. A middle path between these two views seems to provide the answer to the problem. Although cooperation exists between the federal and state governments, and the states often follow the lead of the federal government in enacting new legislation, on the record the state government has not been effective in the control of environment, in that effluent standards have been generally too lenient and often ignored. Therefore, the federal government must take the lead in enacting state legislation if necessary under Article 76 (4) of the federal constitution, which empowers the federal Parliament to enact laws for the state "to ensure uniformity of laws and policy."

2. Enforcement Problems

Legislation is one thing, enforcement of that legislation is another. We may have flawless laws, beautifully worded, with an excellent organizational setup, yet at the same time have pollution in every nook and corner of our homes and cities. If such excellent legislation is not backed up by effective enforcement, it is better not to have any legislation at all.

Being new in the field of environmental quality, Malaysia is seriously handicapped by the lack of officers. As of 31 January 1977, there were only nine officers in the Environmental Division of the Ministry of Science, Technology and Environment. These were:

Director-General of Environment	1
Director of Environment	2
Assistant Directors	3
Enforcement Officers	3
Total	9

How do we expect nine officers to combat pollution created by 12 million people, 2,500 industries, and 35,000 corporations? It is a mission impossible. It is submitted that more officers should be added to the establishment, so that at least one officer is located in each state to head the state Department of Environment, to be assisted by one officer per every 100 industries. In addition, there should be adequate staffing at the headquarters. If this proposal is accepted, then the Department of Environment will have a complement of fifty-eight officers, made up from the following:

Headquarters	(Let us say)	20
States		13
Enforcement Officers		25
Total		58

Let it not be taken for granted that there will be no pollution once we have a full complement of 58 officers. What is needed is enforcement, adequate enforcement of the law.

3. Attitudes of the Government

The attitude of the Malaysian government, or any government at all, is such that it never likes pressure. To put it another way, it is not responsive to public opinion. It was only after the July 1978 general election that the Prime Minister came up with a new form of government—"A responsive responsible government of the people." It is too early to predict how responsive and effective is the government of the people. In the past, the cries of the Malaysian people in the following circumstances have fallen on deaf ears. The following are but four examples of inadequate enforcement or non-enforcement.

(1) The Kuala Juru's Battle for Survival (Consumers Association of Penang, 1976 Publication).
(2) Endau-Rompin tragedy, wherein 30,000 acres of virgin forest designated as a wildlife park have been destroyed by indiscriminate logging.
(3) The Sultan of Selangor's anger on the dirty Klang Royal Town.
(4) The Malaysian Environmental Protection Society's battle for clean air in the cities and on the roads.

However, the Malaysian government must be congratulated on the Concorde supersonic ban. Otherwise, we would not only have pollution on the land, roads, rivers, and streams, but also up above in the sky.

4. The So-Called Dilemma

Some greedy industrialists and "get-rich-quick" millionaires have often argued that strict implementation and enforcement of our legislation on environmental quality will conflict with our goal of industrialization and development. Moreover, it will discourage potential investors because rigid enforcement will cause great hardship to the industries concerned. Furthermore, the high cost of rigid control will be passed back to the consumers in the form of additional costs of the goods purchased. The argument seems to be fallacious, for development and pollution control are complementary to each other. We must recognize the fact that limitations have been imposed on our natural resources, and that the vulnerable nature of our tropical ecosystem, together with increasing industrial development, have made conservation of our environment a vital necessity. We must also recognize the fact that clean and litter-free Malaysian towns would attract both investors and tourists, and would raise the national morale and civic pride.

Like the Singapore government, the Malaysian government must have a conviction that "industry has a role to play in safeguarding the environment since they, as a group, formed one of the worst culprits responsible for pollution. Profit could not be seen as the end-all and be-all of their activities. Rather, they owed a social responsibility to channel part of their technological and financial resources towards the control of pollution and protection of the environment."[4]

Physical development with per capita income running to thousands of dollars would be meaningless if half of our population were sick due to inhalation of black smoke in the road, drinking polluted water, and so forth, and the other half were not healthy. Physical development would be more meaningless if we were to cut our trees now and sell them at a "cheap sale" price only to import them back in ten years' time at a very exorbitant rate. It would be more meaningless if we were to destroy our jungles now only to send our children to the forests of Africa to see for themselves what a tiger or an elephant is.

Life would be more meaningful if we could have a balanced diet, live in moderate buildings, travel in comfort, and enjoy Mother Nature's gift of rivers and mountains full of "beautiful people," rather than live in noisy cities with fumes, smoke, and gases, looking at a barren field prostituted by the so-called development.

Notes

1. Robert Arvill, *Man and Environment* (Suffolk: Penguin, 1976), p. 13.
2. *Third Malaysian Plan* (Kuala Lumpur: Government Printers), Chap. XI, par. 661.
3. Information gathered from an interview with a senior officer of the Department of Environment, Mr. Godwin Singam.
4. Lee Tien Tien, "Law and the Protection of the Environment," Faculty of Law, University of Malaya Project Paper, 1976, p. 95.

Development and Environmental Planning in Singapore

Peter S.J. Chen

I. Development and the Environment

Singapore is the smallest and yet the most developed nation in Southeast Asia. It attained internal self-governing status in 1959 and became an independent republic in 1965. Since its independence, the republic has constantly maintained high economic growth rates and implemented a series of innovative development projects that have resulted in rapid urbanization and industrialization.

Development projects may, on the one hand, contribute to rapid economic growth, but on the other hand, produce an unfavorable impact, ecologically and economically, on the environment. For example, technological advances and industrial activity have resulted in the deterioration of the environment due to pollution and depletion of natural resources. Therefore, environmental issues and considerations must be integrated with development planning as part of the overall framework of economic and social planning.

Environmental problems in Singapore have increased in the past two decades as a result of rapid industrial development, urbanization, population increase, and increased need for transport services. The government has been concerned with the possible adverse environmental effects and has sought measures to maintain a balance between rapid industrialization and the enhancement of the quality of the environment. However, anti-pollution measures mean additional costs and less profit for the industries, who are often reluctant to adopt them unless they are forced to. In the early years of industrialization during the 1960s, the government could only concentrate its efforts on achieving high economic growth rates. It was not until 1970 that the government could make a serious attempt to integrate environmental considerations with the overall national development.

In 1970, the Anti-Pollution Unit was set up under the Prime Minister's Office. Two years later, the Ministry of the Environment was created. As stated in its 1973 *Annual Report*, "the accelerated industrial expansion, urban redevelopment, development of private and HDB [Housing and Development Board] estates further away from the city centre, shortage of manpower and small physical area have made it imperative that efforts must be intensified for the provision of better environmental health services and control of pollution. The need for forward planning sound policies, innovative and effective methods of implementing these policies have led to the establishment of a new Ministry in the Republic."[1] Since then, the Anti-Pollution Unit of the Prime Minister's Office and the Ministry of the Environment have maintained a close dialogue and worked closely with the Economic Development Board (EDB) and the Planning Department of the Ministry of National Development, so that both economic and environmental considerations as well as social implications of development projects are taken into account.

II. Industrialization and Environmental Planning

Planned industrialization as a conscious strategy of economic development in Singapore started in 1961, with the establishment of the Economic Development Board, to embark on an intensive campaign to industrialize the country's economy. The initial tasks were to create employment opportunities, to attract foreign investments, and to diversify the traditional economic base centered on entrepôt activities.

The initial phase of Singapore's industrialization program was directed at the necessary infrastructures—communications and transport facilities, public utilities, and industrial estates. From 1961 up to about 1965, when the initial major efforts were exerted, few economic returns were produced. However, in 1965, the manufacturing industry, in terms of number of people employed and in its share of gross domestic product (GDP), began to grow at a fast rate and grew very rapidly after 1968.

In 1965, a massive program was launched to attract export-oriented industries and foreign investments. To further encourage industries in Singapore, the Economic Incentives Act was passed in 1967. Among other measures, it offered a five-year tax holiday for factories manufacturing approved products, and tax concessions for approved export-oriented companies. In 1968, the Jurong Town Corporation (JTC) was established to take over some of the EDB's functions. Its main function is to provide facilities for the management of industrial estates and sites and the provision of amenities for the well-being of the people working and living in such industrial estates.

Industrialization policies and other measures implemented by the government have resulted in a rapid economic growth for Singapore. During the period 1960–77, Singapore achieved an annual growth rate of 12.6 percent at current prices or 9.1 percent at constant prices.[2] The annual growth rate for the period 1968–74 was 20 percent at current prices or 11.7 percent at constant prices. Industrialization has also brought about a rapid change of the economic structure and a rise in the share of the secondary sector in Singapore's GDP from 18 percent in 1960 to 35 percent in 1977. The most important contribution is from the manufacturing industries, whose share rose from 11.9 percent to 24.6 percent during the same period; this was accompanied by a rise in construction from 3.6 percent to 8.0 percent. The share of utilities, however, remained almost unchanged.

In the process of rapid industrialization, the government has been concerned with possible adverse effects this could have on the environment. Singapore has not indiscriminately offered to play host to polluting industries moving out of industrialized countries. As pointed out by the Minister of Finance, "A serious deterioration of the environment is one result of the activities of the less enlightened or the less socially conscious corporations elsewhere which have brought disrepute upon international investments. Here in Singapore we would hope to avoid any possible embarrassment to investors and to ourselves by assessing in advance and rejecting where necessary projects with likely injurious effects."[3] New industries are, therefore, made aware of the need for pollution control and of the existing environmental standards, and these are insisted upon before industries are allowed to be established in the republic.

Applications for the establishment of new industries are carefully examined and screened by the Economic Development Board, whereas the allocation and siting of new industries are carefully planned by the Jurong Town Corporation and the Planning Department of the Ministry of the Environment and the Anti-Pollution Unit of the Prime Minister's Office. At present, there are about twenty-three industrial estates in the republic, which can generally be divided into two types.[4] The first type are heavy industries, which are located in the relatively rural and newly developed sections of the island, as they require extensive land areas and are relatively more pollution-prone. This type is exemplified by Jurong Industrial Estate, Woodlands Industrial Estate, and Sembawang Industrial Estate, among others. The second type, light industries, are in or around high-density housing estates. Kallang Basin Industrial Estate, Redhill Industrial Estate, and Tanglin Halt Industrial Estate are examples of this second type (Fig. 1).

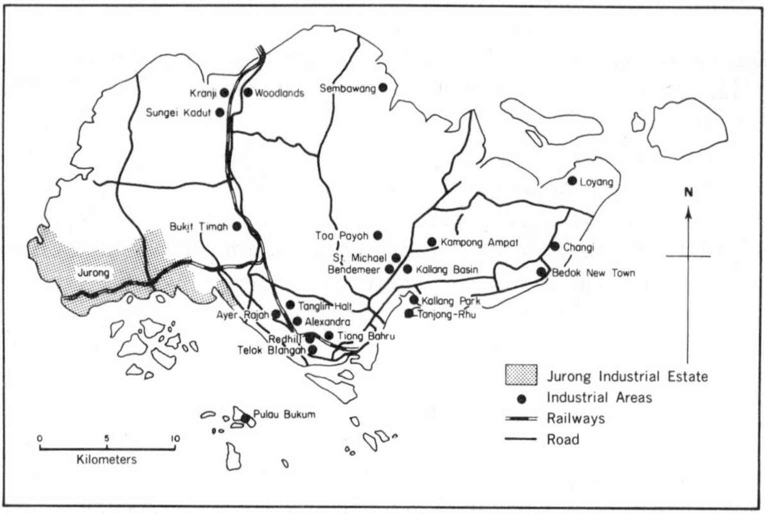

Fig. 1. Distribution of Major Industrial Areas in Singapore. Source: Peter S. J. Chen and Tai Ching Ling, *Social Ecology in Singapore* (Singapore: Federal Publications, 1977), p.7.

Most of the twenty-three industrial estates were set up after 1960 by the EDB and the JTC. The largest of these is the Jurong Industrial Estate, which is also the largest industrial estate of its kind in Southeast Asia. The Jurong New Town has a land area of 5,835 hectares, of which 3,388 hectares or 55 percent of the total area are industrial areas.[5] In 1970, more than half of 262 pioneer firms in the republic were located in the Jurong Industrial Estate. The number of factories in Jurong alone has increased from 202 in 1969 to 866 in June 1978.

Apart from providing jobs for a large number of workers, the town will also eventually accommodate a residential population of about 250,000. To attract workers to live in Jurong New Town, the town has been zoned into various sectors; the industrial, housing and commercial, and parks and recreational. It has been developed into a self-contained town with a full range of social and recreational amenities, including schools, public housing, markets, shopping centers, gardens, recreational facilities, a sports complex, and a good transport system. Pollution problems are kept within manageable limits, and excellent public health standards are maintained.

III. Land Use and Physical Planning

Scarcity of land is a critical problem in Singapore. The republic has a total area of only 616 square kilometers. Of the total land area, in 1977, about 43 percent had been developed for residential, commercial, and industrial usage, and another 17 percent for agriculture. The balance consists of cultivable waste, forest reserves, marsh, and other non-built-up areas. With the severe shortage of land in Singapore, competing demand for land by various sectors of the economy is acute.

Physical planning in Singapore, like other countries, plays a key role in determining the environmental quality. The first comprehensive physical development plan for the whole island was the 1955 Master Plan, which was approved by the colonial government in 1958 and revised in 1960. The plan covered a twenty-year period, from 1953 to 1972. The core policy for urban development as reflected in the Master Plan can be described as one of decentralization. The growth of the existing city was to be limited by a green belt. The population living in the central city was to be reduced by one-sixth to alleviate problems of overcrowding and traffic congestion. Further urban growth was to be accommodated in three new towns at some distance from the central city.

The Master Plan reflects, however, the rather conservative policies and limited aspirations of the colonial government, which could not foresee the rapid political and social changes since 1959, when Singapore attained self-government, nor could it foresee the consequences of these changes for physical planning. The Singapore government, therefore, undertook a major planning project in 1967 with the assistance of the United Nations Development Program (UNDP) to prepare another long-range comprehensive physical plan for the whole of Singapore. Subsequently, after thorough investigations, a concept plan providing for the "ring" development was completed in 1971.

The Concept Plan, which was later referred to as the Comprehensive Plan by government agencies, was projected to 1992, a period of twenty years. The Concept Plan deals mainly with the distridution of major activities, expressed in terms of predominant land uses and organized within a system of structural units, and in terms of transportation links between them. The plan includes a proposed system of expressways, major arterials, airports, major commercial and service centers, a mass transit system, industrial estates, overall settlement patterns for housing of high and low densities, and an open space system.

Unlike the Master Plan, the policy for the central city as proposed in the Concept Plan is to provide for its continued growth as the main commercial and shopping center of the republic. When the final stage of urban development is completed in 1992, there will be seven major urban districts and the Central Area. The population of each district will be from 200,000 to 350,000. Each district will have industries, high-density public housing estates, and a center incorporating main commercial uses and recreational facilities. An expressway system and a mass transit system will link all major activities and urban districts with the Central Area (Fig. 2).

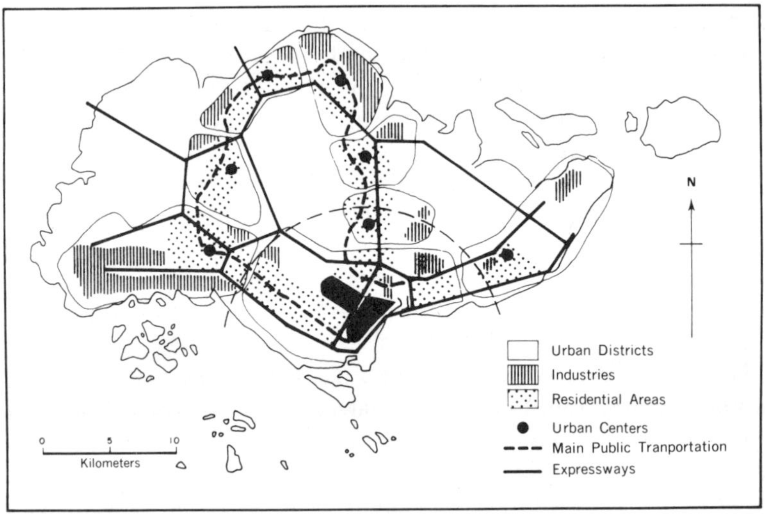

Fig. 2. Proposed Major Urban Areas in Singapore in 1992. Source: Peter S.J. Chen and Tai Ching Ling, *Social Ecology of Singapore* (Singapore: Federal Publications, 1977), p. 13.

The Concept Plan provides guidelines for the overall planning and policy for urban and environmental developments in Singapore, bearing in mind the need to create an ideal and healthy environment for social, residential, commercial, industrial, and recreational activities. The implementation of the plan will definitely affect the quality of the environment as well as the ecological distribution of the population, public and private housing estates, and industrial estates in the whole island.

IV. Population, Housing, and the Social Environment

In planning physical development, the size of Singapore's population and its limited land area are two major and interrelated factors which determine the options of Singapore's urban development plan. The population of Singapore has increased about ten times since the beginning of this century, while the area of land in Singapore remained at 582 square kilometers until 1966, after which the reclamation program succeeded in adding to our land area by some 34 square kilometers (by 1977). The density of population has, therefore, increased from about 390 persons per square kilometer in 1901 to around 3,870 persons per square kilometer today. It is projected that Singapore's population will stabilize at about 3.5 million by the year 2030.[6] The average population density by then will be about 5,800 persons per square kilometer.

The rapid population growth rates during the years before 1960 posed serious problems to the economic and environmental development, especially the problems of acute housing shortage, urban slums, and squatter settlements. Before 1960, many people in Singapore were living in totally inadequate houses. In 1954, a survey of low-income residents in the city area showed that 84 percent of the sample households occupied accommodations consisting of one room or less. Another survey of a densely populated area found that more than half of the residents lived in cubicles which had no corridors, and sanitary conditions were often inadequate.[7]

To tackle the problems of acute housing shortage and urban renewal, the Housing and Development Board (HDB) was established in 1960 to undertake large-scale public housing programs to provide low-cost high-rise housing for the lower income groups. In 1966, the Urban Renewal Department (URD) was established, within the organizational framework of the HDB, to undertake slum clearance and comprehensive redevelopment of the central area of Singapore. The Urban Redevelopment Authority (URA) was constituted in 1974 as an autonomous statutory body to take over the functions of the URD. Urban renewal programs undertaken by the URA and public housing programs by the HDB have been very successful. This is partly due to the firm commitment made by the government on the one hand, and, on the other, to the institutional framework in Singapore which gives the government the authority to acquire any private land for public use of redevelopment purposes.

The city center is at present undergoing very rapid changes on a comprehensive basis through urban renewal programs undertaken by the URA. The urban renewal program aims to reconstruct areas covered by slums and to provide new roads, public utilities, markets, food centers, public housing, car parks, landscaped open spaces, and so forth. The urban redevelopment program also includes the sale of urban renewal sites for investors to develop hotels, entertainment centers, shopping centers, and medium-cost apartments, as well as other projects which promote tourism.

Public housing in Singapore is undertaken by the Housing and Development Board, which concentrates mainly on multi-storyed flats in the city and suburban areas. Since 1960, the HDB has completed three five-year building programs (1961–65, 1966–70, and 1971–75). The fourth five-year building program (1976–80) is under way. By March 1977 the HDB had built a total of 272,420 units of high-rise flats; about 1.3 million persons or 56 percent of the total population in Singapore were living in public housing estates. At present the HDB is building about 30,000 housing units a year. It is estimated that by 1980 about 65–70 percent of Singapore's population will be living in public high-rise flats. By 1992 when the urban development program as proposed in the Concept Plan is completed, about 80–85 percent of the total population will be living in HDB flats (Fig. 3).

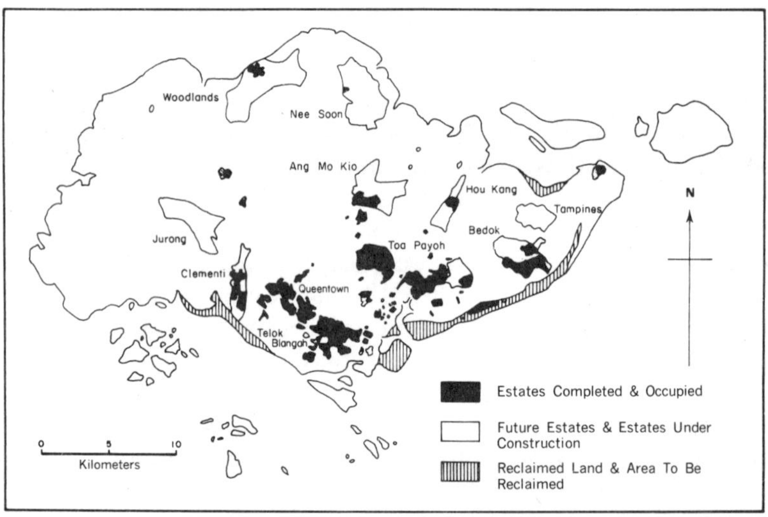

Fig. 3. Location of Public Housing Estates and Reclaimed Land in Singapore. SOURCE: *HDB Annual Report 1977/78* (Singapore: Housing & Development Board, 1978), pp. 18–19.

The physical environment, especially housing and recreational areas, cannot be considered in the isolated context of design and planning. The needs and aspirations of the people must also be considered. Therefore, in the planning and development of housing estates, adequate facilities and amenities to ensure a healthy social environment must be provided.

This involves measures to provide for more and better housing, health and community services, commercial and recreational facilities, as well as to increase the opportunities for intellectual, cultural, and community development. As stated by Mr. Liu Thai-Ker, the deputy chief executive officer of the HDB, "Public housing is not just building, but a way of life."[8] The ultimate objective of the public housing program is to provide a healthy living environment, both physical and social, for the population in Singapore.

V. Comprehensive Environmental Control

The history of advanced industrial countries indicates that there is a close relationship between economic growth and environmental pollution. This relationship, however, need not necessarily be repeated in the growth experience of developing countries today. As discussed in the preceding sections, Singapore is a "late starter" in the development process, having experienced rapid industrial growth, strictly speaking, only after 1968. One of the advantages of being a late starter is that one can learn from the mistakes of others. If sufficient attention is given to the maintenance of a clean environment, economic growth need not be accompanied by rapidly rising pollution levels. In the planning for economic and environmental development, the Singapore government has been consciously concerned with the limited land area, the increasing number of people, and the need for a rapid industrialization process, as well as the interaction process among these variables and their implications for the quality of the environment.

The successful control of environmental pollution demands, among others, the following prerequisites: (1) suitable legislation to ensure effective enforcement of pollution control measures; (2) a system to promote environmental education among the public; and (3) an appropriate organizational structure to coordinate and supervise the various areas of activities in relation to environmental quality control.

The most significant attempt made by the Singapore government to tackle environmental problems is the setting up of the Anti-Pollution Unit under the Prime Minister's Office in 1970. The main functions of the Unit are to survey and identify the nature and extent of pollution problems and to suggest methods of solving them, to formulate policies on and to draft legislation for the control of pollution, and to promote environmental education. In 1972, the Ministry of the Environment was established to assume the responsibility of maintaining the general hygiene and sanitation of the republic, including the provision of sewage facilities and the construction of flood alleviation schemes. The Ministry also works closely with the Economic Development Board and the Anti-Pollution Unit in screening new industries to ensure that they comply with environmental regulations.

In addition to the Anti-Pollution Unit and the Ministry of the Environment, several other government agencies are responsible for environmental control, as follows:

Ministry of National Development	Physical development planning, particularly land-use planning and building control
Housing and Development Board	Development and management of public housing estates
Urban Redevelopment Authority	Development program of the city center
Jurong Town Corporation	Development and management of industrial estates
Economic Development Board	Screening new industries to ensure that they will not cause damage to the environment
Port of Singapore Authority	Prosecuting ships for polluting Singapore waters or for emitting excessive smoke, soot, and ash
Traffic Police Department	Apprehending owners of vehicles with smoky exhausts
Industrial Health Unit (Ministry of Labor)	Environmental conditions of the industries and health of industrial workers

Since the late 1960s, a series of environmental laws has been passed to allow effective enforcement of anti-pollution measures. Among others, the following are some important acts which empower the relevant authorities to take appropriate actions against environmental pollution and to maintain the quality of the environment.

1. The Planning Act, which was passed in 1960 and revised in 1970, regulates the patterns of land use in the republic as well as the control and requirements of all types of buildings. This is to ensure that all types of land are used in accordance with the guidelines provided in the overall long-term urban development plan and that all buildings meet the minimum requirements of the authorities.

2. To combat air pollution. the Clean Air Act 1971 was passed by

Parliament. Subsequently, the Clean Air (Standards) Regulations 1972 was passed, specifying acceptable levels of various air pollutants. The Clean Air (Prohibition on the Use of Open Fires) Order came into effect in 1973. To curb air pollution further, the Clean Air (Amendment) Act 1975 was passed by Parliament. This amended act is to further strengthen control over air pollution and to impose stricter penalties for offenders.

3. Water pollution control in Singapore is achieved with the provision of sewerage and sewage treatment works, and the pretreatment of trade and industrial wastes to prescribed standards before discharge into sewers or water-courses. In 1963, the Local Environmental Integration Ordinance was passed, but the corresponding regulations were not passed until 1970. This was because at the early stages of industrialization, the nature of different types of effluents discharged from different industries was not known, and there was a lack of technical know-how to justify legislation and enforcement of regulations. With more experience gained, the Environmental Public Health Act was passed in 1968 and the Environmental Public Health (Prohibition on Discharge of Trade Effluents into Water Courses) Regulations were passed in 1971. The Local Environmental Integration Regulations 1970 and the Environmental Public Health Regulations 1971 were combined, with modifications, into the Trade Effluent Regulations 1976 under the Water Pollution Control and Drainage Act 1975. These regulations are administered by the Ministry of the Environment.

4. Action against emission of smoke from motor vehicles is taken under a regulation in the Road Traffic Act which is enforced by the Vehicles Department. As a result of the rising affluence among Singapore's population, the number of motor vehicles has increased rapidly and the traffic congestion in the Central Business District (CBD) has become a serious problem. To curb the increase of car ownership, such measures as high road tax rates with progressively higher tax for larger cars, heavy import duties, and high petroleum tax are imposed. To cope with the problem of traffic congestion in the CBD, the Area Licensing Scheme (ALS) was introduced in 1975. Under the Motor Vehicles (Restricted Zone and Area Licensing) Rules 1975, as of 2 June 1975 an area of 620 hectares covering the central business district was cordoned off as the restricted zone between the hours of 7:30 A.M. and 10:15 A.M. during week days. Under this scheme, passenger vehicles of carrying capacity of less than twelve are not allowed to enter the restricted zone unless they possess an Area License (which costs S$4 per day or S$80 per month) or if they are carrying four or more persons including the driver. Contravention of the regulations carries a fine of up to S$1,000.

Since its inception, a significant reduction in private car traffic—over 70 percent during the restricted hours—has been observed.

5. Singapore is the fourth biggest harbor in the world. The threat of oil pollution in the harbor and territorial waters has grown in recent years. In 1971, the Prevention of Pollution of the Sea Act was passed. By an amendment to this act and the new Civil Liability (Oil Pollution) Act 1973, ships are made liable for any damage caused in the area of Singapore from pollution by refuse, waste matter, trade effluent, or oil.

6. Regulations protecting the health of industrial workers have been formulated by the Industrial Health Unit under the Ministry of Labor. The quarry Licensing Regulations 1973 make it compulsory for quarry workers to have annual chest X-ray examinations. Based on a survey carried out in 1975 about occupational cancer, the Labor Ministry will soon introduce an occupational cancer prevention program to control and prevent the disease among workers. The program is to minimize the risk of workers exposed to known cancer-causing agents in the various industries. It will include: (1) drawing up of codes of practice to be used as guidelines for industry; (2) environmental monitoring and engineering control of work places with cancer hazards, where feasible: (3) health education of workers and management on the hazards; (4) medical surveillance of exposed workers by regular specific medical examinations to detect early evidence of occupational cancer; and (5) setting up an informal occupational cancer registry.[9]

To complement regulations combating environmental pollution, the government has carried out a series of campaigns to promote environmental education among the public. Campaigns, such as Keep Singapore Clean, Anti-Littering, Anti-Infectious Diseases, Anti-Drug, Anti-Smoking, Industrial Safety, Save Water, and Save Energy, all aim at educating the public. These campaigns are very successful and are not only initiated by the Ministry of the Environment, but are also initiated or supported by other ministries, statutory bodies, community centers, voluntary organizations, commercial organizations, and other institutions. All these efforts aim at enhancing the quality of our environment and maintaining a healthy social environment for Singapore's population.

Notes

1. Singapore Ministry of the Environment. *Annual Report 1973* (Singapore: Ministry of the Environment, 1974), p. 1.

2. Singapore Ministry of Finance, *Economic Survey of Singapore 1977.* (Singapore: Ministry of Finance, 1978), pp. 51–52.
3. Chor Yeok Eng, "Economic Progress and Environment: No Dilemma," in *Industrialisation and Environment*, ed. Dieter Bielenstein, (Tokyo: Friedrich-Ebert-Stiftung, 1974), pp. 217 27.
4. Peter S. J. Chen and Tai Chin Ling. *Social Ecology of Singapore* (Singapore: Federal Publications, 1977), pp. 22–24.
5. Hew Chow Sin, et al., eds., *Proceedings of Symposium on Our Environment* (Singapore: Nanyang University, 1977), p. 66.
6. Chen and Tai, *Social Ecology*, p. 27.
7. Ibid., pp. 13–18.
8. Pen Chye Chua, ed., *Planning in Singapore* (Singapore: Chopmen Enterprises, 1973), p. 29.
9. *The Straits Times*, 28 August 1978.

Bibliography

Bhathal, R. S. and Chen, Peter S. J., eds. *The Singapore Environment.* Singapore: University Education Press, 1973.

Chen, Peter S. J. "Population and Environmental Factors of Development in Singapore." In *Performance and Perspectives of the Singapore Economy*, edited by K. E. Shaw, et al., pp. 107–32. Tokyo: Institute of Developing Economies, 1976.

———. "Public Housing and Urban Development in Singapore." *Journal of the Singapore Institute of Planners* 6 (1976–77):59–71.

Chia, Lin Sien and Wong, Jenny M. L. "Atmospheric Pollution and Its Control in Singapore." In *Proceedings of Symposium on Our Environment*, edited by Hew Chow Sin, et al., pp. 100–123. Singapore: Nanyang University, 1977.

Lim, B. P. Bill. "Environmental Considerations of Urban Settlement." *Journal of the Singapore Institute of Planners* 2 (1972): 51–54.

Liu, Thai-Ker. "Designing for Highrise Living." In *Towards a Better Singapore*, edited by Tan It Koon, pp. 8–16. Singapore: Singapore Professional Centre, 1976.

Ministry of Health (Singapore). *Population and Trends.* Singapore: Ministry of Health, 1977.

Tan, Hsu Haung. "Some Aspects of Planning for Industries in Singapore." *Journal of the Singapore Institute of Planners* 6 (1976–77):47–54.

National Policy Trends on Environmental Protection and Pollution Control in the Philippines

Perfecto V. Fernandez

I. Organization and Administration

Before 1964 there was no specific public agency entrusted with the administration and enforcement of the laws on pollution or environmental protection. Enforcement was limited to prosecution of offenders or violators through criminal proceedings in the regular courts of justice. Inevitably, this method of enforcement posed many serious obstacles to the regularity and certainty of compliance. The shortcomings of the criminal process as a method of exacting compliance with social legislation are well known.

In 1964, the National Water and Air Pollution Control Commission was created under Republic Act (R.A.) 3931. The commission had seven members, of which five were part-time and two full-time. The part-time members were the chairman of the National Science Development Board, who was also chairman of the commission; an officer of the Department of Health designated by the Secretary of Health; an officer of the Department of Agriculture and Natural Resources, designated by the Secretary of Agriculture and Natural Resources; the remaining two represented the private sector and were appointed by the President with the consent of the Commission on Appointments, one on recommendation of the Philippine Council of Science and Technology and the other on recommendation of the Chamber of Industries of the Philippines. The two full-time commissioners were appointed by the President of the Philippines with the consent of the Commission on Appointments. One of the full-time commissioners must be a sanitary engineer; the other must be a lawyer.

Apparently, problems were posed by the organization of the commission; conceivably, the part-time members could not give enough time to the work of the commission; the number of members posed difficulties in securing a quorum to do business; responsibility was too diffuse; the inevitable result was delay in carrying out the work of the commission. In 1976, during marital law, the commission was reorganized. Membership was reduced to three, with a full-time commissioner assisted by two full-time deputy commissioners: one for standard setting and monitoring, and the other for enforcement. To assist the commission in policy formulation, an Inter-Agency Council was attached to the commission. The council consisted of representatives designated by ministers of nine ministries, and the heads of four special agencies, and was presided over by the commissioner (Secs. 3 and 4, Presidential Decree [P.D.] 984).

Under its original charter (R.A. 3931), the commission was assigned broad functions, powers, and responsibilities. These may be classified as follows: (1) research and studies, directed to amassing adequate and reliable information on pollution in the country; (2) plans and programs, directed at pollution control; (3) standard setting, directed at standards and guidelines for its operational functions of licensing, approval of plans and systems, issuance of specific orders to control pollution, and determination of violations of the law or its own orders; (4) Monitoring, directed at current information and developments as a basis for administrative decisions in discharge of its functions; (5) Investigation, directed at a determination in specific situations either of pollution, or violations of the law, specific permits, orders, or regulations; (6) Enforcement, directed at prevention or abatement of pollution through specific orders, and at the imposition of sanctions upon offenders in the form of cancellation or suspension of permits, criminal penalties, and payment of damages. All these functions, duties, and responsibilities are continued under the amending decree, some with substantial modifications.

With the creation of the Ministry on Human Settlements, which embraces all agencies concerned with environmental protection, the commission is likely to be removed from the Office of the President, in which it has hitherto been situated, and will become part of the ministry, either in its present form or as a bureau on pollution control.

II. Research and Studies

Under its original charter, the commission was to determine if pollution exists in any of the water and/or atmospheric air of the Philippines

(Sec. 6 (1), R.A. 3931). Under the amending decree, this function was greatly broadened, as the commission is to

> Determine the location, magnitude, extent, severity, causes, effects and other pertinent information regarding pollution of the country . . . and conduct continuing researches and studies on the effective means for the control and abatement of pollution (Sec. 6 (a), P.D. 984).
>
> The Commission may conduct scientific experiments, investigations and research to discover economical and practical methods of preventing water, air and land pollution. To this end, the Commission may cooperate with any public or private agency in the conduct of such experiments, investigations and research, and may accept sums of money, for and in behalf of the National Government, given by any international, national or other public or private agency for water, air and land pollution control activities, surveys or programs (Sec. 5).

Ancillary to this broad function are its powers of monitoring conditions relating to pollution in general, and the investigation or inquiry into specific situations of pollution, for the purpose of formulating remedial orders or issuing regulations.

III. Plans and Programs for Pollution Control

Under its charter, original as well as amended, the commission is required to formulate plans and programs for pollution control. Under R.A. 3931, the commission was directed to prepare and develop a comprehensive plan for the abatement of existing pollution and the prevention of new and/or imminent pollution of the waters and/or atmospheric air of the Philippines (Sec. 6 (b)(5)). Under the amended charter, this function of the commission is now subjected to the requirements of national development. It shall

> Develop comprehensive multi-year and annual plans for the abatement of existing pollution and the prevention of new or imminent pollution, the implementation of which shall be consistent with the national development plan of the country (Sec. 6, P.D. 984).

The significance of the qualification introduced under the amended charter should not be missed. The plan for national development of the country has top priority; hence, its requirements will be pressed as a matter of national policy, even at the risk of serious pollution. In brief, the matter of new or imminent pollution, even if serious, must be subordinated to the demands of industrialization. This aspect of current policy deserves careful study, for the reason that in particular projects, the risks of serious pollution may well outweigh the gains to the nation. In such cases, a long view of the national interest may well compel sacrifice of the goal of industrialization, in order to avoid serious damage to the environment and/or to the population. Rather than a policy of inflexible insistence on industrial projects regardless of social cost, an adaptive approach should be adhered to, aimed at a rational decision favoring a positive net gain to the nation, according to a pragmatic, life-enhancing process of reasoning.

IV. Standards and Guidelines

Under both the original and amended charters, the commission is empowered to fix and promulgate standards and guidelines for the proper performance of operational functions relating to the control of pollution. Under the original law, standards were to be fixed for guidance in: (a) the approval of plans and specifications for sewage works and industrial waste-disposal systems and (b) the issuance of permits required by the act (Sec. (b)(6), R.A. 3931). Under the amended charter, such functions were broadened. Apart from standards for the above stated purposes, the commission is required to set up effluent, stream, ambient, and emission standards and promulgate rules and regulations therefor. It is recognized that local governments, development authorities, and other similar government agencies may, with the approval of the commission, set up higher standards, which shall then prevail in areas subject to their jurisdiction (Sec. 6 (1), P.D. 984).

V. Monitoring, Investigation, and Inspection

As a supplement to its general research and studies, the commission undertakes regular monitoring of events and developments relating to pollution generally, as well as the investigation and inspection of places and establishments, for various purposes: (1) to ensure an adequate basis for adoption of plans and programs, and the grant of remedial orders and permits; (2) to aid in determination of any violation of any particular order or permit; and (3) to aid in the prosecution of any specific violation of law, its orders, or regulations.

Under the original charter, the commission is empowered to collect and disseminate information relating to water and atmospheric pollution and the prevention, abatement and control thereof (Sec. 6 (b)(7),

R.A. 3931). It is also authorized to undertake, through its representatives, the inspection of places and investigation of conditions relating to pollution anywhere in the Philippines (Sec. 6 (b)(8), R.A. 3931). To ensure compliance with approved plans the commission is likewise authorized to inspect the construction and maintenance of sewage works and industrial waste-disposal systems (Sec. (a)(2), R.A. 3931).

All these functions are retained under the amended charter and extend now to pollution on land (Sec. 6, P.D. 984).

VI. Licensing System

In order to minimize or to prevent substantial increases in or additions to already existing pollution, certain activities that are definitely known, in our national experience, to add to or to increase pollution, may not be undertaken or performed without a prior permit or license from the Commission. Under both the original and amended charters, the commission is empowered to issue, renew, or deny such permits, on reasonable grounds and conditions. This was a function given to city and district engineers under standards and guidelines set by the commission.

The amended charter states:

> No person shall perform any of the following activities without first securing a permit from the Commission for the discharge of all industrial wastes and other wastes which could cause pollution:
>
> 1. the construction, installation, modification, or operation of any sewage works or any extension or addition thereto;
> 2. the increase in volume or strength of any wastes in excess of the permissive discharge specified under any existing permit;
> 3. the construction, installation or operation of any industrial or commercial establishments or any extension or modification thereof or addition thereto, the operation of which would cause an increase in the discharge of waste directly into the water, air and/or land resources of the Philippines or would otherwise alter their physical, chemical or biological properties in any manner not already lawfully authorized (Sec. 8, P.D. 984).

The exception from the permit requirement of sewage or other works that discharge only domestic or sanitary wastes from a single residential building, provided for under the original charter, has now been modified and broadened, thus:

> That the Commission, by rules and regulations, may require subdivisions, condominiums, hospitals, public buildings and other

similar human settlements to put up appropriate central sewerage system and sewage treatment works, except that no permits shall be required of any sewage works or changes to or extensions of existing works that discharge only domestic or sanitary wastes from a single residential building provided with septic tanks or their equivalent. The Commission may impose reasonable fees and charges for the issuance or renewal of all permits herein required (Sec. 6 (9), P.D. 984).

VII. Remedial Orders and Enforcement Proceedings

Using the criterion of expeditious action, the commission, as an administrative agency, has distinct advantages over the regular courts. First, it has the power to initiate action for the purpose of preventing or abating pollution, without the necessity for a complaint or charge of violation. Second, its hearing and determination procedures are considerably less subject to the technicalities of law and procedure, hence more speedy and expeditious. Third, it has an administrative staff, with a data bank and technical expertise at their disposal.

Express jurisdiction and authority are vested in the commission for taking the following measures for pollution control:

1. Issuance of remedial directives for pollution control, in the form of injunctive, or cease-and-desist, orders. Such directives may be issued upon the initiative of the commission itself.
2. Suspension or cancellation of existing permits, due to violations.
3. Prosecution of specific violations of the law, or its own remedial directives.

Under the original and amended charter, the commission was empowered to issue specific orders requiring the discontinuance of pollution through the discharge of wastes of any kind, and specifying the conditions and the time within which such discontinuance must be accomplished (Sec. 6 (a)(4), R.A. 3931). Such an order is remedial, because it seeks to prevent new or abate existing pollution. However, since private rights will be affected, generally, a hearing is required before its issuance. Only under exceptional circumstances, where remedial action is urgently needed, is an *ex-parte* injunctive order authorized.

Under the amended charter:

Public hearings shall be conducted by the Commissioner, Deputy Commissioner or any senior official duly designated by the Commissioner prior to issuance or promulgation of any order or decision by the Commissioner requiring the discontinuance of discharge of sewage, industrial wastes or other wastes into the water, air or land resources of the Philippines as provided in this Decree: Provided, That whenever the Commission finds a *prima facie* evidence that the discharged sewage or wastes are of immediate threat to life, public health, safety or welfare, or to animal or plant life, or exceed the allowable standards set by the Commission, the Commissioner may issue an *ex-parte* order directing the discontinuance of the same or the temporary suspension or cessation of operation of the establishment or person generating such sewage or wastes without the necessity of a prior public hearing. The said *ex-parte* order shall be immediately executory and shall remain in force until said establishment or person prevents or abates the said pollution within the allowable standard, or modified or nullified by a competent court (Sec. 7, P.D. 984).

There are two sets of sanctions provided for under the charter of the commission. The first is administrative, which is directed at the suspension, cancellation, or non-renewal of permits issued by the commission, for violation of the law, the applicable regulations, or the conditions and terms of the permit itself. The second is criminal prosecution for violation of the law or orders of the commission.

The commission under the amended charter has acquired greater authority for the enforcement of its own decisions. While under the original act the imposition of sanctions, including fines and penalties, required institution of court action, under the amended charter the commission is empowered to try violations of the law or its orders, and to enforce the same through its own processes. It is believed, however, that the imposition of penalties in the form of prison sentences requires the institution of criminal actions in the regular courts of justice.

The amended charter states:

1. Any person found violating or failing to comply with any order, decision or regulation of the Commission for the control or abatement of pollution shall pay a fine not exceeding five thousand pesos per day for every day during which such violation or default continues; and the Commission is hereby authorized and empowered to impose the fine after due notice and hearing.

The fines so imposed shall be paid to the Government of the Philippines through the Commission, and failure to pay the fine in any case within the time specified in the above-mentioned Order or Decision shall be sufficient ground for the Commission to order the closure or the stoppage in the operation of the establishment being operated and/or managed by said person or persons until payment of the fines shall have been made. The Commission shall have the power and authority to issue corresponding writs of execution directing the

City or Provincial Sheriff or other peace officers whom it may appoint to enforce the fine or the order of closure or stoppage of operations.

Payment of fines may also be enforced by appropriate action in a court of competent jurisdiction. The remedies provided in this subsection shall not be a bar to nor shall affect any other remedies provided for in this Decree but shall be cumulative and additional to such remedies.

2. Any person who shall violate any of the provisions of Section Eight of this Decree or its implementing rules and regulations or any Order or Decision of the Commission, shall be liable to a penalty of not to exceed one thousand pesos for each day during which the violation continues, or by imprisonment, and in addition such person may be required or enjoined from continuing such violation as hereinafter provided.

3. Any person who shall refuse, obstruct, or hamper the entry of the duly authorized representatives of the Commission into any property of the public domain or private property devoted to industrial manufacturing, processing or commercial use during reasonable hours for the purpose of inspecting or investigating the conditions therein relating to pollution or possible or imminent pollution shall be liable to a fine not exceeding two hundred pesos or imprisonment of not exceeding one month, or both.

4. Any person who violates any of the provisions of, or fails to perform any duty imposed by this Decree or its implementing rules and regulations or by Order or Decision of the Commission promulgated pursuant to this Decree thereby causing the death of fish or other aquatic life, shall in addition to the penalty above prescribed, be liable to pay the government for damages for fish or aquatic life destroyed.

5. In case the violator is a juridical person, the penalty shall be imposed on the managing head responsible for the violation.

While the present enforcement set-up is certainly a distinct improvement over the previous one, there are weaknesses or vulnerabilities that adversely affect its overall efficacy. For one thing, in relation to the powerful and massive interests that will confront it in the process of enforcement, the commission as a body of technical experts will be facing pressures that will be difficult to resist. Second, unlike the judiciary, the commission is subject to continuing executive control, with or without formalities of appeal or petition for review, not only at the ministerial level but also at the highest executive level. Third, all kinds of problems and pressures at the level of actual execution are likely to arise. For these reasons, it might be best if the commission were limited, in terms of the enforcement process, to filing its orders for enforcement with the Court of Appeals. Upon the filing of an order of the commission, calling for injunction or imposition of penalty, the solicitor general will seek a court judgment providing for appropriate relief. The party affected, of course, shall have the right to oppose the same but only on grounds of substantive invalidity. Once the Court of Appeals renders judgment, the same will be remanded to the Court of First Instance of the district where the offender resides or can be found, for appropriate execution, according to the Rules of Court. In this way, the commission will be left to take care of its area of expertise, that is, pollution control, without being enmeshed in technicalities of judicial enforcement.

Environmental Problems in Thailand

With Special Reference to a Case Study of Lead Poisoning and the Environmental Laws

Twesukdi Piyakarnchana, Sunee Mallikamarl, and Mattaya Jarupan

Thailand is an agricultural country in which about 80 percent of the population earn their living by growing rice or engaging in other small farming practices. Bangkok, the capital, is a good example of a primary city, with about 4.5 million inhabitants. Since the implementation of the First Economic and Social Development Plan (1961–65), Thailand has invited industrialists, both local and foreign, to invest in its industry. The initial objective was primarily to substitute for imported goods and materials those produced locally, both for local consumption and for export. Export-oriented industries have been in operation since 1966, but their number is still small. The most significant policy change of the government in promoting export industries occurred during the Third Plan (1972–76). Increased industrialization during the previous periods had a severe impact on quality of the environment. From 1970 to 1976, for example, the sugar mill industries along the Mae Klong River discharged untreated waste water into the river, causing damage to clean and potable water, and also killing a large number of fish and shellfish along the river basin and at the river mouth. A rough estimate of the loss of shellfish at the river mouth alone was nearly 30 million baht (US $1.5 million).

In 1973, the sub-committee for the study on marine pollution in Thai waters reported that there was a remarkably high amount of total mercury in the water and sediments at some locations in the upper portion of the Gulf of Thailand. Such a high accumulation of mercury in the marine environment was due to the discharge of waste waters from the caustic soda manufacturers located along the coast line and on the Chao Phraya River. Fortunately, after the above report was published, the government authorities compelled the factories to remove the mercury in the waste.

The destruction of forests is yet another matter. It was estimated that at the start of the first plan forested areas covered about 50 percent of the kingdom. However, in the early phase of the Fourth Plan, the total area had been reduced to about 38 percent. These lands are used for agriculture. Areas affected by such destruction are subject to severe and frequent floods and drought.

I. Lead Poisoning

The only severe case of industrial pollution affiecting human beings in Thailand concerns an instance of lead poisoning. A large outbreak in which twelve persons were ill was reported in 1970.[1] The outbreak occurred in a village near the Bangkok Metropolitan Area. Four or five children became seriously ill. The physician reported that the cause of the illness was lead poisoning. The lead originated from the fumes and ashes of fireplaces that used car-battery casings as a fuel for coconut sugar production. After being treated in the hospital, the seriously ill children were sent back home. No further follow-up study was made. Occupational disease officers gave general advice to the villagers on the harmful effect of lead from the fumes and how to avoid it. No other serious action to prevent the repetition of such incidents was ever taken.

Six years later, in August 1976, a baby girl about two years old was admitted to Chulalongkorn University Hospital and died a few days later.[2] The doctor diagnosed the case and found that she had died from acute lead poisoning. Interestingly, she came from the same village mentioned above. The case was brought to the attention of the Institute of Environmental Research, Chulalongkorn University, where a research team composed of environmental scientists, environmental engineers, social scientists, medical doctors, and pharmacists was set up by the Institute.

The group spent about three months on their research. The results of their findings may be summarized as follows.

1. Background and Analysis of the Case

Tambon ("village") Bangkru is one of the thirteen villages of Ampur ("district") Prapradaeng, Samut Prakarn Province. It used to be a quiet agricultural village prior to 1960 and its main products were rice, coconuts, and various kinds of fruit. Since 1960, the area has been developed as one of the industrial sites of Samut Prakarn Province.

According to the statistics for 1976, the total population of this village was 11,093, with 5269 males and 5824 females. There were 122 industrial plants. About 49 percent of these plants were textile industries, 20.5 percent were metal and tool industries, and only 1.6 percent (two plants) were lead smelting plants.

In the community affected by lead poisoning, there were 186 inhabitants, with 95 males and 91 females. There were twenty-five wooden houses, with 56.0 percent having two stories, 12.0 percent one and a half stories, and the rest one story. There were two types of families in the community. The first, accounting for 85.7 percent, can be called a nuclear or conjugal family type, and the rest (14.3 percent) can be classified as the extended or consanguine family type. The monthly income of the head of the family and his wife is shown in Table 1. This indicates that the people in this community are in a low-income bracket. Most of them earned their living mainly on a day-to-day hire-wage basis. It was also learned that men who were also head of a family could find jobs more easily than their wives.

Table 1. Monthly income in Tambon Bangkru

Income	Head of the family		Wife	
(Baht)	Number	Percent	Number	Percent
Less than 500	—	—	7	35.0
501–1,000	7	21.2	7	35.0
1,001–1,500	10	30.3	6	30.0
1,501–2,000	4	12.1	—	—
2,001–2,500	5	15.1	—	—
2,501–3,000	6	18.2	—	—
3,001–3,500	1	3.0	—	—
Total	33	100.0	20	100.0

Source: The Institute of Environmental Research, Chulalongkorn University, "Case Study of Lead Poisoning." Bangkok, 1977.

Nearly 90 percent of the housewives in the lead-contaminated village went shopping for food and prepared the meals for their families. Nearly all of them (94.0 percent) went to the market every day. Besides the food from the market, 82.99 percent of the villagers harvested edible vegetables in the lead-contaminated area. Some of these vegetables were analyzed for their lead content by environmental scientists.

For about 3 to 6 hours a day, 57.7 percent of the children between 2 and 12 years old played on the road, which was paved with contaminated lead. The rest played on the road from 1 to 3 hours a day. Among the 25 families examined, 7 families drank rain water, 12–15 families drank tap water, and the rest drank either rain water and tap water or rain water and shallow well water.

More than 74 percent of the children did not wash their hands before taking their meals. Only 11.7 percent always washed their hands before their meals, and the rest (13.8 percent) occasionally washed their hands before meals. Sixty-five percent of the children did not wear shoes while playing on the road and only 21 percent wore shoes every time.

The analytical results indicated that the main source of the lead was the earthen road in front of the houses. Within the previous three years the surface of the road had either been covered or had had holes filled many times by the asphalt-type material from the old car-battery casings, from which some of the lead had been extracted in a recycling process by the factories nearby. Gradually, the spread of lead into the surrounding environment increased. The results are shown in Tables 2

Table 2. Lead level in the soil, water, fish and edible vegetables

Material	Location	Range (ppm)	Average (ppm)
Soil	Pavement surface	3695–4000	3758.3
	Along the roadside	1833–950	1892
Water	For washing	—	0.01
	In the ditch nearby	—	0.12
Vegetables	In the areas around the community	13.2–36.5	23.5 (Fresh)
Fish (*Trichogaster sp.*)	In the canal and ponds near the community	16.5–33.6	25.1

Source: The Institute of Environmental Research, Chulalongkorn University, "Case Study of Lead Poisoning." Bangkok, 1977.

Table 3. Lead levels in the air

Date	Amount ($\mu m/m^3$)*	
2 Oct. 1976	129.5	While the lead smelting plant was in operation
14 Oct. 1976	105.1	When the plant had stopped operation

*Measured during the afternoon hours

Source: The Institute of Environmental Research, Chulalongkorn University, "Case Study of Lead Poisoning." Bangkok, 1977.

and 3. The results from Table 3 also show that about 23 percent of the lead came from the activities of the lead-smelting plants nearby.

Two scientists from the Institute of Environmental Research, Menasweta and Wattnakorn, investigated the amount of lead in the blood and hair of the children.[3] The amount recorded in the blood of 69 children was in the range of 0.15 to 5.40 ppm, with an average of 1.28 ppm. The amount of lead in the hair of the 49 children between 4 and 10 years old ranged between 47.5 and 1875.0 ppm, with an average of 468.1 ppm. In a control group of 18 children who lived in the Bangkok Metropolitan Area, the range was between 16.5 and 122.0 ppm, with an average of 48.6 ppm. It can be seen, then, that the amount of lead in the hair of the children in the contaminated community was ten times higher than that found in the children outside the area.

In her preliminary report on the intellectual development of the sixty children in the lead-contaminated community, Dr. Wasna Sornmanee concluded that the first group (0–3 years old) showed signs of severe language defects which could lead to an impairment in cognitive and verbal function.[4] In the second group (3–6 years old), an impairment of visual motor function and some speech problems were observed. Among the third group (6–15 years old), she found no significant differences in general intelligence, except for the general feature of prominent visual motor impairment.

2. Responses to the Case

Copies of the report were distributed to the government agencies responsible and also to the Samut Prakarn Provincial Authority. The news of the findings of the Institute of Environmental Research was released to the mass communication media. Some leading newspapers in Bangkok published reports of the case in detail. Unfortunately, during that period, a student uprising occurred which later led to the coup d'état of 6 October 1976. Consequently no serious attention was given to this matter either by the government or the public. However, a few newspapers continued to publish articles on lead poisoning, and the Department of Industrial Inspection (Ministry of Industry) sent inspectors to investigate a lead-smelting plant near the community. It was later announced that this plant was operating illegally and it was closed down. The office of the National Environmental Board sent a letter of acknowledgment to the Institute of Environmental Research. No other measures were taken in order to correct the environmental contamination of the ill-fated community.

As a result of a questionnaire given to the housewives in the lead-contaminated communities, it was learned that prior to the incident of the death of the young child, none of them had any knowledge about the health hazards presented by lead. After being informed by the researchers, they seemed to react quickly: 97.1 percent of them supported the proposal to remove the contaminated earthen road surface. They promised to help the authorities as voluntary workers. Some of them told the researchers that they were willing to contribute money in order to improve the environment. Many of them were worried about their children. They also realized that in order to stop the illness, the lead-contaminated road should be removed as quickly as possible.

It is safe to assume that the improvement and correction of the environment of this community would not have taken place if the newspapers at home and abroad had not given publicity to this matter. A year after the outbreak, a few children were seriously ill again and were admitted to Chulalongkorn University Hospital. This was reported in the *New York Times* in an article entitled "Thai village finds tragedy on a road paved with lead."[5] Similar stories were also published in newspapers in Canada and in England. The *Bangkok Post* raised the issue in an article, "Lead poisoning threat to children."[6] This article was brought to the attention of the former Minister of the Interior, Mr. Samak Sunderavej. He visited the "death village" and immediately ordered the government officers concerned to rectify the situation. It is noteworthy that most of the suggestions and recommendations made by the Institute of Environmental Research to correct the environmental deterioration of the community one year before were accepted.

In less than a month the contaminated earthen road surface was completely removed and a new concrete pavement was constructed. The Department of Public Welfare printed a poster advising the public how to prevent lead poisoning. At present, the Institute of Environmental Research is still making follow-up studies on the physiological and mental recovery of the children affected by chronic lead poisoning.

3. Legal Resolution of the Case

The most relevant law dealing with this problem is the Civil Code (section 420). It provides that any person causing damage willfully or negligently to the life, body, health, liberty, property, or any other right of another person is considered to have committed a wrongful act and is required to make compensation for such an act. However, it is difficult to establish the wrongdoer's guilt since his negligence may be concealed, or his errors of omission may not even be realized. According to the present process of litigation, the injured person bears the burden of proof in convincing the court that he is damaged by the wrongdoer's commission or omission and has to establish whether the wrongdoer has acted willfully or negligently. With reference to the case discussed above, the entire problem seems to depend on whether the owner of the factory (the wrongdoer) can show that he has kept his poisonous materials in the proper place. If he can do so, he may be exempted from the charge.

According to the Factory Act, B.E. (Buddhist Era) 2512 (1969), as amended by B.E. 2518 (1975), section 39(6), it is the duty of the licensee of an industrial business to dispose of waste and to provide good drainage and ventilation according to the minimum standard set by the Ministry of Industry. Section 20 calls for the disposal and destruction of waste or surplus materials containing poisonous elements or flammable materials and makes it the duty of the owner of the factory to provide such measures in the interests of public safety and good order. The penalty for violating this provision is rather low—specifically, imprisonment for up to one month or a fine of up to 10,000 baht (U.S. $500), or both.

In addition, the government official concerned is required to give warning to the owner of the factory in order to make him conform to the law, should the factory owner still continue to violate the regulation regardless of the official's order. Furthermore, injured parties have to institute a tort case to collect compensation for alleged damages.

In the case of lead poisoning, no legal action had ever been taken except for closing down the lead-smelting plant in 1976. The people who were critically contaminated by the lead poisoning never understood their legal rights. Public funds were used by the Department of Public Welfare (Ministry of the Interior) to help the victims, and also to clean the contaminated environment, rather than being used to prosecute those directly responsible for the unfortunate situation. It is also relevant to note that legal action against the wrongdoer in cases involving environmental hazard is not popular among the people or the jurists themselves in Thailand.

II. Attempts to Solve Environmental Problems Through Legal Means

In an attempt to solve its environmental problems, Thailand has to face three basic obstacles:

(1) There is a lack of public consciousness regarding the seriousness of environmental problems.

(2) Since Thailand is a developing country, the Thai government has

to take economic development, especially promotion of investment, as the first priority.

(3) No specific environmental laws have been enacted in Thailand. The experts and technicians concerned are exerting efforts to devise measures to put a stop to, or at least to relieve, the deterioration of the environment. One of the significant measures is to keep the public well informed of the seriousness of environmental hazards in order to promote cooperation from society at large. However, the most significant move required to solve such problems is for the Thai government to immediately formulate its policy and aims regarding the conservation of the environment. Fortunately the Thai government is becoming aware of the problems involved and is trying to solve them.

One of the effective measures used by the government is to hand down summary prison sentences to those who destroy the nation's natural resources. By virtue of section 27 of the Constitution for the Administration of the Kingdom (B.E. 2520 [1977]), the government, through its Prime Minister, is empowered to give a summary punishment of any nature, including execution. It should be pointed out that, in cases involving the destruction of forestry resources, only terms of imprisonment have so far been given by the Prime Minister. For instance, on 2 August 1978, three men were sentenced to jail terms ranging from five to fifteen years. A man was sentenced to fifteen years' imprisonment for attempting to float 665 small boats made entirely of teak; another two men received sentences of five years each for acting in collusion in this case.

The forestry area in Thailand has been reduced from 50 percent to 38 percent, which has meant that land which used to be prosperous, bright, green, and suitable for planting all kinds of tropical trees has become extremely arid. Evidence of this is particularly notable in the northeast of Thailand, where a lot of money has to be spent each year to replant trees, and a great deal of time and energy has to be expended in order to preserve them.

Industrial plants are also another factor contributing to environmental problems because almost all waste matter is released into rivers and nearby canals or into the air. Though a solution to this problem exists, it costs a lot of money to buy the necessary equipment for waste matter treatment. Generally speaking, factory owners in Thailand are not willing to accept responsibility for waste matter treatment. The government itself is reluctant to enforce its environmental policy by compelling owners to ensure waste-matter treatment, for fear that strict enforcement of such a requirement might discourage foreign investors as well as local businessmen. Under such circumstances, the only solution is to make factory owners realize that prevention of pollution is their duty in the interests of the environment and the quality of human living. As there have been no specific environmental laws enacted in Thailand, individuals are themselves responsible for the quality of the environment.

1. The Present Situation

Without any specific environmental laws, only a few indirect laws exist to help conserve the environment. These were passed under various acts and they are generally ineffective in ensuring the conservation of the environment. The reason for this is that at the time of the enactment, environmental problems were not appreciated. They were only intended to safeguard public health, promote clean surroundings, and prevent "nuisances." It should be pointed out that there is no provision in such acts clearly providing remedies for the injured party suffering from toxic chemicals. Moreover, in practice these laws have not been fully enforced, as is obvious from the fact that three major resources—air, water, and soil—continue to deteriorate.

The most significant law aiding environment conservation is the Improvement and Conservation of National Environmental Quality Act, B. E. 2518 (1975), enacted by virtue of the Kingdom of Thailand B. E. 2517 (1974). As a result of its enactment, the National Environmental Board was set up in order to resolve environmental problems and to submit a policy of environmental quality to the Council of Ministers. The office of the board carries out the recommendations of the Board itself, acts as a coordination and public relations center in matters regarding local environmental quality, and maintains liaison with foreign countries. Another role of the National Environmental Board is to consider and to seek a remedy for any petition of any person who has been aggrieved or damaged by an act which has had an adverse effect on environmental quality.

The recent enactment of this law is an indication that the Thai government is giving more attention to environmental problems. However, it should be pointed out that the National Environmental Board does not have a very significant role, because every project studied by the board has to be submitted to the Council of Ministers before any action can be taken.

2. Laws Aiding Environmental Conservation

As has been pointed out, Thailand does not have a specific environmental law, but there are nevertheless over fifty acts and regulations applicable to the protection of the environment. Some acts relate to the control of air pollution and some to prevention of water pollution. There is very little legislation relating to the conservation of the environment, regarding either soil, water, or air. There are no control measures. In some acts, only one or two sections relate to the conservation of the environment.

There are significant acts that are worth considering as examples, namely, the Improvement and Conservation of National Environmental Quality Act, B. E. 2518 (1975), the Factory Act, B. E. 2512 (1969) and the Public Health Act, B. E. 2484 (1941). The Improvement and Conservation of National Environmental Quality Act has been discussed earlier.

a. Factory Act, B. E. 2512 (1969)

The purpose of this act is to control the factories through directives issued by the Ministry of Industry. This ministry has the power to control a factory during the entire period of its operations. When first enacted, this law did not have provisions for dealing with problems of deterioration caused by industrial plants. But a later amendment in 1975 does contain clauses relating to the conservation of the environment.

The Factory Act, B.E. 2512, (1969) as amended by B.E. 2518 (1975), consists of four chapters dealing with establishment and operation, control, licensing, and penalties and includes certain transitional provisions. Nowhere does the act specifically mention the conservation of the environment. It gives directions for applying for permission to operate a factory. As stated in section 8, "A factory may be established only when a license to operate a factory has been granted by the Under-Secretary of State or the person entrusted by him to grant the license."

In granting a license to establish a factory, a set period for the completion of the factory is prescribed. The rules, procedure, and conditions for the application for a license to establish a factory are prescribed in the ministerial regulations. These regulations provide for safety of the building and for proper ventilation, and that the location of the factory should not be hazardous or cause a nuisance or damage to people or property. The factory must be equipped with an effective waste-water treatment plant, for which plans and details must be submitted. If the applicant does not act in compliance with the requirements, the license is not granted, and violations of the regulations incur penalties.

It can, then, clearly be seen that a factory is under statutory control from the time of its inception. If the ministerial regulations are not followed with regard to the prevention of pollution, the license is not granted. Also, the Factory Act vaguely empowers the under secretary of the Ministry of Industry and its officials to take into consideration the standard requirements with respect to the quantity of the discharge from the factory. However, only waste water standards are prescribed in the regulations.

Order No. 2 of the ministry, issued in 1970 under the Factory Act of 1969, reads in part as follows: "No. 22. No waste water can be let out of the factory unless the following stipulations are observed: (1) The pH value should be between 5 and 9; (2) The permanganate value should not be more than 60 milligrams/liter; (3) Dissolved solids should not be more than 2,000 milligrams/liter; (4) The H_2S should not be more than 1 milligram/liter; (5) The HCN should not be more than 0.2 milligram/liter; (6) The amount of zinc, chromium, arsenic, silver, copper, mercury, cadmium, barium, selenium, lead, or nickel should not be more than 1 milligram/liter; (7) There should be no tar; (8) There should be no oil and grease; (9) The formaldehyde content should not be more than 1 milligram/liter; (10) Phenols and cresols should not be more than 1 milligram/liter; (11) Free chlorine should not be more than 1 milligram/liter; (12) There should be no insecticide or radioactive elements; (13) If the ratio between the spoiled water and the good water (river, canal, etc.) is between 1: 8 and 1: 150, the mixed floating elements must not be more than 30 ppm.; if the ratio is between 1:151 and 1:300, the mixed floating elements must not be more than 60 ppm.; if such a ratio is between 1:301 and 1:500, the mixed floating elements must not be more than 150 ppm; (14) The BOD (Biochemical Oxygen Demand) value must not be more than 20 milligrams/liter; (15) The temperature of the waste water to be let off must not be higher than 40 degrees centigrade; (16) The color or the smell of the waste water after flowing into the natural water must not be unpleasant."

Air pollution control is also vaguely prescribed in sections 24 and 25 of the same ministerial regulations: "No. 24. Ventilating measures must be taken by providing enough working space with doors, windows and wind-slots, i.e., not less than 1 out of 10 parts of the whole area. In other words, ventilation must be provided for not less than 0.5 cubic meter per minute per one worker for a general factory where no poisonous materials, chemical elements, inflammable materials, explosives, or other dangerous materials or particles of dust are kept.

"No. 25. Workers who have to work in a stale place without ventilation shall be provided with a ventilator and there should be at least one person working at the entrance door in order to help other persons working inside."

It is further recommended that standard requirements should be reviewed in the future.

The Factory Act does not provide for claims for compensation in the case of damage caused by factory pollution. People who primarily suffer from pollution are those who live in the vicinity, including workers. Legal remedies for workers are available by claiming worker's compensation as provided by the Labor Law. Injured parties other than workers are entitled to claim damages by virtue of tort. However, if the damages incurred cannot be shown to have a direct relationship to the alleged cause, the claim might be dismissed; and if the injured party lacks financial support, legal proceedings are out of the question. The government should take responsibility for such proceedings, since it is stipulated in the constitution that every citizen is entitled to his or her personal liberty and has property rights. Claiming compensation by means of tort is difficult as it is known that the consequences of pollution on human beings are not immediately apparent. If Thailand does not tackle these problems, it could lead to protest demonstrations such as have already occurred in other countries as a result of an unsatisfactory resolution of such issues.

The way the government always deals with environmental problems caused by industry is to close down the offending factory if it does nothing to correct the pollution. This creates other types of problems. For instance, in 1972, the Mae Klong River was polluted because many sugar refinery factories discharged their waste water into the river. Thousands of people were suffering from a lack of water for their daily use as well as for their farms. The quantity of waste water discharged was too much to be treated naturally, and complaints were made to the government. By order of the Environment Control Division (Department of Factory Control), these factories were required to install waste-water treatment plants. However, some factories ignored the order due to the fact that they would have to spend enormous sums of money in order to install proper waste-water treatment plants. Therefore, orders were issued by the Minister of Industry to close them down. This resulted in a demonstration by the sugar cane farmers as they were unable to sell their crops and had to suffer a big financial loss. Unemployment problems also ensued, and consequently the government was forced to change its measures and to allow the factories to continue their operation, providing them with technicians to instruct them in the techniques of waste disposal utilizing a central waste-water treatment plant. Since then, the quality of the water in the Mae Klong River has improved.

b. Public Health Act, B.E. 2484 (1941)

The purpose of this act is to maintain public health. Although it has nine chapters covering various subjects, the essence of this act, insofar as it concerns the environment, is in Chapter I, Part 5—Nuisances. A definition of nuisances is given and such nuisances are prohibited. Many types of nuisances are described, relating to such topics as buildings, animals, factories, smell, noise, vibration, dust, soot, ash, and so forth. The local authorities are given the power to abate such nuisances, including the power to remove the building creating them. This provision is not very practical due to the fact that there is an overlap of this power between municipal officers and the police authorities, without any regulations prescribing clearly the power to be exercised by each authority.

3. The Effectiveness of Environmental Laws

Though there are over fifty acts and regulations which are more or less concerned with the conservation of the environment, the application of such laws is not satisfactory because:

(1) They lack a real understanding of the requirements for environmental control;
(2) Some of the laws reflect outmoded ideas and have not yet been amended;
(3) There is a lack of manpower to enforce the laws;
(4) The National Environmental Board, which is the administrative body, has insufficient authority under the National Environmental Quality Act; and
(5) There are no provisions for remedies for injured parties in these laws.

At the time of the enactment of the early laws concerned with the environment, the problems were not fully appreciated. The public was not aware of such problems or of the seriousness of pollution. This may be due to the fact that the majority of Thais belong to the lower income class. For most of their time they have to concentrate on making a living, so environmental problems tend to be ignored. Moreover, when the laws were enacted, no case of pollution-induced injury had been reported by the news media. The early laws, therefore, do not include provision for effective protection of the environment. Nevertheless, these laws are the main legal recourse open to the environmentalist.

Some of the laws related to the conservation of the environment are a hundred years old. For example, in the Canal Conservation Act, B.E. 2446 (1903) (Section 6), it is provided that, "if some alternative is possible, it is prohibited to dispose of waste or refuse in any canal, ditch, or waterway flowing downstream to a canal. Whoever commits such an offense shall be liable to a fine not exceeding 20 baht (approximately U.S. $1) or one month imprisonment or both." This section is still in effect without any amendment having been made to it. Another law having a low penalty, thus making it easy for the violator, is the Public Health Act, which provides a fine not exceeding 100 baht (approximately U.S. $5) and not less than 10 baht (approximately U.S. 50 cents) per day throughout the period during which the offense continues. However, there are laws which have been amended due to the fact that they were out of date. For example, the Factory Act, B.E. 2482 (1939), was amended by the Factory Act, B.E. 2512 (1969) and finally by the Factory Act, B.E. 2518 (1975). In each case the penalties provided (both fines and imprisonment) were made more severe. The second amendment also empowered the court to issue an order to discontinue the operation indefinitely or until the license expired. These laws can only be of use to the conservation of the environment if they are suitably amended.

To control the environment effectively, manpower is the main requirement. At present, when a problem arises there is inadequate manpower to enforce the laws. Police authority is the sole resource for enforcement, and their responsibility includes receiving complaints, making enquiries, and making arrests. The police at present lack personnel due to the increasing rate of all types of offenses. However, a division of municipal police has been set up recently whose function is partly to oversee the conservation of the environment in the municipal area.

At present, the Improvement and Conservation of National Environmental Quality Act does not actually empower the National Environmental Board to the extent that the board can administrate at its own discretion. Its role, therefore, is to provide information for and seek coordination from the government office. However, this obstacle has been taken into consideration by the Environmental Law Drafting Committee, and it is expected that a revision of the role of the National Environmental Board will be made so as to give it more authority.

Human beings suffer from many forms of pollution, mostly in the form of nuisances, such as the deafeningly loud noise of the traffic, exhaust fumes from automobile engines, airborne particles from industrial factories, and offensive smells from discharges and refuse. The fact that serious damage can be caused by poisonous chemicals, such as in the case of lead poisoning, is not generally realized by the public.

However, though remedies are not set forth in the laws on environmental conservation, the injured parties are entitled to compensation by virtue of the provisions specified in the law concerning "wrongful acts," but only if the party deemed to be committing such a wrongful act can be clearly identified. On the other hand, the offending party may not be identifiable or identification may be very uncertain. For example, if the river has been polluted by waste water discharged from many factories situated nearby, causing an epidemic of diarrhea to break out, it is a matter of speculation as to which factory the court case should be brought against. In such instances, the government should take the responsibility for making compensation. Up until now, the Thai government has never been sued for compensation as a result of environmental problems.

It is obvious that environmental problems are of a serious nature and the government should take the responsibility for them. Funds and time are required to resolve such problems as well as to prevent them. The Thai government is also in need of expertise to help in this matter.

The most significant point to be emphasized is that at present Thailand does not have specific environmental laws. Enactment is not an easy matter due to the fact that advances in science and technology affect the environment a great deal. Public acceptance of pollution also adversely affects the situation. Inefficiency in the enforcement of new laws could arise due to the lack of public knowledge and understanding.

III. The Trend of Future Environmental Laws

Since Thailand does not have any specific environmental laws, the majority of Thais have little awareness of environmental problems. This is probably due to the fact that Thailand is an agricultural country, consisting mainly of forest and vegetation. As agriculture alone would not improve the economy, Thailand has to bolster its economy through industrial development. Thus, industry has been expanding at an increasing rate every year. At the same time, the Thais have never before experienced environmental problems or appreciated the gravity of such problems. The treatment of factory discharges has not been considered a high priority because the Thai government always has many other immediate problems of a different nature to solve.

In 1961 it came to the attention of the government, thanks to the smog incident in England, that pollution is a very serious problem. This incident helped to draw the attention of the subsequent government to pollution problems, and it is to be hoped that this trend will continue in future administrations. Policies against pollution have indeed been set up by some previous administrations. These policies resulted in the 1975 environmental law (Improvement and Conservation of National Environmental Quality Act), which was discussed above. However, this act cannot be considered a specific environmental law. Morever, as pointed out earlier, there are approximately fifty acts and regulations which could be considered conservation laws. The authority for administering these laws is not vested in one office, but rather is spread over many offices, such as local municipalities, the Ministry of Industry, the Ministry of Public Health, and so on, which results in an overlap of responsibilities.

Consequently, it is obvious that Thailand is in need of a single government office dealing directly and solely with the control and protection of the environment. The most suitable office, and one which is already in existence, is that of the National Environmental Board established under the Improvement and Conservation of the National Environmental Quality Act. As things stood in the past, this Board was not empowered by the law to effect enforcement. In order to make this law more effective, it was amended and was proclaimed as a law on 31 December 1978.[7] This new amendment gives more authority to the Prime Minister in dealing with environmental problems.

However, there is still room for discussion as to the extent of the power which should be given to the National Environmental Board. If this board is vaguely empowered, it could impede industrial investment and find its authority still overlapping with that of other agencies. Furthermore, it would produce more red tape which would be an inevitable burden for business operators and also might lead to unfairness. The status accorded to the National Environmental Board needs to be carefully considered, and its power of enforcement might well be subject to the approval of the Council of Ministers, at least in certain cases.

As a sign that the Thai government is growing more concerned about pollution, the Environmental Law Drafting Committee was formed in 1977. This committee consists of many legal experts and is expected in the near future to draft specific environmental laws controlling the quality of air, water, noise, and other environmental concerns. It can be predicted that the pattern of such laws will be similar to those at present enforced in Japan. In this connection, Japan is a good example to follow since it has accomplished many phases of industrial and economic development as well as having encountered various environmental problems. Such being the case, the Thai participants at this conference are pleased to have this opportunity of exchanging technical opinions on various aspects of environmental problems and feel there will be general benefit to all participants in the interest of maintaining and improving the quality of the environment.

Notes

The authors wish to thank Chulalongkorn University for providing traveling funds to Ms. Mattaya Jarupan to attend the conference. Thanks to Dr. Colin R. Elliott of the Scientific English Division, Science Faculty, Chulalongkorn University, who kindly read the manuscript, and to Ms. Chamaiporn Premsoonthorn, the Institute of Environmental Research, Chulalongkorn University, for typing the manuscript.

1. Chaiyoth Chavalithikul, "The lead village," *Journal of Thailand Industrial Hygiene* 8(2):17–20 (in Thai).
2. The Institute of Environmental Research, Chulalongkorn University, "Case study of lead poisoning," Bangkok, 1977 (in Thai with English abstract).
3. P. Menasweta and G. Wattnakorn, "An investigation on lead in the environment of the village that used battery jar residues for filling up the land," Seminar Proceeding No. 2, Pollution Problems of Heavy Metal in the Environment in Thailand, 1978, 165–75 (in Thai with English abstract).
4. Wasana Sornmanee, "Preliminary study on the intellectual development of the children who lived on the road overlaid with the old battery casing, Bangkru, Samut Prakarn," Seminar Proceeding No. 2, Pollution Problems of Heavy Metal in the Environment in Thailand, 1978, 248–49 (in Thai with English abstract).
5. *New York Times*, 5 June 1977.
6. *Bangkok Post*, 30 August 1977.
7. 95 Government Gazette (Part 156) 1 (1978).

Water Pollution in Indonesia from the Aspect of Industrial Development

R. Tjang Mushadji Sutamihardja

Recently in Indonesia, environmental problems and environment pollution, especially water pollution, have become alarming as a result of the rapid increase in population and economic development during the First Five-Year Development Plan (1969/70–1973/74) and the Second Five-Year Development Plan (1974/75–1978/79), compared with development in the years before. Pollution will increase during the Third Five-Year Development Plan (1979–1984). The present views on Indonesian environmental pollution are quite diverse. One group of scientists claims that Indonesia now is still free from environmental pollution so it is not necessary to worry. Another group feels that pollution is a consequence of the increase in economic development achieved by a developing country such as Indonesia, while a third group suggests that the environmental problem should be tackled seriously as soon as possible.

The economic development basically should be examined from the phenomena of urbanization, industrial product development, increase in agricultural achievement and yield, transportation and infrastructure, and many others, in increasing the society's per capita income. Within this context there is an increasing demand for land, water, energy, and other resources which exceed presently available resources, with consequences of increasing quantities of waste and effluent which could cause environmental hazards and deterioration. Such phenomena have occurred in many places and regions in Indonesia.

This presentation will mainly focus on and discuss the impact of industrial development on our water system and exclude the problems of air and soil pollution.

I. Indonesia's Industrial Development

In accordance with the Outline of the Basic Guidance of State, one of the targets of the long-term development plan is how to change the fundamental structure of Indonesian economics. The goal is to have a greater proportion of the national product outside the agricultural sector, and on the other hand, to increase the number of people who are independent of the agricultural sector.

To achieve such long-term targets, and to make industry the backbone of economic development, a stepwise approach to development of the industrial sector is expected. In the First Five-Year Development Plan priority was given to industrial development which supported the agricultural sector, and during the Second Five-Year Development Plan was focused on industries which convert raw materials into half-finished products. The Third Five-Year Development Plan emphasizes an increase in manufacturing, such as light and heavy industries. By such stepwise development, it is hoped that in the long-term plan structural equilibrium can be achieved by focusing on industrial strength supported by a stable agricultural sector.

Industrial development in Indonesia has achieved enough promising results, especially during the implementation of the First Five-Year Development Plan, which is already finished, and during the Second Five-Year Development Plan ending in 1978/1979. Quantitatively, economic development is expected to increase 7.5 percent per year, comprising the agriculture sector, 4.6 percent; industry, 13 percent; mining, 10 percent; construction, 9.2 percent; transportation, 10 percent; and other sectors, 7.7 percent. From the figures presented, the industrial sector is expected to have more potential for increasing Indonesian economic development than the other sectors.

A forecast of industrial development during the Second Five-Year Development Plan, showing the breakdown by various industries, is given in Table 1.

To accelerate such industrial development, aside from domestic sources, the Indonesian government has invited outside investors to invest capital in Indonesia. This could be accommodated by the Indonesian government through the Foreign Investment Capital Law and the Domestic Investment Capital Law enacted in 1966 and 1967, respectively, which year by year since their promulgation have fast increased achievement.

According to data from the Department of Industry, during the Second Five-Year Development Plan, in the year 1977, throughout Indonesia foreign and domestic investment totaled 2,327 projects: 1,843

Table 1. Development Growth Rate of Main Industries, 1974/75–1978/79

	Rate increase/year (%)
Light industry	10.4
Textiles	12.0
Leather	53.1
Wood processing	18.2
Paper	38.0
Chemicals & pharmaceuticals	23.4
Rubber processing	8.1
Nonmetal mining	21.1
Metals	24.1
Manufacturing	30.0

Source: Second Five-Year Development Plan 1974/75–1978/79, Industrial Sector.

projects for the domestic capital investment and 484 projects for foreign capital investment. Almost 82.9 percent of these projects are concentrated in the island of Java, with percentages as follows: West Java 31.1 percent, Jakarta area 19.5 percent, East Java 16.5 percent, and Central Java 7 percent. In comparison, in 1976 almost 72.1 percent were concentrated in Java.

The size of Java (including Madura) is only 6.7 percent of the total Indonesia area, but Java's population in 1978 was projected to be 89 million, compared with the total population of Indonesia of nearly 142 million. This means that 62.7 percent of the total population live and are concentrated in Java, and as mentioned before, about 80 percent of industrial projects are also concentrated in Java. So it is not surprising that though the effects of population problems and the stress of industrial development are found everywhere, they are especially evident in the island of Java, with respect to water, soil, air, and human settlements as well as socioeconomic problems.

There is a dilemma: on one hand economic development is necessary, but on the other hand the environmental side effects are creating some problems.

II. Pollution Cases in Indonesia

Water pollution cases have occurred in several places in Indonesia, e.g., water pollution by textile industries in Bandung, West Java, damage to paddy fields caused by oil drilling in the Indramayu area (West Java), damage to catfish in pond cultures by petrochemical industrial wastes in East Java, damage to fishes in Kapuas River by insecticide accidents from wood products and processing in West Kalimantan.

Water pollution also occurred in 1975, 1976, and 1977 during the dry season in Surabaya River, East Java, mainly caused by industrial and domestic wastes. In 1977 the municipal water supply of Surabaya was suspended for several days because the water quality had deteriorated. In the Semarang area (Tugu district), in August 1978, 40 hectares of paddy fields and hundreds of hectares of milkfish pond culture were damaged by chemical industrial waste producing calcium citric acid.

1. Case Study: Surabaya River Pollution

During the dry seasons of 1975, 1976, and 1977, serious water pollution occurred in the Surabaya River three times.

The main causes of the Surabaya water pollution could be described as follows: 1. The low water flow during the dry season. During the dry season, the water flow of the Surabaya River in Mojokerto was only 40 m^3/s. This water is used for irrigation in the Brantas Delta, for industries, and other purposes, and upon entering the Surabaya River the flow became only $\pm$ 7 m^3/s. It is no wonder that the pollutants were very dense during that time.

2. Industrial waste. On the basis of the survey conducted on the industries which lie along the Brantas River, and especially those along the Surabaya River, it was found that a few industries had inadequate waste treatment plants, and practically all the remaining industries discharged their effluents directly into the river stream without any waste treatment at all.

Along the Brantas and Surabaya rivers, there are many industries, such as those concerned with sugar refining, sodium glutamate, alcohol, pesticides, textiles, paper, metal, leather, and chemicals. These industries discharge their effluents directly into the river. The industries are located in the upper part of the stream, and in the lower part is located the municipal water supply plant. It was the lower part of the river which was polluted, and where the fish were killed or poisoned during the serious pollution accidents in 1975, 1976, and 1977.

3. Industrial location. The industrial location lies on the upper part of the Surabaya River, and its water is supplied from the Surabaya River. On the other hand, the Surabaya River is also still used by the people for domestic purposes, and technically this is an unsuitable location for industry. Also, there is a limited water flow (7 m^3/s) during the dry season, and this amount must be divided between the industrial

supply and the municipal water supply. As for the municipal water supply share, the water coming from the upper part of the Surabaya River, which has been polluted by untreated industrial wastes, could be damaged or deteriorate as a water resource. Further industrial development in such a location should be carefully considered because of the burden placed on the river by industry and the resulting interference with self-purification of the river itself.

The Biochemical Oxygen Demand (BOD) level increased in Perning after receiving a high load of pollutants from the Marmoyo River due to discharge from the sugar refining industry. After passing the Legundi area in which there are many industries near Driorejo and Sepanjang, the BOD levels increased again.

The levels of Dissolved Oxygen (DO) along the river indicated a decrease because of the high BOD levels. Even our investigation during the rainy season (in December 1977) in many parts of the Surabaya River in Surabaya indicated that its DO levels were very low, almost all below 2 (see Table 2).

Table 2. Levels of Dissolved Oxygen in Surabaya River (December 1977)

	Dissolved oxygen level (ppm)
Kepanjaran	5.77
Perning	6.59
Jrebeng	1.65
Karangpilang	1.34
Gunungsari	1.30
Sonokarimun	0.41
Jalan Mustajab	1.84
Jalan Kapasan Jepun	0.62
Dana Karya	1.63

Source: Water Quality Studies Team, Center of Natural Resources Management and Environmental Studies, Bogor Agricultural University, 1978.

The resulting level of ammonia content was increased compared with the normal levels.

The effects of the water pollution could be reported as follows: Since the pollution in the upper part of the Surabaya River could damage the fishes, it could decrease the income of the fishermen. Since the raw water supply was damaged by the pollutants, the moderate water supply treatment was not enough, resulting in a lowering of the water quality as to odor, color, and taste. Further treatment of the water by the Surabaya municipal water supply would be very costly and could also increase the cost of water to the consumer. Other effects, such as toxicological or ecological effects, are still unknown because of insufficient data.

2. Other Water Pollution Cases

By carefully studying some cases of water pollution in other parts of Indonesia, such as in the JABOTABEK area (Jakarta, Bogor, Tanggerang and Bekasi), Ciliwung and Cisadane rivers, Garang River in Semarang, Cikapundung River in Bandung, and Musi River in Palembang, the causes of water pollution can be explained as follows:

(1) uncontrolled industrial development without considering proper land use planning;
(2) rapid urbanization, resulting in change of the original city plan;
(3) lack of proper waste treatment;
(4) increase and diversification of industrial development;
(5) insufficient supply of municipal water;
(6) lack of consciousness by industry that industrial wastes can have hazardous effects on biological organisms (acute and chronic effects);
(7) different capacities for self-purification of each river;
(8) seasonal pattern, low water flow during the dry season, and erosion;
(9) lack of serious measurement action (sectoral or integrated), and lack of integrated coordination;
(10) weakness in law and law enforcement.

III. Necessity for Anti-Pollution Programs

Since industrial activities can decrease the environmental quality or create environmental pollution, measures should be taken as follows:

(1) establishment of suitable industrial locations or an industrial zone, and relocation of unsuitable industries on a long-term basis;
(2) proper industrial management, including suitable production methods, conservation of chemicals and water, reuse and recycling of chemicals or used water, elimination of pollutants to the least amount possible; proper waste treatment plants, and proper drainage of liquid waste;
(3) consideration of human settlement around the industrial location, by supplying enough safe water, and by protecting the

ground water from infiltration by industrial pollutants or waste;

(4) in the long run, consideration of the total amount of industrial waste water in an industrial zone, and the cost of operational techniques.

Since there is wide utilization of water resources in Indonesia for domestic uses (washing, bathing, and drinking), irrigation, fisheries, industry, recreation, navigation, and transportation, research programs on water standards should be conducted from now on. It is necessary to start research on the present status of water quality in Indonesia regarding surface water (rivers, lakes, dams) and ground water, which are consumed widely and intensively in the urban areas.

Some standards have been officially promulgated by the central government or by local governments, e.g. Regulation by Minister of Health (No. 01/BIRHUKMAS/I/1975) in 1975 for drinking water quality requirements and supervision. This was expanded by the Regulation by Minister of Health (No. 173/Men.Kes/Per/VIII/77) regarding the supervision of stream water according to its use in relation to health aspects.

In 1971 the local government of Jakarta set up a regulation (Regulation No. 12, 1971) on the prevention of pollution of the air, water, and coast in the Jakarta area, followed by another regulation (Regulation No. 382, 1977) forcing industry to check its industrial waste. Still another regulation was made by the Jakarta governor (No. 484 in 1977) regarding water quality criteria for streams in accordance with their respective uses. In early 1978 the Department of Industry issued a decree signed by the Minister of Industry (No. 12/M/SK/I/1978) for prevention and measures on environmental pollution caused by industrial activities, but so far there have been no concrete results.

From Indonesia's point of view it is not enough to adopt foreign countries' standards, or even WHO standards, since the condition in Indonesia itself may be different and the standards unsuitable. It is necessary that our institutions collect data intensively and create models which are suitable to the local conditions.

Environmental management strategy should be created, and it is time for the enactment of Indonesia's environmental laws since we feel that the existing regulations are very weak. Measurement action by a sectoral/ departmental approach is necessary, but it would be more beneficial if it were strengthened by an integrated approach.

In 1978 a state minister of Development Supervision and Environment was created. The results of a seminar on environmental development under the supervision of the minister, which was conducted in

Jakarta in June 1978, and which discussed environmental aspects and problems in Indonesia, could be used as a basic strategy for creating a better environmental condition in Indonesia.

IV. Conclusion

Economic development by industrialization is absolutely necessary, but we realize that such side effects as industrial waste or industrial pollution should be considered. Prevention is more valuable than to cure the environmental hazard or damages.

Environmental law and governmental regulations for industry to install waste treatment plants are necessary, since only a few industries are equipped with waste treatment plants.

By careful studies on the spread and diversification of industries, prediction of the possibility of environmental deterioration should be made, and measurements should be established. Since industrial spreading in Indonesia is most concentrated in Java and around big cities, attention should be given to such places.

The number and type of industries and natural self-purification are different among regions in Indonesia, so measurement actions should also be different. It is therefore necessary to take inventory of all the environmental qualities concerned.

By considering all of the aspects, environmental pollution could be minimized in order to achieve environmental protection.

Bibliography

Chanlet, E. T. *Environmental Protection*, McGraw-Hill Series in Water Resources and Environmental Engineering (New York: McGraw-Hill 1973).

Lund, H. F. *Industrial Pollution Handbook* (New York: McGraw-Hill, 1971).

Ministry of Public Works and Electric Power (Indonesia). "The Development of Water Resources in Indonesia," March 1976.

Ministry of Public Works and Electric Power (Indonesia). Directorate General of Water Resources, Water Pollution Control Effort. *Water Pollution Supervision and Water Quality Management* (*Special Report*), April 1978.

Ministry of Public Works and Power (Indonesia), Sir M. MacDonald & Partners and Directorate General of Water Resources Development. *Brantas Pollution Study*, July 1978.

Ministry of Public Works and Power (Indonesia), Sir M MacDonald & Partners and Directorate General of Water Resources Development. *Lower Brantas Pollution Study*, September 1977.

Ouano, E. A. R., B. N. Lohani, and N. C. Thanh, eds. "Water Pollution Control in Developing Countries," *Proceedings of the International Conference on Water Pollution Control in Developing Countries*, Bangkok, 21–25 February 1978.

Simpson, M. "Water Quality Management System Design and Implementation:

Lecture Notes Pre-Conference Short Course," International Conference on Water Pollution Control in Developing Countries, Bangkok, 19–21 February 1978.
Sutamihardja, R. T. M. "Water Quality Management Program for the Third Five-Year Development Plan," Support Paper on National Environmental Development Seminar, Jakarta, 5–6 June 1978.

Japan

Japanese Environmental Policy and Law

Akio Morishima

Japan has a long history of environmental pollution beginning with its industrialization in the late nineteenth century. As early as 1877, Osaka issued an ordinance in order to regulate polluting factories. In 1895 a copper-smelting plant moved from a coastal area to a small isolated island for no other reason than to avoid polluting neighboring farmland. However, during the wars and after World War II, priority was put first on industrial production in order to continue fighting, and later to restore the economy, which had been destroyed by the wars. Industry, and the government as well, did not pay any serious attention to the effect of industrial pollution. Beaches were reclaimed and farmlands were changed into industrial sites. Factories were built next to residential areas. During the 1960s the country recorded an increase in the growth rate of the gross national product in excess of 10 percent each year. However, by the end of the 1960s Japan had become the most polluted country in the world.

The Organization for Economic Co-operation and Development (OECD) Secretariat's report on Japanese environmental policies, which was submitted to the OECD conference for a country survey held in 1976, pointed out that five major factors had aggravated the effects of pollution: (1) economic indicators, such as industrial production, energy consumption, and the number of automobiles, are high compared to world levels; (2) production growth rates have been extremely high in Japan (for example, the production of plastics increased ten times between 1960 and 1970); (3) economic activities concentrate in relatively small areas, consequently industrial output per square kilometer of inhabitable area in Japan is more than twenty times as much as in the United States and nearly eight times that in the United Kingdon; (4)

public investments in social overhead had been small in Japan; and (5) the economic growth-oriented social attitudes and values in Japan resulted in the neglect of competing goals, such as environmental protection.

These factors caused serious pollution. Water pollution and air pollution resulted in health injuries. The existence of patients with a peculiar bone ailment was reported by a local doctor in 1955. The patients cried "Itai-itai" (ouch-ouch) because of severe pains. The cause of the disease was identified later as cadmium discharged from a mine. The next year victims of mercury poisoning were found in Minamata in Kyushu, a southern area of Japan. The mercury was discharged into Minamata Bay by a chemical factory. It had accumulated in the bay for a long period and was taken into human bodies through eating fish. Despite this sad experience, victims of the same disease were again found in 1965, nine years after the Minamata incident, in Niigata Prefecture in northern Japan. Many patients having respiratory diseases due to air pollution were found in Yokkaichi after a huge chemical industry complex was completed in the area.

I. Action by National Government

The government was slow in establishing policies for the prevention of pollution. However, when health injuries caused by industrial pollution became a serious social and political problem, the government was forced to take countermeasures against pollution. In other words, establishment of Japanese environmental policies dates from the beginning of actual occurrence of injury to victims due to pollution. This was a very serious, immediate, and realistic problem; it was the starting point. But legislators and administrators usually took measures on a case-by-case basis, mainly from the standpoint of the prevention of health injuries. Thus, the environmental policy has not been comprehensive and has been developed sporadically. For example, in the case of air pollution, much effort was exerted for the control of sulfur oxides, considered to be the cause of bronchitis and asthma in Yokkaichi and other industrial areas, and not much consideration was paid to visibility and other factors. In water pollution, the toxic substances, such as mercury, were the central focus of endeavors, and indices, such as Biochemical Oxygen Demand (BOD) and Chemical Oxygen Demand (COD), which do not have direct relevance to health injuries, were not the subject of great concern. In this context, the Japanese environmental policy and legislation can be said to be created only after damages actually occur.

In 1967, the Basic Law for Environmental Pollution Control was enacted. As a matter of fact, however, it was established because many resident groups objected to the construction of large-scale chemical complexes since they were afraid of the occurrence of pollution. They developed major citizen movements against pollution and were very successful. As a result, the government feared that unless it took comprehensive measures, industrial sites might become very difficult to find in the future. This was the real motivation for the Basic Law. Therefore, it can be said that the environmental regulations in Japan have been stringent in the fields where problems actually occurred and, on the other hand, environmental concerns have not been integrated into industrial development plans under a comprehensive pollution control plan. It is only recently that the conservation of nature has become a part of environmental policy. The main target of the Japanese environmental policy has been the prevention of health injuries. As the OECD report pointed out, as far as that objective is concerned, the Japanese environmental policy has been very effective. However, ours has not been a comprehensive system including land use control. And at the present stage, the idea of integrating environmental concerns into development plans has not actually institutionally materialized.

II. Action by Local Governments

Another feature to be considered is the role of local governments in the development of Japanese environmental policy. In Japan, under the traditional legal system, the national central government has strong controlling power over local governments. Japanese constitutional law provides that local governments, that is prefectures, cities, and other municipalities, can enact ordinances within the scope or authorization of national law. The Local Autonomy Law prescribes the power of local government under the assumption that the central government has a preemptive power over local governments. Local government officials are considered subordinate to the national government, except in the case where they implement inherent tasks for local people. However, with the inception of the environmental problem, the traditional legal system has been through a great change. When the local governments were faced with serious pollution problems, they found that the national regulations were far from being sufficient. In some areas where the national government enacted regulations, they felt that those regulations were too lenient.

Therefore, even at the risk of jeopardizing the traditional legal system, the local governments had to enact pollution control regulations. Among residents of local municipalities, there were many victims, one after another, and complaints became numerous. And in local election campaigns, pollution problems became an important issue. Thus, the local government officials responsible had to tackle pollution problems as a matter of realistic politics, despite some difficulties in the legal system. They justified their actions for pollution regulation by saying that it was the primary and inherent obligation of the local government to exert its authority in order to preserve the safety and health of the residents. They tried to avoid as much as possible direct confrontation with the national government, but frequently they took very stringent attitudes on pollution control. Concerning that general tendency, at the beginning the central government asserted that such local autonomous ordinances were illegal in relation to the national law. However, they now succumb to forces of public opinion and actually recognize such ordinances. Furthermore, the Air Pollution Control Act and Water Pollution Control Act were revised to expand widely the rights and authority on the part of local governments to enact environmental ordinances and to enforce pollution control. The Local Autonomy Law itself was revised and now recognizes that pollution control and environmental preservation are within the scope of the inherent authority of local government.

The total emission control of sulfur dioxide is an example. This system was first applied to Yokkaichi by Mie Prefecture, and the central government employed it later in the Air Pollution Control Act. Thus, in environmental policy, the local governments are leading the central government both in legislation and administration, and this has had a very great impact upon the national legal system.

III. Administrative Compensation Law

The third feature of Japanese environmental law is the fact that the strict tort liablity of industry for personal injuries caused by air or water pollution, and an administrative compensation system for these injuries, are incorporated in the pollution law. The Compensation Act for the Victims of Pollution-Related Health Injury is the first administrative compensation scheme in the world. Under the act, victims of specific pollution-related diseases in designated areas may receive medical care, living allowances, and some other expenses, if they are certified by local governments as the victims of pollution. All expenses except some of those for administration of the scheme are incurred by the polluting industry. This scheme might be considered a kind of charge system, but it is a system for allocation of costs compensating for damages which occurred in the past. It may, however, have the effect of preventing pollution, since expenses are allocated every year to each factory on the basis of the amount of pollutants discharged during the previous year.

IV. Procedural Problems

1. Role of the Public

In addition to the above-mentioned aspects of substantive environmental law, other procedural problems can be pointed out. With regard to public participation in decision making, the environmental impact assessment procedure has not been institutionalized in Japan. None of the environmental legislation prescribes that the public can be involved in the environmental decision-making process. At the background of this feature there lies a tradition of the superiority of governmental administration. Japanese bureaucracy has a long tradition of recruiting capable young university graduates and bureaucrats as experts in policy making and administration. They have maintained superior power over private enterprise and the public. They believe that none of the others can make effective and fair judgments to protect national interests. They are confident that, even though they may negotiate with industry and members of parliament, they ultimately represent the public interest. From their viewpoint, therefore, public participation brings in unnecessary confusion, which in turn results in distortion of decision making.

After World War II democratization of the administrative process took place, and the notion of the superiority of the governmental administration has somewhat changed. Public hearings, however, are held only in extremely limited cases in a rather formalistic way. Advisory councils or committees are expected to reflect opinions of the public, but in fact they are led by the bureaucrats. After all, the public has no formal access to the governmental decision-making process nor to information which governmental agencies have. Japan does not have such legislation as the U.S. Freedom of Information Act. Such an administrative process may be accepted so long as the public trusts the government. However, when industrial pollution has become serious as a result of the governmental policy where priority was placed on industrial development, and when the delay of governmental reactions against pollution has made the situation worse, the public has lost confidence in the government and now insists on keeping watch over the administrative process and participating in it. Despite the change in public attitudes toward the governmental administration, the bureaucrats are still hostile to public participation in the administrative process. Being deprived of the institutionalized channel to reflect their own opinions, the public often resorts to such direct but not necessarily reasonable means as demonstrations, sit-ins, or violence.

It is often said that in Japan decisions are formed on the basis of consensus among parties. While the consensus method, in which negotiations are repeatedly carried out and an agreement is gradually formed as a result of negotiations, still exists between the government and industry, it no longer exists between the government and the public. More accurately, from the beginning the public has not participated in the policy decision-making process and, therefore, has not been a party to an agreement. At the present time a new way to achieve consensus between the public and the government or industry is being sought, but the Japanese legal system has not yet solved this question. The U.S. experience, particularly under the National Environmental Policy Act (NEPA), may provide valuable examples for Japan.

In Japan the notion of due process has not been well established except in the field of criminal procedure. But the importance of the concept of due process is to be recognized in the present day when value judgments vary among people. When value systems conflict, it is most important to respect opinions of the minority group through due process, and the opposing party should respect the results attained through due process. The traditional consensus method can be applied only to a society where mutual reliance exists. Present-day Japan is somewhat similar to to the United States where a variety of values coexist. The legal system should be reformulated to cope with changes in society.

2. Limitation in Administrative Litigation

The next feature of the procedural problem is limitation in the administrative litigation. Before the war, administrative power superseded that of other branches, and the judicial court had no authority to review administrative decisions. That system changed after World War II and, in theory, all administrative decisions can be reviewed by the court under the new Administrative Litigation Act. However, in practice, the court has avoided intervening in the administrative power. For example, the court has interpreted very narrowly with regard to problems of standing to sue, ripeness to sue, and illegality of administrative decision.

Governmental administration still maintains wide discretionary power, and the public is prevented from checking the government through administrative litigation. The reason that in Japan private law suits, such as negligence tort suits and nuisance-type injunctions, have been much utilized to protect the environment is that there are various restrictions in the administrative litigation. While the attitudes of the court have gradually changed recently, the court is still not so free as the U.S. court. To improve the environmental legal system in Japan it is vitally necessary for the court to review freely administrative actions.

V. Enforcement

Enforcement of the law is the last feature to be mentioned. By and large, Japanese statutes prescribe rather simple and general provisions and leave details to governmental regulations. The role of law is not to confine administrative power to the framework set forth by the legislator but rather to give authority to the administration with wide discretion. The government often takes administrative measures without any specific legal authorization. This type of executing administrative power is called "administrative guidance." It is implemented by administrative agencies by persuading industry to follow their directions. Readers may recall the traditionally superior power of the government over industry. If a private corporation does not comply with the administrative guidance of an agency, it will be treated unfavorably by it in the future, explicitly or implicitly; on the other hand, so long as industry follows guidance the government will take care of it.

In environmental administration this form of administrative guidance has been fully utilized. Even though no law requires industry to control pollution, the government may exert administrative guidance to regulate industry if it seems necessary. On the other hand, even though the law prescribes punishments for noncompliance with legal regulations, the administration seldom indicts violators. Instead the administration gives technological suggestions for meeting regulations and even subsidizes or makes financial arrangements to install control devices. The administration believes that industry will cooperate more easily with it in prevention of pollution by administrative guidance than by punishments. Local governments as well have made full use of administrative guidance. By using this measure they can avoid direct confrontation with the national government when they regulate industry more stringently than the national law requires. They have covered the shortcomings of the national environmental laws through administrative guidance by relying upon public support for environmental preservation. Industry has so far followed stringent guidances more than national laws. It has seldom filed a lawsuit against a local government on the ground that the latter violated the constitutional law. This is because public opinion against pollution which caused injuries to humans has been so strong that industry is afraid of having a bad reputation in a commutity resulting from the lawsuit. It is also because industry has been able to absorb the costs of pollution control during its stage of high economic growth. However, enforcing environmental regulations in this way may be dangerous. Administrative guidance may easily fail to enforce without legal grounds if it loses public support. For example, the public may be interested more in unemployment than in the quality of the environment.

VI. Conclusion

Japanese environmental law and policy is now at a turning point: from the first stage, where prevention of human injuries caused by pollution is a matter of most serious concern, to the second stage, where amenity of life is also an important factor for policy consideration. On the other hand, low or zero economic growth may prevent enormous investments in pollution control. Policy considerations will not be so simple as in the previous stage. The legal framework must be comprehensive to meet complex needs. To attain a new type of consensus, public participation in policy formulation must be incorporated into the environmental legal system. These tasks are not easy to achieve, but in order to survive to the twenty-first century we must find solutions.

Recent Tendencies and Problems of Court Cases on Environmental Protection in Japan

Nobuo Kumamoto

There have been many court cases on public nuisance (hereinafter referred to as *kōgai*) problems in Japan since the Osaka Alkali case in 1961.[1] The four *kōgai* cases—Itai-itai disease,[2] Niigata Minamata disease,[3] Yokkaichi Asthma,[4] and Kumamoto Minamata disease[5]—are major examples of these cases. These *kōgai* cases are fundamentally different from cases on environmental protection; the latter are the cases for protecting our environment or surroundings before damages or injuries occur, and for enjoining a cause of actions against pollution. These types of court cases are seen not only in civil injunctive suits but in administrative suits.

On the other hand, the *kōgai* cases, such as the four major *kōgai* suits mentioned above, are the ones in which compensation after injury has occurred is sought. There are also civil suits which were brought to court based on tort laws. These *kōgai* compensation suits expanded new theories on cause-effect relationship, fault, limitation of endurance, and joint tort action. These suits also had an important role in giving legal remedy to *kōgai* victims. This type of court case is, however, a suit brought after injury has occurred, and does not help recover the lost lives or the lost fresh air or water, even though the plaintiffs might win.

In order to improve such a situation, theories of "From *kōgai* to protecting the environment" or "From compensation to injunctive suit" have been widely advocated and supported. This conversion of view has been realized in the legal field as "From *kōgai* compensation suit to environmental protection suit." Furthermore, a suit for protecting the right to enjoy good surroundings has been recognized as more and more important than before. The report submitted herein deals with this type of legal suit for environmental protection rather than *kōgai* suits.

Kōgai compensation suits and environmental protection suits have different objectives in courts. In the *kōgai* compensation suits, it is argued in court that air pollution, water pollution, noise problems, vibration, ground subsidence, offensive odors, in addition to the blocking of sunshine or scenic views occur over a considerable area as the result of industrial or other human activities. In environmental protection suits, the arguments also include natural resources, such as forests, seas, good scenery, beautiful spots, or cultural assets, in addition to the items stated above. At this point, we shall turn our attention to the recent tendency and problems of legal cases on environmental protection in Japan.

The main difference between *kōgai* suits and environmental protection suits is that plaintiffs in a *kōgai* suit mainly seek compensation for injuries resulting from the defendant's activities, while plaintiffs in environmental protection suits seek injunctive actions against such activities of the defendant. In other words, plaintiffs in environmental protection suits expect to enjoin any kind of activity which may cause harmful results to the plaintiffs. In order to bring such a suit to court, plaintiffs face several difficulties, which will be pointed out in the following sections.

I. Civil Injunctive Suit

We have two types of legal suits: a civil injunctive suit and a legal suit in administrative law. Although there are injunctive suits and suits seeking compensation in civil law, we shall first discuss a civil injunctive suit. Generally speaking, an injunctive suit has a preventive effect for protecting the environment, whereas a suit for compensation is usually brought to court after an injury has been done by polluters. It mainly aims to give remedy or compensation to the injured person. In such an injunctive suit, standing to sue, cause-effect relation, illegality, reason for injunction, and so forth will be the points to be discussed here. Among them, the problem of illegality is considered by far the most important one, for almost all of the court cases deal with this type of problem.

1. Standing to Sue

In contrast to an administrative case suit, there are few cases on standing to sue in civil litigation because the problem of standing to sue in civil litigation appears in relation to a claim of the case itself. In other words, the sphere of interest of plaintiffs who apply for an injunctive suit is generally limited by a regional standard.

For example, competence for application for an injunctive suit for a temporary decision to prohibit construction of a building was decided on the basis of a regional limitation. This was also the basis for decision in cases seeking the prohibition of construction of a sanitary center,[6] a crematory,[7] a pipe line settlement,[8] and a dumping reclamation center.[9] The most important problem in these cases is how we decide the sphere of the limitation itself. We may say in general a polluted area or an affected area.[10] Then we may modify it case by case. For instance, we have examples such as 1.5 kilometers in the sanitary center case, 500–600 meters in the crematory construction case, or 5,500 meters in the pipe line settlement case. The reclamation center case may suggest to us the settlement of a temporary regional limitation, when the court decides a temporary disposal. The court admitted 443 plaintiffs within about 1,200 meters from the spot where the center was to be constructed.

Standing is admitted not only to individuals but to groups.[11]

2. Illegality

Illegality is one of the main problems in an injunctive suit and a temporary disposal suit, while fault is a principal issue in a compensation suit. It is said that, generally speaking, an injured party can seek an injunctive claim against an offender where there is a probability that he may injure the victim beyond the limitation of endurance, if the cause-effect relationship is admitted. This limitation of endurance theory has been cited in many cases seeking not only an injunction but compensation. The limitation of endurance sometimes reflects the degree of illegality. This limitation, however, is merely a general, abstract expression of legal standards which are applied to decide the illegality of a defendant's activities. Problems in this situation, therefore, should be analyzed as to what kinds of concrete elements are to be the basis for deciding a polluter's responsibility. The focus of discussion should be on the degree of his responsibility to submit proof to the courts. The comparison of interests should also be considered.

In other words, a general conception of the limitation of endurance itself is substantially a flexible, relative, and compound conception which consists of various elements—procedural, regulative, or substantial. Therefore, anyone who wants to determine the illegality of injunctive suits should know the contents of these elements and conceptions.

In this paper we cannot examine all of these cases to analyze these elements and conceptions. Therefore, we shall consider one example, through which we may see how a court in Japan examines fundamental elements for admitting an injunctive suit.

One typical example, the construction of the sanitary center in a town, shows us these elements to be considered in admitting an injunctive suit, as follows:[12]

(1) probability of the character and degree of interests which will be be infringed;
(2) standards set in public laws to regulate discharges;
(3) degree of consideration of the opinions stated by people at the hearing who will suffer from the construction;
(4) extent of exchange of opinions with the people on the disposition for compensation and monitoring system for pollution;
(5) degree of thoroughness of efforts to find the best alternative site for the construction;
(6) substantial planning and consideration for finding the best pollution-preventive facilities;
(7) social value and character of publicity about the facilities;
(8) degree and character of injuries to the defendant by admitting an injunction; and
(9) financial responsibility and investigative ability of the defendant.

From these elements examined in this court, we may say that the court has paid much attention to procedural problems, such as in items (3) hearing of residents. (4) exchange of opinions, (5) responsibility for finding the best alternative site, or (6) responsibility for substantial planning of the best pollution-preventive facilities. From this case, we can say that procedural processes have been widely considered and evaluated by the court. This indicates the future tendency of the examining process in a court.

Thus, when a court decides a limitation of endurance problem, the following elements have also been reviewed by the courts in many other cases:

(1) character and degree of infringed interest;
(2) standards settled by public laws;
(3) loss by defendant of an injunctive suit;
(4) character of publicity;
(5) responsibility of making assessment;
(6) examination of alternative planning; and
(7) opinions of residents who live near the construction site.

We can say again that procedural elements have been considered extremely important. Thus we can also say that a court has reviewed such procedural elements in deciding a limitation of endurance case.

II. Administrative Cases

1. Role of Administrative Litigation

Another type of legal case relates to administrative litigation, which has been brought by residents who live around the site of a facility or construction, or by interested groups who support them. A person who wants to contest an administrative decision should ask for legal relief under provisions of the Administrative Litigation Act of 1962, which was originally drafted in 1947. The Act provides four types of litigation:

(1) a suit contesting an administrative decision;
(2) a suit between parties provided by law;
(3) a suit between administrative functions; and
(4) a suit raised by citizens (Populace suit) (Art. 2).

Among these suits, a suit contesting an administrative decision (hereinafter called a contesting suit) and a suit raised by citizens (hereinafter called a popular suit) have actually been used and will take an important role in the future.

These types of litigation have some disadvantages over civil procedures for litigation, such as an exclusion of temporary disposition (Art. 44), restrictive suspension of execution (Art. 25), or a short term for bringing litigation (Art. 14). But they also have some advantages, not only of making interested persons, in a broad sense, directly contest administrative action at a comparatively early stage, or seek administrative responsibility, but also of giving a general effect or influence to a judgment of revocation or a judgment of executive suspension.

In a real function of these litigations, however, it seems that they do not yet function well enough to give a legal remedy to people of a region who seek *kōgai* prevention and environmental protection.

2. Administrative Decision as Objects of Litigation

We now examine a contesting litigation as a legal injunction for protecting environments. First of all, the sphere of administrative decision should be discussed here before analyzing the meanings of contesting litigation and an appeal for executive suspension. Courts in Japan take it in a comparatively narrow sense; sometimes they interpret it more rigidly. Namely, an object of "Litigation for revocation" or "Torikeshi-Soshō" (Art. 3, 2, 3), "Confirmative litigation for nullification" or "Mukō Kakunin-Soshō" (Art. 3, 4), and "Suspension of execution" or "Shikkō Teishi" (Art. 25) is "an action which was considered as an administrative decision or some other action which was done by a public authority" (Art. 3, 2). Corresponding to it, a temporary disposition which was provided in the Civil Procedure Code (Art. 44) is denied for an administrative decision. Having excluded some public facilities which make *kōgai* or destroy our good environment from the objects of administrative action, the courts have a tendency to deny a protesting litigation or an appeal for suspension of execution.

3. Examples of Objects of Administrative Decision

We have several types of court cases on administrative decision relating to *kōgai* or environmental protection, such as those relating to dumping disposal,[13] a pedestrian bridge,[14] highway construction,[15] airport management,[16] and reclamation.[17] The courts admitted some of these cases as objects of administrative decision and denied others. Even having carefully read these cases, we face the difficulty of setting uniform standards for making administrative dispositions legally admitted enough to be brought to court. Thus far, we must say that it should be decided case by case.

In these cases, we expect to find some uniform standards for admitting them as administrative dispositions. If a case is admitted as an administrative disposition, people may bring it to court to contest its character; in other words, if it falls within the sphere of administrative disposition in connection with legal requirements for a legal suit. Traditionally, standards for judgment of administrative disposition by the courts rely on whether it forms directly the legal duty of a citizen by an exercise of the power of public authority, or whether it is legally allowed to limit its legal sphere.

From this standpoint, we may say that if we apply such standards to cases before the courts, all of the "managing power in an act of the administrative agency" is taken away from the legal interests which should be protected by the courts. Thus far the sphere of selection by the citizen for seeking legal remedies will be narrowed.

4. Administrative Action in Formal Meaning

Considering such a tendency, we may take note of a recent theory on admitting objects for a protesting suit or a suspension of execution about administrative actions, which have factual controlling power, as having been seen as administrative disposition. It is called an administrative action in formal meaning.[18] We find such a theory in the pedestrian bridge case as "it is administrative action by an administrative agency, and moreover it relates more widely to the daily life of the the people around the site."[19] It is a flexible interpretation of the court, which demonstrates exactly an administrative action in formal meaning.

This problem focuses on what kind of actions by an administrative agency should be taken to court to provide a legal remedy for citizens under the procedures of the Administrative Litigation Act. We may say, from this point of view, that a conception of administrative action has been merely adopted by a court conveniently or in legal terminology in order to determine its meaning. In other words, it is required to find an interpretation for properly fixing the purpose. Thus, we may say that it is supported to admit the theory in an administrative action in formal meaning.[20]

5. Examples of Administrative Action in Formal Meaning

As stated above, the theory of administrative action in formal meaning helps a person who wants to bring an action against administrative decisions which may do him substantial injuries or damages. Though these administrative decisons do not form any legal rights or give any influence to legal duties of citizens, we may admit a legal right to the person who wishes to bring a case to court, because such administrative actions are considered administrative dispositions.

For example, the Tokyo district court flexibly interpreted an action taken by the Tokyo Metropolitan Bureau relating to the construction of an over-street pedestrian bridge in Kunitachi City as "an administrative action by an administrative agency which closely and broadly relates to the daily life of residents in the city."[21] This is a perfect example of administrative action in formal meaning. On this point, an opposite interpretation was made by a high court. The opinion of the court denied its character of administrative disposition because it belongs to an action *de facto* but not to legal action.[22] Though we have two types of court cases on the character of administrative disposition in this example, the theory of administrative action in formal meaning helps us to bring a case to court based on this theory.

Another example relates to construction of a highway, which was decided as an administrative action because the decision was made by an agency based on a city plan and several statutes concerning highways.[23] A tentative decision sought by a plaintiff was denied in this case because it was an administrative action. (Article 44 of the Administrative Litigation Act denies a tentative decision to an administrative action.) The same opinion was adopted in a case concerning the reclamation of Lake Biwa.[24] As to the character of administrative disposition, there are cases relating to airport construction and reclamation. There is no objection as to the character of administrative disposition of providing facilities for an airport and its management. Courts in these airport cases clearly denied an application seeking a tentative decision brought by a plaintiff.[25]

As to a license of reclamation which was given by a local governor, courts decided it as an administrative action, arising from a privilege based on the Public Surface Water Reclamation Act of 1921.[26] Therefore, it was considered an object of appeal litigation[27] or a suit for a suspension of execution.[28] The reason that courts have taken the cases cited above as administrative actions stems, in my opinion, from the fact that the intention of the courts is to extend the opportunities to bring cases to court. In other words, whether or not a plaintiff may bring a case of appeal litigation or a suit for suspension of execution depends, with relation to legal elements, upon whether or not it is considered as an administrative action. Standards of decisions on this point taken by a court are to be whether or not it forms rights or duties of citizens by the execution of administrative power, or whether or not it is admitted by law to define the sphere of its limitation.

Courts in Japan, however, have not been so severely or rigidly bound by the above standards. Their posture is flexible enough to extend the standing to sue to a citizen whose rights might be invaded by an administrative decision *de facto* or by a substantial execution of public power. They have been, in this logical extension, wrapping up the decision with the words "administrative action in formal meaning." From this standpoint, we may say that the theory of administrative action in formal meaning has given citizens more opportunities to seek a remedy in court.

6. Ripeness for Review

We have discussed the limitation for sphere of administrative action based on court cases. This is a matter of crossing the sphere of the problem of administrative action. We must, however, see the vertical side of the sphere of this problem, too. Namely, it is a matter of the proper time to bring a case to court. We may simply say, the sooner the better, to prevent any kind of damages or invasion by administrative decision. Courts in Japan adopted the idea of ripeness of issue for review from the Anglo-American legal system.[29] The first case relating to this notion appeared in 1966 concerning a land readjustment plan.[30] Several precedents of this concept show a rather rigid attitude, which analyzed a case as to whether or not it was ripened or concrete enough. These precedents suggest that we consider a case as to how it is ripened, but not as to whether it is ripened or not.

The main problem of ripeness for bringing a case to court relates to the original planning of a project. The reasoning of a court which denies the ripeness of a case for review usually points out that the original planning itself does not harm any right or interest of a person whose property or interest will be affected by the project. When a court admits the ripeness, it is generally a step of extending the process of the project, where a right or interest of a person may be concretely infringed upon or invaded by an action of the executive function.[31]

Examples of this interpretation of the courts are as follows. In a case where a project for the construction of an industrial zone and a new harbor was argued at court, the opinion of the court rejected a plaintiff's statement. The court said, "The project before this court is not clear enough to recognize what kind of entrepreneurs are to be invited. Moreover, as far as this court acknowledged above, no harm or invasion to plaintiffs beyond the limitation of endurance is admitted, because the occurrence of *kōgai* is merely presumable, but not reliable according to the contents of the project itself."[32] A similar attitude of interpretation of a lower court appeared in the Narita Shinkansen line case, where twelve plaintiffs sought revocation of a license given by the government to construct the line.[33] The plaintiffs argued this case based on the reason that when the Shinkansen was in operation, noise, vibration, smoke, dust, interference with sound waves, wind damage, blocking out of sunshine, and so forth, would occur. The court, however, rejected this argument of the plaintiffs, stating that at the time the license for executive planning of the construction was given, the ripeness had not matured enough in this case, because no concrete sphere of interested persons under this planning would be defined. In other words, even though the location of the rails was indicated on a map with a one-millimeter wide line, the court stated that if the line were actually drawn on the ground it would be a 200-meter wide zone, which does not indicate clearly where an actual line would be located. The high court sustained this opinion.[34]

Opportunity for judicial review in these two cases was denied in this way. We may presume that the courts expected to make a clear distinction between a concrete invasion of citizens' rights and mere planning. Surely without any concrete indication of damage to a plaintiff by an administrative decision, no one can bring a case to court. Later, however, even if the plaintiff brings a case to court, he often loses it for the reason that most of the planning process has been completed, and that therefore no order should be issued to revoke the decision.[35]

One of the recent cases, however, shows us a more flexible consideration relating to the ripeness. Plaintiffs in this case sought revocation of a governor's decision to change a residential area to a quasi-industrial area under a new town plan.[36] The court, accepting the plaintiff's argument, stated that the indication in this case was to regulate a certain area where plaintiffs would suffer from it, though such an indication itself is usually a general disposition to the public. This flexible interpretation of the court, however, was revoked at the second instance, by reasoning that the object of a revocation suit is limited to an invasion or regulation of a concrete legal right of a certain person by an administrative disposition. This court, relying upon a traditional theory on standing, concluded its opinion by saying, "the indication of zoning area of the city planning act is not a disposition to a certain person, but a mere decision of a certain purpose for a certain area. This does not directly effect any concrete change to a resident by it, though it imposes a legal regulation to an owner of land and houses within the area."

7. Legal Interest

In addition to the problem of ripeness for review, a matter of legal interest as a standard for standing to sue should be discussed here. Though this standard had been considered in a rather narrow sense, which required an invasion of legal rights, cases occurring since the adoption of the Administrative Litigation Act in 1962 had denied it and showed an "interest legally protected."[37] This "from right to interest" flow is a reflection of tort law, where we can see the "from invasion to right to illegality" flow.

Recent cases in courts under the Administrative Litigation Act seem rather to proceed by admitting a tendency toward "all interests which should be protected in suits."[38] Cases relating to environmental protection, however, still seem to take an old-fashioned attitude in admitting the new tendency on standing stated above.

Relating to the protection of a group of giant Japanese cedars (estimated to be 5,000 years old), a court required a concrete invasion of a plaintiff's interest rather than a general interest of protection for such natural monuments.[39] Moreover, in a case where protection of Seto Inland Sea water was sought, a court rejected a plaintiff's argument, saying "such an interest stated by the plaintiff does not directly relate to his concrete interest . . . and he does not show enough interest to claim its illegality."[40] The plaintiff in this case expected to enjoin construction of a nuclear power plant along the coast of the sea, stating that if it were constructed and an accident occurred, the sea water would be polluted by radioactivity and would no longer be recoverable for our culture and economics.

Another example of denying a plaintiff's standing relates to his interest in protecting special scenery by the Cultural Property Protection Act. The plaintiff in this case brought a suit to revoke permission given by the Cultural Property Protection Commission, which allowed the building of a dam for an electric power plant. The interest or right which the plaintiff expected to protect was his right to appreciate the special beauty which would be protected by the act. The court, however, denied it, reasoning that the designation of special beauty by the act did not give any legal right or interest to anyone else and that it gave a mere "reflecting interest" to him.[41]

The above cases show us a certain tendency of opinions of courts concerning legal interest for standing in protecting the environment. Some courts, however, gradually indicate a direction toward admitting another legal interest. In a case for protecting the scenic beauty of a town, standing for application to enjoin the execution of a decision was admitted, though the merit of the case itself was denied.[42] The high court, however, denied the scenic beauty of the town as a legal interest of the plaintiff, because maintaining a healthy living environment for a person varied depending upon time and place. In my opinion, the court refrained from setting standards for the scenic beauty of the town.

The interest of a person who should be protected from any kind of invasion of his rights beyond limitation of endurance relating to his living environment has been affirmed as a legal interest by the first instance of the pedestrian bridge case.[43] Another affirmative example for legal interest relates to the construction of a bowling center which was to be located in a residential area, stating that the interest of those living around the center, which should be protected through proper operation of architectural regulations, was not a mere "reflecting interest *de facto*" but an interest which should be protected by law.[44]

New progress in this area appeared in 1975. As to the living interest of a citizen in a town, a court clearly took it as a legal interest, which should be protected by a court based on the living right of Article 25 of the Constitution when it is invaded by an action of administrative power.[45] The court, denying the defendant (the governor), declared its philosophical background that citizens who should be protected by a court, based on Article 25 of the Constitution, were invaded by the governor's action beyond their limitation of endurance.

Another important development in legal interest relates to the problem of protecting life, body, property, or safety for living from accidents or casualty. A high court admitted the legal interests of residents around a proposed nuclear reactor site because their rights or interests might be indirectly invaded by an administrative action taken by the local government for a private company which intended to build the reactor.[46] A similar opinion was adopted by a court which admitted legal interest to citizens who alleged revocation of permission to a private sector which intended to construct a nuclear reactor.[47]

In these two cases, the citizens living around an intended power plant were given standing to sue though their rights or interests were not directly invaded. The courts only required that they live there, stating it was experimentally clear that rights of residents around the reactor would be infringed on if the reactor were not reliable enough and an accident occurred. The interest of beneficiaries of a forest reserve was also admitted as legal interest under the Forest Act, when they argued against intended construction of a military base, because the construction would force a certain part of the forest to be cut down, affecting the residents substantially for the worse in regard to their water supply or in case of flood.[48] The appeal court, however, limited legal interest to those plaintiffs who would be directly affected.[49]

8. Illegality

At the final stage of standing to sue, a survey for illegality should be introduced. We may clearly recognize two patterns of illegality in environmental protection suits: illegality as to the violation of established procedure, and illegality as to the process of exercise of discretional power.

The lower court dealing with the reactor construction revoked an administrative decision, for a procedure provided in the Building Standard Act was ignored. In this case, the defendant, a local examination board on construction, had dismissed an appeal by the plaintiffs, residents around the intended construction site of the reactor, who alleged that the construction permit was illegal because there was no oral examination. They claimed that the act was intended to check the construction of the building itself but not of settling the reactor in it, and that the plaintiffs were asking for safety of the reactor, which was not covered by regulations of the act.

We can say without doubt that no one can separate any danger of the construction of a building from the settlement of the reactor in it. Though there is a provision relating to the revocation of permission of the settlement of a reactor in the Act Regulating Atomic Energy Materials, Fuel, and Reactors, and though Article 70 of the act allows a citizen to raise a suit separately, this does not provide any excuse to deny the revocation suit for permission to construct the building.

As to the procedure in the act stated above, several problems have been raised in Japan.

Article 23 of the act requires a constructor to obtain permission and to hear an opinion from the Atomic Power Commission, which was settled by Article 14 (II) of the Act to Establish an Atomic Energy Commission. The commission then is to order a survey on safety of the nuclear reactor by the Atomic Power Safety Technical Examining Board, which consists of scientists. The commission, after having received the result of the survey from the board, is to send its affirmed opinion on the matter before it to the defendant.

Plaintiffs in this case raised the points concerning procedures stated above. The court, however, rejected all of the points raised. The main points of the statements by the plaintiffs are summarized as follows: Because of an extremely dangerous problem, an administrative agency should be required, according to Article 31 of the Constitution and the purport of the fundamental law, to obtain the consent of residents who live around the reactor, to make available to them all of the materials concerning its safety, to have a public hearing on it, and to provide notification of the hearing to them, even though there are no special concrete provisions which require the above items. This argument fundamentally relates to the acceptance of due process of law in Japan.[50] The court naturally denied the plaintiffs' argument, saying that the procedures which the plaintiffs requested were not required in the procedure of the law, and that therefore they were left to the discretional power of the administrative function.[51]

On the illegality of the discretional decision used by the administrative function, it is left to the executive function because it belongs to a conception of discretion, when laws provide an equivocal, inclusive conception such as "proper" or "reasonable" in order to define the elements of administrative decision. In such a case, a court should refrain from making its own decision in replacing the decision by the administrative function.

The process of discretional decision by an administrative function, however, has been an object of judicial examination. Courts have revoked an agency's decision because of its illegality on discretional decision, when the object is improper, or when the elements which should not be essentially considered were included in it. It is the case when Article 30 of the Administrative Litigation Act provides "abuse of discretional decision" as the reason for revocation of a disposition.[52] The problem, however, is what the concrete standards are for a decision of illegality.

Court cases relating to this point show a variety of reasons, which indicate several elements affecting the conclusions, such as direct or indirect damages to the sufferers, pollution of water and air by the operation of factories to be constructed on the reclaimed land, or the favorable effect of the productive activity of the factories.[53]

Another case which denied a plaintiff's statement on illegality counted several reasons which relate to it, such as a defendant's obligation for a survey on the character and extent of the effects on fishery, contents of the *kōgai* prevention agreement among concerned parties, and situations of the scenery and environment around the location for reclamation, which was not considered as a special place to be protected.[54]

From the conclusions of these cases, we may admit that courts have intended to find more detailed and precise elements which might affect the illegality done by the administrative function.

III. Conclusions

This short survey on the recent tendencies and problems of court cases on environmental protection in Japan indicates several important aspects of arguments in courts. Some other problems in law remain to be introduced at another opportunity, such as constructions and elements of illegality in environmental protection suits, analysis of difficult damages to be recovered, causation links between a disposition and a result in administrative litigations, and others. The following are, however, to be pointed out as conclusions of this survey.

Not only in the civil injunctive suits but also in the administrative cases, we may recognize that courts tried to find procedural, regulative, or substantial elements in detail which affect conclusions of these suits or cases.

The courts which we have examined have quite prudently but affirmatively given their attention to the procedural elements adopted by a defendant's side (mostly the side of an administrative function). The courts, however, prudently and not so affirmatively show a refraining from examination through a substantial part of the cases; the problems such as why an administrative function promotes an intention or why the function permits construction of such a facility have been left aside.

This substantial part is surely left to the decision-making function of the three separated powers. We should, needless to say, admit that governments (including local ones) have a kind of duty to promote welfare administration for the people. This is the reason that the judicial function of the three powers has prudently refrained from using its power except in examining the procedural process. This is a matter of the limitation of the judicial function. The function, however, has affirmatively used its power to examine the procedural process which was done by its counterpart function in detail and with precision. In this meaning, we say that the social role of the judicial branch has been, is, and will be expected to protect our good surroundings.[55]

Notes

1. Taishin'in (Supreme Court under the Imperial Constitution), Taishō 5 (1916).12. 22, 22 *Minroku* 2474 (1916).
2. Toyama District Court, Shōwa 46 (1971).6.30, 22 *Kasai Minshū Bessatsu* 1 (No. 5.6) (1971); Nagoya High Court, Kanazawa Branch, Shōwa 47 (1972).8.9, 674 *Hanrei Jihō* 25 (1971).
3. Niigata District Court, Shōwa 46 (1971). 9.29, 22 *Kasai Minshū Bessatsu* 1 (No. 5.6).
4. Tsu District Court, Yokkaichi Branch, Shōwa 47 (1972).7.24, 23 *Kasai Minshū Bessatsu* 1 (No. 7) (1972).
5. Kumamoto District Court, Shōwa 48 (1973).3.20, 696 *Hanrei Jihō* 15 (1973).
6. Hiroshima Kankyō Eisei Center Case, Hiroshima District Court, Shōwa 46 (1971).5.20, 22 *Kasai Minshū* 640 (No. 5–6) (1971).
7. Izumi Kasō-jō Case, Osaka District Court, Kishiwada Branch, Shōwa 47 (1972). 4.1, 663 *Hanrei Jihō* 80 (1972).
8. Chiba Pipe Line Case, Chiba District Court, Shōwa 47 (1972).7.31, 676 *Hanrei Jihō* 4 (1972).
9. Chiba Gomi Umetate Shorijō Case, Chiba District Court, Shōwa 51 (1976).8.31, 836 *Hanrei Jihō* 18 (1976).
10. This means a region which has the probability of being polluted or affected. Nomura Yoshihiro, "Gendai no Shakai Mondai to Hō," [Contemporary social problems and the law] in 51 *Gendai Hōgaku Zenshū* [Modern Law Series] (Tokyo: Chikuma Shobō, 1978), p. 24.
11. Nagoya Toshi Gas, Gas Holder Case, Nagoya District Court, Shōwa 52 (1977). 6.17, 867 *Hanrei Jihō* 19 (1977).
12. Hiroshima District Court, Shōwa 46 (1971).5.20, 22 *Kasai Minshū* 640 (No. 5.6) (1971); Hiroshima High Court, Shōwa 48 (1973).2.14, 693 *Hanrei Jihō* 28 (1973).
13. Tokyo District Court, Shōwa 36 (1961).2.23, 12 *Gyōsai Reishū* 27 (No. 2) (1964). Tokyo High Court, Shōwa 36 (1961).12.14, 12 *Gyōsai Reishū* 2575 (No. 2); Supreme Court, Shōwa 39 (1964).10.29, 18 *Minshū* 1809 (No. 8) (1964).
14. Tokyo High Court, Shōwa 49 (1974).4.30, 743 *Hanrei Jihō* 32 (1974).
15. Kobe District Court, Amagasaki Branch, Shōwa 48 (1973).5. 11, 702 *Hanrei Jihō* 19 (1973).
16. Niigata District Court, Shōwa 48 (1973).8.4, 297 *Hanrei Times* 204 (1973).
17. Tsu District Court, Shōwa 44 (1969). 9.18, 601 *Hanrei Jihō* 81 (1969).
18. Kaneko Masashi, "Gyōsei Soshō Hō" [Administrative Litigation Act] in *Gyōsei Tetsuzuki–Gyōsei Soshō Hō* [Administrative Procedure–Administrative Litigation Act] (Tokyo: Chikuma Shobō, 1973), p. 276.

19. Tokyo District Court, Shōwa 45 (1970).10.14, 21 *Gyōsai Reishū* 1187 (No. 10) (1970).
20. Nomura Yoshihiro, "Kankyō Mondai" [Environmental Problems] in 51 *Gendai Hōgaku Zenshū* 115.
21. Kunitachi Hodō Kyō Case, Tokyo District Court, Shōwa 45 (1970).10.14, 21 *Gyōsai Reishū* 1187 (No. 10) (1970).
22. Kunitachi Hodō Kyō Case, Tokyo High Court, Shōwa 49 (1974).4.30, 743 *Hanrei Jihō* 32 (1974).
23. Hanshin Kōsoku Dōrō Case, Kobe District Court, Amagasaki Branch, Shōwa 48 (1973).5.11, 702 *Hanrei Jihō* 19 (1973).
24. Biwako Umetate Case, Ōtsu District Court, Shōwa 40 (1965).9.22, 16 *Gyōsai Reishū* 1557 (No. 9) (1965).
25. Niigata Kūkō Case, Niigata District Court, Shōwa 48 (1973).8.4, 297 *Hanrei Times* 204 (1973); Osaka Kūkō Case, Osaka District Court, Shōwa 49 (1974). 2.27, 729 *Hanrei Jihō* 4 (1974); Osaka High Court, Shōwa 50 (1975).11.27, 797 *Hanrei Jihō* 37 (1975).
26. Toba Wan Umetate Case, Tsu District Court, Shōwa 44 (1969).9.18, 601 *Hanrei Jihō* 81 (1969).
27. Usuki Wan Umetate Case, Ōita District Court, Shōwa 46 (1971).7.20, 265 *Hanrei Times* 105 (1971); Fukuoka High Court, Shōwa 48 (1973).10.19, 300 *Hanrei Times* 154 (1973).
28. Ibid. 265 *Hanrei Times* 109 (1971); 300 *Hanrei Times* 170 (1973).
29. Louis L. Jaffe and Nathaniel L. Nathanson, *Administrative Law: Cases and Materials* (Boston: Little, Brown, 1963), p. 290.
30. Shōwa 41 (1966).2.23, 20 *Minshū* 271 (No. 2) (1966).
31. Ibid., p. 271.
32. Fukui Konbināto Case, Nagoya High Court, Kanazawa Branch, Shōwa 47 (1972).4.14, 4 *Kankyō Hakai* 39 (No. 3) (1972).
33. Tokyo District Court, Shōwa 47 (1972).12.23, 691 *Hanrei Jihō* 8 (1973).
34. Tokyo High Court, Shōwa 48 (1973).10.24, 722 *Hanrei Jihō* 52 (1973).
35. Article 31 of the Administrative Litigation Act provides that even if an administrative decision is illegal, the court may turn down a demand when the revocation of the decision does not conform to the public welfare, taking into consideration the degree of damage to be incurred by a plaintiff, the indemnification of damage on the degree and method of prevention and all other conditions.
36. Tokyo High Court, Shōwa 53 (1978).4.11 (1978).
37. Article 9 of the act provided that "legal interest with respect to seeking the revocation of said disposition or decision" which includes "persons having legal interest still to be recovered by the revocation of disposition or decision even after the effect of the disposition or decision has ceased due to the elapse of the period thereof or any other person."
38. Harada Naohiko, *Uttae no Rieki* [Interest for bringing a suit] (Tokyo: Kōbundō, 1973), pp. 8–9.
39. Nikkō Tarō Sugi Case, Utsunomiya District Court, Shōwa 44 (1969). 4.9, 20 *Gyōsai Reishū* 373 (No. 4) (1969). Tokyo High Court, Shōwa 48 (1973).7.13, 710 *Hanrei Jihō* 23 (1973).
40. Ikata Genshiryoku Hatsudensho Case, Matsuyama District Court, Shōwa 53 (1978).4.25 [A case for revocation of permission for the construction of a nuclear power plant]; Matsuyama District Court (Decision), Shōwa 53 (1978).4.25, [A case for suspension of permission for the plant], 49 *Hanrei Jihō* 891 (1978).
41. Sandan Kyō Case, Tokyo District Court, Shōwa 30 (1955).10.14, *Gyōsai Reishū* 2370 (No. 10) (1955).
42. Kunitachi Hodō Kyō Case, Tokyo District Court (Decision), Shōwa 45 (1970). 10.14, 21 *Gyōsai Reishū* 1187 (No. 10) (1970).
43. Tokyo District Court, Shōwa 48 (1973).5.31, 24 *Gyōsai Reishū* 471 (No. 4, 5) (1973).

44. Tokyo District Court, Shōwa 48 (1973).11.6, 737 *Hanrei Jihō* 26 (1974).
45. Utsunomiya District Court, Shōwa 50 (1975).10.14, 796 *Hanrei Jihō* 32 (1976).
46. Mitsubishi Genshiryoku Case, Tokyo High Court, Shōwa 47 (1972).9.27, 23 *Gyōsai Reishū* 729 (No. 8, 9) (1972).
47. Ikata Genshiryoku Case, Takamatsu High Court (Decision), Shōwa 50 (1975). 7.17, 325 *Hanrei Times* 161 (1975); Matsuyama District Court (Decision), Shōwa 50 (1975).5.24, 786 *Hanrei Times* 3 (1975).
48. Naganuma Naiki Kichi Case, Sapporo District Court (Decision), Shōwa 44 (1969).8.22, 565 *Hanrei Jihō* 24 (1969); Shōwa 48 (1973).9.7, 712 *Hanrei Jihō* 25 (1973).
49. Sapporo High Court, Shōwa 51 (1976).8.5, 27 *Gyōsai Reishū* 1175 (No. 8) (1976).
50. Kumamoto Nobuo, *Gyōsei Tetsuzuki no Kadai* [Problems of administrative procedure] (Sapporo: Hokkaido University Press, 1975), p. 135.
51. Article 31 of the Constitution of Japan has a provision similar to Amendment V to the Constitution of the United States of America, which provides *due process of law*, while Article 31 states *procedure established by law*. This requires government officials in Japan to adopt the procedure provided in the laws concerned. Substantially, therefore, this invites a negative attitude of the officials to interpret it without consideration of *due process of law*.
52. Article 30 provides "With respect to a discretionary disposition of an administrative agency, the court may, insofar as it has gone beyond the purview of its discretional right or it has abused its right, revoke such disposition."
53. Usuki Wan Umetate Case, Ōita District Court, Shōwa 46 (1971).7.20, 22 *Gyōsai Reishū* 1186 (No. 7) (1971).
54. Funka Wan Umetate Case, Sapporo District Court, Shōwa 51 (1976).7.29, 22 *Shōmu Geppō* 1991 (No. 8) (1976).
55. Much of this paper was suggested to the author by Nomura Yoshihiro's article, "Kankyō Mondai."

Summary Procedures for the Settlement of Pollution Cases

Shōzō Kondō

I. Alternatives to Judicial Proceedings

It is needless to say that the judicial courts play very important parts in the formation of the environmental law with their decisions on the pollution litigation cases. The decisions of the four big *kōgai* litigation cases (Itai-itai, Niigata Minamata, Yokkaichi Asthma, and Kumamoto Minamata; see preceding Nobuo Kumamoto paper), for example, have made essential contributions to the development of our anti-pollution legal system. Our courts are deemed by the people to be the ultimate relief when they suffer damages from environmental pollution as well as in other kinds of tort cases.

However, the judicial relief depends on such a process as is suitable to resolve an individual conflict where both parties contest at law on an equal footing. It takes much time and money to obtain justice within the judicial process.

These characteristics of the judicial proceedings do not always make it possible to provide redresses for the social conflicts caused by environmental pollution. A great number of victims may be involved. They are in general resourceless, while the polluter happens to be a giant industrial entity or a large-scale public project. The substances which cause the damages may not be scientifically proved. The chain of causation may be uncertain. Often those responsible for the damages cannot be identified easily. We need nevertheless to stop as soon as possible the proliferation of the miserable consequences of pollution, and to find some settlement for social conflicts caused by it.

On the other hand, Japanese people tend to be reluctant to have their disputes settled by the law courts. They rather prefer an agreed settlement. This attitude results from their sociopsychological nature, which is worth observing for itself, but we are not concerned with this problem here.

Thus, since early times, the persons who have some influence in the local community have been invited to use their good offices for the settlement of disputes caused by the environmental disruption in their region. Those persons were often the mayor, prefectural governor, or other persons related to the public administration, according to the social conflicts in question. This is hardly a source of wonder in such an administration-oriented society as ours. Indeed, it was the governor of Tochigi Prefecture who had tried to act as an intermediary between the polluter company and the victim farmers in the Ashio Copper Mine case of 1891. To cite a more recent case, the victims of the Minamata disease had once tried to satisfy themselves with the mediation provided by the administrative officials, though they decided afterward to bring actions against the polluter company.

II. Establishment of the Administrative Procedures

When our national anti-pollution law system emerged in the late 1950s and 1960s, the laws relating to water and air pollution introduced procedures for the settlement of pollution disputes in which administrative committees are engaged to encourage the parties to compromise. This kind of non-judicial settlement procedure had been set up for Ashio mine damage disputes and other cases for a long time; thus it was more easily accepted for the pollution disputes.

The Basic Law for Environmental Pollution Control of 1967, which establishes our anti-pollution policy, has obliged our government to take the necessary steps to establish a system for the summary settlement of pollution disputes (Sec. 21). Under this Basic Law, the government should promote preventive and curative countermeasures against environmental pollution. The settlement of the pollution disputes depends on the curative measures, which consist of prompt reduction of the increasing damages, restoration of the original situation, prompt relief for the victims, and so forth. The Compensation Act for the Victims of Pollution-Related Health Injury was enacted in 1974 to offer victims prompt and fair compensation by the administrative process. The rapid settlement of pollution disputes is another kind of relief that the Act for the Settlement of Pollution Disputes of 1970 should ensure for the profit of the victims.

This act of 1970, as amended in 1972, has three objectives:

(1) to set forth uniform procedures for the summary settlement of the disputes related to those kinds of pollution specified by the Basic Law—water, air, and others;
(2) to establish administrative collegial bodies—a kind of administrative tribunal—which are charged to handle these procedures; and
(3) to institutionalize the treatment of the pollution grievances by the local governments.

The pollution grievances presented by the local residents had been received and treated by local administrative officials as a part of their daily business for a long time. To formalize this voluntary procedure, the Law requires prefectural governments and municipalities of a certain size to have counsellors for the pollution grievances. This counselling system must be used to obtain the related information from the residents, to avoid the pollution disputes, and to improve the necessary countermeasures. With this system, the public authority touches the actual sensitiveness of the people regarding environmental quality.[1]

The administrative collegial bodies set up by the act of 1970 are the Environmental Dispute Coordination Commission on the national level and the Environmental Dispute Councils on the local level. The former consists of members nominated by the Prime Minister with consent of both Houses of the Diet. The members of the latter are nominated by the governor with consent of the prefectural assembly. These members are guaranteed independence in the exercise of their functions.

Their functions are to settle disputes by means of reconciliation, mediation, or arbitration between the parties involved in the pollution. Concerning these procedures of agreed settlement, the central commission handles in general only the serious and wide-ranging cases, while the other cases are handled by each local council of the prefecture in which the pollution takes place. As for the central commission, it also has exclusive jurisdiction to adjudge the pollution cases. To accomplish these functions, both the central commission and the local councils nominate a committee for this purpose from among their own members.

The reconciliation procedure aims to encourage the parties to engage in the negotiation and to facilitate a compromise based on mutual concession. In the mediation procedure, the committee proposes a mediation plan to be accepted by the parties. To draft this plan, the committee hears the parties, and orders them to propound their documents and other materials related to the case. It is also empowered to visit the factory, construction site, or other places concerning the case. These investigations may be made ex officio by the committee. To play a more active role in the mediation proceeding, the committee is allowed to determine the deadline for the parties to accept the plan proposed by it, and even to publish this plan with its reasoning. If neither of the parties refuses explicitly to accept this plan within the time limit, they are considered by the law to have implicitly agreed to the solution formulated in the mediation plan. This proceeding is expected to put pressure upon the parties, who are not indifferent to public opinion.

The proceedings of reconciliation and mediation are in general commenced upon the application of one of the parties. But the central commission and the local councils may engage *proprio motu* in the reconciliation, and also in the mediation afterward, in order to try to settle the cases in which the pollution causes extensive and remarkable damages and the dispute thereof seems not susceptible to early solution, inciting serious social troubles.

The arbitration procedure is governed by the application *mutatis mutandis* of the related provisions of the Civil Procedure Code. It should be added only that the arbitrating committee is empowered to make the same ex officio investigation as that of the mediation procedure indicated above.

Beside these agreed settlements common with the local councils, the central commission has the adjudicative jurisdiction to decide on the liability of the polluter upon the application of a victim as well as to declare the causation of the damages the victim of the pollution suffers. This procedure of adjudgment is a quasi-judicial one. The committee examines the case at the public session under the adversary principle, and renders its adjudgment according to its own convictions and findings, which may be formed with the facts, evidence, and arguments on law presented by the parties. An ex officio investigation may also be made by the adjudicative committee. When the case is ready to be decided, the commitee gives the adjudgment sought for by the applicant victim. This adjudgment contains the full reasoning in almost the same form as the final decision of our judicial court. We might say the Environmental Dispute Coordination Commission is a true "Pollution Tribunal."

It should be noted, however, that its adjudgment has an odd and peculiar effect. If the parties do not bring a lawsuit concerning the "adjudgment on the liability" in due course of time, they are considered by the law, as in the case of the mediation plan accepted, to have made an agreement of the same import as that of the adjudgment. This lawsuit will be the civil action for the compensation of the damages in the case of the victim-plaintiff. It will be the civil action for confirmation that no obligation of that compensation exists in the case of the polluter-plaintiff.

In these cases, the court will proceed to the *de novo* trial on the matters of fact and law. Thus, the committee's adjudgment has only a persuasive authority to the court and anyone else who may be concerned with it. This is particularly true for the "adjudgment on the causation." Proceedings of this type of adjudgment are commenced not only by the application of the victim or the polluter, but also by the adjudicative committee itself in the proceeding of the liability adjudgment. Moreover, it may be commissioned by the judicial court before which a civil litigation related to the pollution is pending.

Indeed, by the "adjudgment on the causation" the committee pronounces the expert opinion with regard to the factual chain of cause and effect involved in the environmental pollution damages. It is certain that this adjudgment is useful for settling the disputes in which the clarification of the causation is the key issue. But the adjudgment has only a persuasive effect. Whether or not the adjudgments of the committee have a moral authority of some importance remains to be seen. It might be interesting to ask now if the liability adjudgment can rely upon equity rather than the law. Such a possibility has already been discussed in the doctrine of arbitration judgment, which has an effect equivalent to the irrevocable final decision rendered by the judicial court according to the Civil Procedure Code. On the other hand, it is recommended to appeal to *bon sens* ("right reason") and equity rather than to the rigid law for the settlement of the dispute by means of reconciliation and mediation. Following our observation here, the effect of the liability adjudgment seems to have some similarity to the mediation project accepted by the parties. If the liability adjudgment is able to grant more flexible relief than the judicial decision can, it might help to establish and to consolidate its moral authority questioned above.

III. Operation of the Administrative Procedures

It has been seven years since our system was put into operation. In these years, 230 cases were filed to the central commission, 142 of which have been settled. The local councils received 162 cases, 137 of which have reached settlement. In other words, these bodies have all together registered 394 cases in their rolls and settled 279 cases during these seven years. Classification of the cases is given in Appendix A.

To observe some details of the handling of the disputes, let us examine the examples of the central commission.[2] (See also Appendix B.) It may be remarked that the mediation procedure is utilized to cope with the mass disputes in which from hundreds to about twenty-two thousand victims are involved and the largest amount of the claims is about 1.5 billion yen. As to the time elapsed until the settlement, it takes one or two years (about eighteen months on the average) to conclude the proceedings before the central commission. If we compare it with the judicial solution, which takes at least several years in the first instance for the mass pollution cases in Japan, we could safely say that the parties have their disputes settled in a relatively short lapse of time. In particular, the mediation of the Ashio Copper Mine case set at peace the central issue of the most difficult disputes which had been repeated for eighty years.

The flexible operation of the procedures and the active role of the commission should be much appreciated regarding the steady and rapid settling of the disputes. Adjudgments were demanded in three cases. Two of them were finally settled by mediation, the procedure having been changed. The commission has therefore adjudged only one case thus far. In this instance, a restaurant owner and his wife complained of noise, vibration, and land subsidence caused by the construction of a subway line in Tokyo. They claimed 23 million yen as compensation for the business loss and moral injury. The adjudicative committee took ex officio the documents and other materials as significant evidence. It also commissioned a research institute to carry out the related investigation. As a result of twenty-eight months' examination of the case, it admitted the compensation of 4.5 million yen for business loss and moral injury. The defendants have brought an action related to this adjudgment and the case is now pending before Tokyo District Court.

As for the costs of these administrative proceedings for the summary settlement, they impose fewer burdens upon the parties. Expenses for expertise and witnesses, travel fees of the commissioner and others, costs of summons and service, costs related to evidence produced under the committee's order—these expenditures are altogether charged to public funds. The stamp is exempted for the reconciliation procedure. The stamps necessary for the other procedures are much less expensive than those for the judicial civil action. Suppose someone claims 10 million yen before the district court. He must pay 54,000 yen for the stamps. If he chooses mediation by the committee, he has only to spend 6,000. When he seeks the adjudgment, he will have to pay 11,000 yen for the stamps.

To conclude this rapid observation, we should mention some problematic aspects of our summary settlement system for pollution disputes. As mentioned above, the principal items of the procedural fees are defrayed out of the public funds, namely the national and the local treasuries. These coffers are not, of course, inexhaustible. Whereas a special item of appropriation is assigned to the central commission in the national budget, the expenditures of the local councils might be mingled in the items assigned for the general anti-pollution measures in the local budgets. If financial strictures limit the activities of these bodies, especially their costly investigations, their moral authority, which relies upon the exact and trustworthy finding of fact related to the environmental pollution in question, might be irretrievably lost. Without such investigation, without sufficient appropriation to that effect, our summary settlement system would become an authoritarian intervention of the administration into social troubles. At the beginning of this observation, it was noted that our summary settlement system is established in order to grant relief for victims of pollution by way of rapid treatment of the disputes. But the adjudgment procedure might become an additional step to the ordinary course of the civil tort action, if the parties always refuse to accept its settlement, denying its authority.

On the contrary, if this authority is established firmly, it should be recommended to introduce the substantial evidence rules for the committee's finding and also to omit the instance of the district court in the litigation cases related to the committee's adjudgment on the liability. This reform would ensure considerable abridgment of the related civil proceeding. As for the agreed settlements, it must be insisted upon that their rapidity cannot justify departure from the justice the law court dispenses in similar cases. If the weak accept the rule of the stronger, the disputes can be settled with ease and promptness in agreed settlements. In this sense, the summary settlement procedures are not independent of the ordinary justice of the court.

Notes

1. *Kankyō Hakusho* [White Paper on the Environment] (Tokyo: Printing Bureau of the Ministry of Finance, 1978), p. 403. The Act for the Settlement of Pollution Disputes provides that prefectural governments and municipalities of more than 100,000 population must have counsellors for pollution grievances. The municipalities of less than 100,000 population may have them. It places upon them these duties: 1) to hear the pollution grievances presented by the residents, 2) to make investigations, directions and counselling necessary to resolve these grievances, and 3) to notify the related administrative authorities and to take other necessary measures to handle these grievances (Sec. 49). As may be seen from the following tabulation, the number of diverse grievances received by the counsellors has been slightly decreasing since 1973, having increased until 1972:

Year	Number of Grievances	Percent of Change
1970	63,433	—
1971	76,107	+20.0
1972	87,764	+15.0
1973	86,777	− 1.0
1974	79,015	− 9.0
1975	75,531	− 3.0
1976	70,033	− 8.5

2. Kuroda Naoyuki and Misumi Hisashi, "Kōgaitōchōsei-iinkai ni okeru kōgaifunsō shori jirei" [Cases treated by the Environmental Dispute Coordination Commission], 836 *Hanrei Jihō* 13 (1977). A compilation of the cases reported by these members of the office of the Environmental Dispute Coordination Commission is found in Appendix B.

Appendix A

Classification of Cases by Cause of Conflict and Settlement Procedure

	Reconciliation	Mediation	Arbitration	Adjudgment	Total
Air pollution	5	23(1)	2	1(1)	31(2)
Water pollution	6	208(193)	3(1)	1(1)	218(195)
Noise & Vibration	15	104(23)		4(4)	123(27)
Earth pollution	1	8(2)		1(1)	10(3)
Foul smell		8			8
Land subsidence		1		3(3)	4(3)
Total	27	352(219)	5(1)	10(10)	394(230)

( ) indicates cases settled by the central commission.
Source: *Kankyō Hakusho* [White Paper on the Environment] (Tokyo: Printing Bureau of the Ministry of Finance, 1978), p. 399.

Appendix B

The cases reported by members of the office of the Environmental Dispute Coordination Commission are compiled below.

Key to numbering of items: 1) Dates of application and settlement
2) Main cause
3) Applicant
4) Defendant
5) Claim
6) Main items of the settlement

Group I. Mediation case concerning the water pollution in Kagawa Prefecture
1) 11 October 1971–17 October 1972
2) Water pollution caused by liquid waste
3) 1,390 fishermen
4) Seventy paper and pulp companies
5) Compensation of 1 billion yen for the damages to the fishery, evacuation of the bottom sediment, 50 percent reduction of the productive operation until the implementation of the evacuation
6) Compensation of 113 million yen for applicants

Group II. Mediation case concerning Minamata disease in Kumamoto Prefecture
1) First application 24 November 1971–27 April 1973 and after
2) Water pollution by organic mercury
3) 773 applicants, 620 of which have been settled
4) One chemical industry company

5) Compensation for the material and mental damages
6) Consolation money per capita of 18 million, 17 million, or 16 million yen according to the degree of the illness, monthly allowance per capita of 60,000, 30,000, or 20,000 yen

Group III. Mediation case concerning Ashio Copper Mine in Tochigi Prefecture
1) March 1972–11 May 1974
2) Water and earth pollution by heavy metals
3) 971 farmers
4) Copper mining company
5) 3,877 million yen for the damages caused during 1952–1971
6) Compensation of 1,550 million yen for the applicants

Group IV. Mediation case concerning damages to the fishery at Tokuyama Bay in Yamaguchi Prefecture

Subgroup A.
1) 29 November 1973–2 June 1976
2) Water pollution by liquid waste
3) 234 fishermen
4) Soda industry company and other eleven companies on the east coast of the bay
5) Evacuation of the bottom sediment, abeyance of the water effluence by the factories until the construction of the public sewage treatment facility, compensation of 1,007 million yen for the damages to the fishery
6) Compensation of 200 million yen for the damages to the fishery

Subgroup B.
1) 9 April 1975–24 August 1976
2) Same as A
3) 377 fishermen
4) Soda industry company and nine other companies on the west coast of the bay
5) Evacuation of the bottom sediment, abeyance of the water effluence by the factories until the construction of the public sewage treatment facility, compensation of 1,114 million yen for the damages to the fishery
6) Compensation of 214 million yen.

Group V. Mediation case concerning Osaka Airport
1) First application 15 February 1973–October 1975 partial settlement
2) Noise pollution by aircraft
3) 20,138 residents
4) National government
5) Abolition of Osaka Airport, noise abatement until that abolition, consolation money per capita of 500,000 yen, monthly allowance of 10,000 yen until that abolition (the last item is claimed by almost 66 percent of applicants)
6) Implementation of the noise abatement measures which are the accomplishment of the plan concerning the aircraft-noise environmental standard, improvement of machines and aviation practice, arrangement of the operation of the airport, adjustment of the related land use, betterment of the related public facilities, reconsideration of the designated area for the noise countermeasures; items concerning the abolition of the airport and the noise abatement are still pending

Group VI. Arbitration case concerning subterranean water pollution in Fukuoka Prefecture
1) 4 December 1975–26 April 1976
2) Pollution of a well by train cleaning water waste
3) One resident
4) National Railways Corporation
5) Compensation of 54 million yen for health damage
6) Rejection of the claim

Group VII. Adjudgment case concerning earth pollution in Nagano Prefecture
1) 20 September 1974–12 May 1976 (changed ex officio into mediation procedure)
2) Water and earth pollution by liquid waste containing cadmium
3) 445 farmers
4) Optical glass company
5) Compensation of 81 million yen for the damages to the agriculture
6) Payment of 21 million yen by the company to the applicants

Group VIII. Adjudgment case concerning air pollution in Saitama Prefecture
1) 27 June 1975–11 June 1976, changed ex officio into mediation procedure
2) Air pollution
3) Chemical industry company
4) Forty-eight residents
5) Clarification of the causation of the damages to health and agriculture attributed by the defendant residents to the applicant
6) Payment of 2.5 million yen by the applicant to the residents

Group IX. Adjudgment case concerning noise pollution and other environmental problems in Tokyo Metropolis
1) 5 August 1974–29 November 1976
2) Noise, vibration, and land subsidence caused by the construction of a subway line
3) Two residents
4) Construction company and Tokyo Metropolis
5) Compensation of 23 million yen for business loss and moral injury
6) Compensation of 4.5 million yen for business loss and moral injury

Land Reclamation and the Protection of the Sea and Seashore Surrounding Japan

Yasutaka Abe

The sea and the seashore that surround Japan have supplied the Japanese with foods that are indispensable for our existence from time immemorial. People in continental nations would have difficulty conceiving how great a role marine products play in our diet. But the sea and the seashore have been polluted and destroyed extensively during the last two decades by the economic and industrial development that has made Japan the second-ranking nation in terms of gross national product (GNP) among the capitalistic states. As a result of this process the ecosystem, one of the fundamental elements of our existence, was also seriously affected.

Therefore, the Japanese should now first find out why the sea and the seashore were destroyed and polluted and then find the way to protect and, if possible, to restore them.

I. The Value of the Sea and the Seashore

Human nature, unfortunately, is such that we become aware of the value of a thing that we have enjoyed as a matter of course only after we lose it. The sea is closely connected with the life of mankind. The Japanese are very fond of taking walks along the seashore, enjoying the beauty of the sea, fishing, swimming in the sea, gathering shells at low tide, picking up floating branches, planting seaweed, and so on. Much of the food on which Japanese live depends on fishing. We are given so many gifts by the sea. The role that the sea plays in our recreation and food is very great.

The Japanese have appreciated the beauty of the sea in poems, pictures, and so on for a very long time. This cultural value of the sea is also precious. According to folklore, the sea is the place that connects the present world with that after death; it is the entrance and exit from and to which the gods of the ancestors come and go, and the sacred place in which the impurity of mankind is purified.

The seashore builds an ecologically very complex system as a connecting place between the land and the sea. The activity of the living matter along the seashore is very productive. In the tidelands, shallow-sea nourishment is so rich that many sorts of living matter lay eggs and grow up there, and migratory birds stop there to eat.

The sea, especially the shallow sea, can purify polluted matter by the function of tides, waves, and the activity of the living matter (self-purifying capacity). So if the shallow sea is lost because of land reclamation, the whole sea will stop its activity and lose its self-purifying capacity; the sea will die.

The seashore is the place in which living matter were born at the beginning of the earth. For example, in Kasaoka Bay in Okayama Prefecture, *kabutogani*, a rare species of crab which is called a living fossil, has lived from time immemorial without evolving. For this reason, the seashore is valuable from the biological point of view.

II. The Pollution and Destruction of the Sea and the Seashore

The rapid economic development in Japan that began about 1960 brought us material richness. But on the other hand, our indispensable environment, health, and life were made victims of it to a considerable extent.

At least at first, priority was given to this rapid economic development, so that industrial waste water was not so strictly controlled. Legal control of the pollution was insufficient so that often industry was allowed to pollute the environment. Examples are the pollution of the Tagonoura Harbor by paper-manufacturing factories and the mercury pollution of Minamata Bay by Chisso Company.

The sewerage system in Japan is constructed insufficiently when compared with Western countries. People provided with sewers totaled only 22 percent of the whole population in 1975. Thus not only industrial but also domestic waste water flowed directly into rivers or the sea without being treated. Until 1973 excrement was disposed of in the Seto Inland Sea.

The increase of the sea traffic following extensive industrialization caused more ship collisions and more oil pollution. This also brings to mind the accident of the Mitsubishi Oil Company in Mizushima in Okayama Prefecture at the end of 1974 which caused the Seto Inland Sea great damage.

Land reclamation has deprived many living matters in the shallow sea of their natural habitat. According to research made by the Environment Agency, 20 percent of the whole length of the seashore of Japan was lost through, for example, the construction of harbors and land reclamation. In Tokyo Bay, 80 percent of the seashore, 73 percent in Osaka Bay, and 50 percent in Ise Bay have been artificially changed by the construction of harbors and land reclamation. The tideland in the Seto Inland Sea is decreasing year by year from 251 square kilometers in 1898 to 150 square kilometers in 1969. The sum total of the land that was reclaimed after World War II until 1975 amounts to 121,129 hectares. This is about 0.3 percent of the whole territory of Japan, and half of the capital, Tokyo. There are three reasons why so much land was reclaimed from the sea:

1. Because Japan is very densely populated, large amounts of land can only be obtained from the sea.
2. Reclaimed land is very cheap. Its basic cost consists of the compensation to the fishery, cost of the construction, and only 3 percent of the market price of the reclaimed land as a license fee. According to one estimate, with 500 billion yen (about U.S. $2.5 billion) all the fishery rights in the Seto Inland Sea can be bought. This, however, does not take into account the ecological value of the sea and the seashore. On the other hand, land is very expensive in Japan. So when land is reclaimed from the shallow sea near a big town, very great benefits can be obtained.
3. As Japan lives on foreign trade, its industrial areas are situated near harbors and, consequently, along the seashore.

For these reasons the sea, especially Tokyo Bay, Ise Bay, and the Seto Inland Sea, has been extensively polluted. The COD (Chemical Oxygen Demand) has increased. The water of the sea has been eutrophicated by phosphorus and nitrogen, and the quality of the transparency of the water has also decreased substantially. As a result, fishery has been damaged a great deal by this pollution and the destruction of the sea.

Now, unfortunately, the Japanese people swim in pools at the seaside, and crowds of people rush to artificial beaches that have been constructed in place of the many destroyed beaches. Probably more amateur fishermen than there are fish stand on the quay, but not on the natural seashore, and without success. In shell-gathering at low tide one finds only shells that have been cast artificially the previous night, and moreover, one must pay for them. The bait for fishing that could be found free in the seashore is now imported from a neighboring country. White sands and green pine groves, the beauty of which we once appreciated, can now be rarely seen.

III. Movements to Restore and Protect the Seashore

Over ten years ago *kōgai*, that is, the pollution not only of the environment, but also of human health and life, became a serious social problem. Land reclamation is one of the important causes, as it is said that the map of the pollution coincides with that of land reclamation. Thus people became conscious of the value of the sea and the seashore. Many citizens' movements for the protection of the sea were organized and many suits were instituted. Industrial activities causing pollution, construction of big roads, railways, airports, sewage treatment works, power stations, and projects for regional development are being resisted in many cases by these suits and citizens' movements.

In regard to the protection of the sea and/or the seashore there have been many suits against licenses for land reclamation,[1] and one against the construction of a fishing harbor in Nagahama in Ehime Prefecture (Matsuyama District Court, Shōwa 53 [1978].5.29, 889 *Hanrei Jihō* 3 [1978]). Also, many suits are pending in the first instance, namely:

1. The Red Tide Suit: In Japan there is a phenomenon known as the "red tide." It is presumed to be caused by phosphorus and nitrogen in waste water, and as a result, has killed the fish living in waters affected by it. Therefore, fish culturists are seeking damages from the state and from the industries causing the pollution for the loss of their fish by the red tide, and an injunction against the discharge of waste waters by those industries.

2. Buzen Suit: Inhabitants sought an injunction against the land reclamation for an oil power station on the basis of the right to a healthy environment, but the suit was rejected by Fukuoka District Court (Shōwa 54 [1979]. 8.31, 937 *Hanrei Jihō* 19 [1979]).

3. Himeji LNG Suit: Against a license for land reclamation for a liquified natural gas work, rejected by Kobe District Court (Shōwa 54 [1979].11.20, 954 *Hanrei Jihō* 17 [1980]).

4. Ōita 8 Gōchi Suit: Against a plan based on the Act for Promoting the Establishment of New Industrial Cities that leads to land reclamation. The suit was lost on March 3, 1979, because this kind of plan cannot be challenged in a court (Ōita District Court, 925 *Hanrei Jihō* 3 [1979]).

5. Kōshienhama Suit: Against a harbor plan seeking to reclaim land from a beautiful seashore.

6. Biwako Suit: Injunction against the development of Lake Biwa. These suits were brought at first by fishermen but now also by the citizens, who assert that they have the right of access to the beach (*irihama-ken*). The *irihama-ken* movement originated in a small city, Takasago, in Hyōgo Prefecture. In this city the people could previously swim and gather shells on the beach. But because of industrialization the beach was monopolized by the industries, and the citizens claimed that they had the right of access to the beach.

IV. Legal Defects in the Protection of the Sea and the Seashore

The present legal system of land reclamation benefits only development. According to the Public Surface Water Reclamation Act of 1921, a private person can be licensed to reclaim land from a body of public water and after completion obtain the property. Public property is thus changed through land reclamation into private property. This act is based on the economic consideration that nature has no value and that land reclamation should be actively promoted because it produces very precious land and enlarges the territory by peaceful means.

This act was amended in 1973 for the prevention of pollution. Nevertheless, it has many defects from the point of view of environmental protection. This amendment is not for the protection of the natural seashore. This act does not take into account the security of the living aquatic resources and the recreational value of the seashore, and the environmental impact statement system of this act is insufficiently practiced. Furthermore, the applicant for a license and the authorizer of the license are very often the same person, because the applicant is often the local government and the authorizer is the governor or the chief of the harbor management organized by the local government.

The Harbor and Bay Act of 1950 and the Fishing Port Act of 1950 also facilitate only the development and construction of harbors, not the protection of the seashore.

The legal system for the protection of the seashore is insufficient. The Temporary Act for the Protection of the Environment of the Seto Inland Sea was enacted in 1973. This act succeeded in decreasing the allowed amount of COD to half of that in 1972, but not in preventing other pollution. This act provides that the characteristics (the scenic beauty and rich marine products) of the Seto Inland Sea must be sufficiently taken into account when an application for land reclamation is examined. However, after the enforcement of this act many licenses were granted, one after another. One of the reasons lies in the insufficiency of the environmental impact statement. The Natural Parks Act of 1967, the Nature Conservation Act of 1972, and the Living Aquatic Resources Protection Act of 1951 provide that areas to be preserved must be designated. As a consequence, areas that are not so designated are open to development. In effect, the present legal system is not sufficient to protect the sea and the seashore.

The present legal system is also insufficient regarding the procedural formalities in a suit. Land reclamation is an irreversible alteration of the natural surroundings, so it is necessary to enjoin it in advance, if it is illegal. But there have been cases in which, during the hearings of the disputes in the court, land reclamations were begun and, moreover, were completed, because temporary injunctions were not issued.

Some courts did not examine the illegality of the industrial pollution that would be emitted from the works on the reclaimed land in suits against licenses for land reclamation. The reason lies in the fact that land reclamation only changes the sea into land and has nothing to do with the use of the reclaimed land. But according to this act the anticipated use of the reclaimed land must be entered on the application form and so examined. Further, land reclamation not only changes the sea into land. Land is not reclaimed if it is not needed. If pollution is emitted from the reclaimed land and it cannot be controlled, the land becomes useless. It must therefore be determined in advance whether or not the anticipated use of the reclaimed land will pollute the environment.

The *irihama-ken* is not acknowledged in court. In the Nagahama Fishing Harbor case an injunction against the use of municipal money for the construction of a fishing harbor was sought as a taxpayers' suit, a procedure that was introduced from the United States after World War II. The plaintiff asserted that the construction would destroy the scenic swimming facilities, so that financing it through public funds was illegal. But according to the judgment of the court nobody had the right to swim there. The state permitted inhabitants to swim there only by not prohibiting them from doing so. The present legal system does not take the value of nature into account, although the state is entrusted by the public to manage the seashore appropriately (see the preamble of the Japanese Constitution). Also, the value of the swimming facilities should have been taken into account when the town decided to construct the fishing harbor, even if there was not any explicit reference to it. They should have balanced the value of the swimming facilities against the need to build the fishing harbor. In my opinion, the *irihama-ken* should be acknowledged as a right, at least in this sense.

V. Measures and Proposals for the Protection of the Sea and the Seashore

1. *Irihama-ken*

The people who claim the *irihama-ken* refer to foreign law, for example, the right of common access in Sweden and the Coastal Zone Management Act of 1972 in the United States. They propose the repeal of the Public Surface Water Reclamation Act, the passage of the Basic Bill for the Protection of the Sea and the Seashore and a Bill for Securing the *Irihama-ken,* the freezing of all land reclamation plans until the enforcement of these acts, and the enactment of municipal ordinances for the protection of the sea and the seashore.

Moreover, they have launched a Japanese Neptune Plan. After the model of the National Trust in England, they aim to buy with private funds seashores that are threatened with development. It might be too costly, if not impossible, to buy all such lands with donations from citizens; perhaps it would be better to limit the use of the land along the seashore by law and/or ordinances. But it will be very significant if this plan succeeds in preserving seashores.

2. Activities of the Japan Bar Association

The Japan Bar Association is interested in the protection of the sea and the seashore. It has investigated the actual circumstances of the polluted sea and has done research on the legal countermeasures. According to this association, the present legal system is concerned only with development and takes only simple countermeasures against pollution. Therefore, a comprehensive environment management will be necessary to build a healthy environment in practice. It will be necessary to unify and coordinate all of the individual plans of each administrative branch from the environmental point of view; to establish the right of the citizen to a healthy environment; and to acknowledge the citizens' participation. It is proposed that a Bill for the Protection of the Environment of the Seto Inland Sea should be passed according to the principle mentioned above, and that the Public Surface Water Reclamation Act should be amended into a Public Surface Water Reclamation Control Act, so that land reclamation is in effect prohibited.

3. A Draft of an Act by the Ministry of Construction

There is no act now that designates the management of the coastal zone outside the harbor area which is controlled by the Harbor and Bay Act. A draft of an act regarding the public management of the coastal zone by the Ministry of Construction has been drawn up, and it would fill this legal void. It provides for obtaining permission to occupy the coastal zone, to construct, and so forth. However, this act does not recognize the right to a healthy environment, nor does it extend to the comprehensive preservation of the environment of the coastal zone.

4. Protection of the Seto Inland Sea.

The Special Act for the Protection of the Environment of the Seto Inland Sea was enacted in 1978, supplanting the Temporary Act for the Protection of the Environment of the Seto Inland Sea of 1973. This act inherited the contents of the earlier act and, moreover, introduced some new legal provisions namely:

(1) a prefectural plan based on the basic plan for the Seto Inland Sea Environment Protection;
(2) the decrease in the discharge of phosphorous waste matters by *gyōsei shidō* (administrative guidance) in order to prevent the outbreak of the red tide;
(3) the designation of the natural seashore protection areas by prefectural ordinances.

In addition, the Water Pollution Control Act of 1970 was simultaneously amended. The present system is defective because it controls only the density of the pollution and permits the discharge of large amounts of polluted matter, much more than if the waste water were diluted with fresh water. Thus the purpose of this amendment is to diminish the total amount of pollution. The Prime Minister decides on a basic policy; governors decide on the plan for diminishing the total pollution and the standards for control of the total amount of the pollution, and allocate the permitted level of pollution to each industry. This new system applies not only to industrial but also to domestic waste water.

There are many drawbacks to this act, however. When it was enacted the prohibition of tanker traffic at night and stricter control over the discharge of oil, waste water from ships, and the control over phosphorus by legal order were proposed by the Environment Agency. But these proposals were eliminated because of opposition from the industries and other ministries.

The control of land reclamation has not been strengthened. Designation of the natural seashore protection areas is said to have introduced the spirit of the *irihama-ken*. Although this is true in one sense, it is still insufficient. First, this act will function to promote development outside these narrowly designated areas. Second, not only the prefecture but also the cities, towns, and villages should be able to designate these areas.

This act does not control at present the nitrogen that is said to cause the red tide. Control of the phosphorus is not sufficient because it is not regulated by order, only on the advice of administrative bodies.

Regarding the diminution of the total amount of COD pollution, the target value and the year in which the target will be reached are delegated to the administration absolutely. Citizens' participation and supervision were not introduced.

VI. Conclusion

In principle, everybody agrees that the necessity for protection of the sea and the seashore is urgent. But as far as regional interests are concerned, particularly the people in developing regions eagerly wish to see their respective areas developed. This might be called a North-South problem existing within one country.

In Japan it is said that the local government played a prime role in the protection of the environment. But in this area, local autonomy may lead to the destruction of the sea and the seashore by regional interests in development. Thus it is necessary for the state to regulate the development projects of each region. We cannot rely only on the local autonomy, but on the state level, most of the ministries want to develop Japan. A compromise between development and protection will be necessary.

It is said that theory is pure, but legislation is a product of compromises among several interests. In Japan, the compromises have been, regrettably, too frequently to the advantage of development and industrialization. An effort must be made to change this situation in Japan, and the amendments mentioned above will be a step forward in this direction.

Notes

Please refer to two articles by Kumamoto Nobuo, "Coastal Zone Litigation and Protection by Law in Japan," 13 *Hokkaigakuen Law Journal* 235 (1977), and "On Wetlands and Coastal Zone Protection by Law in Japan," 13 *Hokkaigakuen Law Journal* 121 (1978). These two articles treat almost the same theme.

1. For example, Matsuyama airport (Matsuyama District Court, 23 July 1968), Usuki (Ōita District Court, 20 July 1971), Date power station (Sapporo District Court, 29 July 1976), Okinawa CTS (Naha Dsitrict Court, 4 October 1975), Fukushima nuclear power station (Fukushima District Court, 19 June 1978). The Matsuyama airport and Usuki cases were won, the others lost.

Problems and Concepts in Noise Prevention

Yoshihiro Nomura

Noise, a growing social problem throughout the world, can be classified into the following five types: factory noise, construction noise, highway traffic noise, railway noise, and airport and air base noise. In Japan, two of these types, namely factory and construction noise, are covered by regulatory measures under the Noise Regulation Act, but highway traffic noise, railway noise (especially that of the Shinkansen super-express railway line), and airport and air base noise remain outside the provisions of this law. Measures to prevent airport and air base noise have, it is true, been carried out under the relevant laws, and administrative measures in the form of prohibition of late-night flights have been instituted. Also, while there is no regulation of highway traffic noise as such, the noise level of individual vehicles is controlled to some extent by the Noise Regulation Act and other related legislation. Railway noise, however, has a completely free rein.

In this paper, the problems involved in the present regulations and the desirable form of future controls are discussed for each of the above five types of noise. The inadequacy of the existing legislative system to deal with the large-scale noise problems of the present day is pointed out, and it is recommended that special legislation be introduced to cope with noise prevention.

I. Factory Noise

The Japanese Noise Regulation Act includes regulatory measures governing specified factories and is designed to control noise generated by the operation of factories or other types of work sites which affect a considerable area. These measures, however, contain a number of problem areas which await improvement.

1. Designated Area System

The prefectural governor, seeking to regulate noise produced by specified factories, and so forth, must designate concentrated residential areas, school and hospital zones, and other such areas in which it is deemed necessary to protect the living environment of the residents from noise (Art. 3, Par. 1).

However, in view of the harm caused by excessive noise now being experienced throughout the country, retention of the designated area system in its old form is inconsistent with the requirements of noise prevention, and is also unnatural in view of the approaches already established by the Air Pollution Control Act and the Water Pollution Control Act. Furthermore, in many of the relevant local ordinances, air and water pollution and noise are all covered by a single pollution-control ordinance in which the designated area system is not adopted. Thus this system has also become divorced from the reality of the regulations contained in local ordinances. Improvement of the Noise Regulation Act must begin with the abolition of this designated area system.

2. Regulatory Standards

Article 4, Paragraph 1 stipulates that the regulatory standards for noise in regard to specified factories shall be established by the prefectural governor. In actual practice, however, there is little scope for the discretion of the prefectural governor, who is able to set such standards only within the scope of those established by the Director-General of the Environment Agency according to the necessary degree of noise control for specified hours and zones of designated areas.

Article 27, Paragraph 1 of the Noise Regulation Act allows the adoption by local ordinance of necessary regulatory measures for noise emitted by specified factories in accordance with the particular local physical and social conditions, from a different standpoint from that of the act itself, but it does not go to the extent of allowing the establishment of supplementary regulations by local ordinance.

Moreover, the competent authorities of cities, towns, or villages are empowered to establish independently more stringent regulatory standards than those set by the prefectural governor for all or part of a designated area where special physical or social conditions exist, but this is also restricted to "within the scope of the standards set forth by the director-general of the Environment Agency" (Art. 4, Par. 2; by public notice this scope is set at not less than the lower limit of the regulatory standards established by the director-general of the Environment Agency). Thus in the final analysis these standards amount to nothing more than supplementary standards within the overall framework.

3. Inadequacy of Penal Provisions

The Noise Regulation Act is so designed that penal provisions are not invoked until after recommendations and orders for improvements have been issued (Arts. 12 and 29), suggesting a distinct reluctance to take disciplinary measures. There is a need to provide thorough penal provisions which will allow immediate punishment for violation of the regulatory standards.

4. Lack of a Preventive Approach in Orders for Improvement

The prerequisite for formulating recommendations or orders for improvement is "finding that the level of noise emitted by a specified factory exceeds the regulatory standards, thereby being detrimental to the environment of the surrounding area," that is, the regulatory standards must have actually been infringed upon. This is no more than an *ex post facto* measure. It is to be desired that the issuance of recommendations and orders for improvement should shift in the future toward an approach of prevention before any damage is done. That is, it should be possible to invoke such measures where noise might be found to be in excess of the standards being emitted.

5. Necessity of Compulsory Noise Monitoring

Article 21–1 of the Noise Regulation Act places the responsibility for the monitoring of noise levels in designated areas on the prefectural governor, but does not compel the party responsible for noise emission from a specified factory to conduct noise monitoring. It would be appropriate also to provide an express statement of the duty of the party responsible for noise emission to monitor and record the noise levels.

6. Special Consideration Applicable to Small Enterprises

Article 13 of the Noise Regulation Act stipulates that in applying the provisions of Article 9 (Recommendations for Plan Changes) or those of Article 12, Paragraph 1 or 2 (Recommendations and Orders for Improvement) to operators of small enterprises, the prefectural governor shall give special consideration to the content of recommendations or orders so as not to substantially impede the performance of said enterprises. This is in spite of the extensively discussed relationship between pollution and industrial development, and the deletion by the Sixty-fourth Diet session of the "harmony with sound development of the economy" clause from the Basic Law for Environmental Pollution Control, the Air Pollution Control Act, and so forth. The necessity of retaining Article 13 has become extremely questionable. Other appropriate measures, such as making available loans which favor the relocation of plants or improvement of facilities, should be applied to small- and medium-scale enterprises; to make the contents of the regulatory measures themselves lenient is only to shift the burden onto the affected residents.

II. Construction Noise

The Noise Regulation Act contains regulatory measures for specified construction work in order to control the generation of noise affecting a considerable area which accompanies construction projects. However, these provisions of the act are more problematic than those concerning specified factories. The problems inherent in the designated area system itself have already been discussed in relation to factory noise.

1. Regulatory Standards

The regulatory standards governing noise emission from specified construction sites are set forth separately from those for specified factories. In this case too, however, the standards are to be set by the director-general of the Environment Agency (Art. 15, Par. 1), and, furthermore, unlike the noise standards for specified factories, there is no provision made for the standards set by the director-general to cover a range, and therefore no latitude for choice by the prefectural governor. Also, whereas in the case of specified factory noise it is possible for the city, town, or village authorities to establish qualifying supplementary regulations, not even this possibility exists in regard to the regulatory standards for specified construction work noise.

2. Lack of Direct Penalty Provisions

Direct penalty provisions are lacking in this case as in that of the specified factory noise regulations. Since construction work noise differs from factory noise in often being of short duration, the provision of direct penalties would be a more effective sanction than the use of improvement orders and similar time-consuming measures.

3. Necessity of Orders with a Preventive Approach

Any party who plans to undertake construction projects which involve specified construction work in designated areas is required to report the work to be conducted (Art. 14). However, the recommendations for plan changes (the system for which is stipulated in Article 9 as regards specified factories) and orders for plan changes are not designed to follow upon this reporting. The required technology has been developed to such a level that the prediction of noise levels, based on the details of the planned construction work and the physical and social conditions of the area, is quite feasible. It should therefore be possible to judge in advance whether the proposed "methods of noise abatement" described in the report (Art. 14, Par. 1, Item 4) are adequate. It would thus be appropriate to have available a system of recommendations and orders for plan changes.

At the same time, the *ex post facto* nature of the steps for rectifying a harmful situation by recommendations (Art. 15, Par. 1) and orders for improvement (Art. 15, Par. 2) should be revised to allow these measures to be invoked with a more preventive outlook.

As discussed above in the case of factory noise, so for construction noise also the operator should be made responsible for noise monitoring.

4. Special Consideration for Public Projects

Article 15, Paragraph 3 of the Noise Regulation Act stipulates that in issuing recommendations (Art. 15, Par. 1) or orders (Art. 15, Par. 2) pertaining to specified construction work undertaken for facilities or structures of a public nature, the prefectural governor shall give special consideration so as not to unnecessarily impede the progress of work. This approach places priority on the execution of public works or works of a public nature; therein lies a policy decision that the residents must simply put up with the accompanying noise.

"Standards for Regulation of Noise Generated by Special Construction Work" (Notice No. 1 of the Health and Welfare Ministry and the Construction Ministry, 27 Nov. 1968) brings this out more explicitly. In cases of work carried out at night to ensure the normal operation of railways, and work that the authorities designate to be performed during the night hours under Article 34 of the Road Act or Article 77,

Paragraph 3, of the Road Traffic Act, partial exemption is granted from the actual regualtory standards themselves.

III. Highway Traffic Noise

Today, with the expansion of the national highway network throughout the country, traffic noise has become a major social problem, the third most serious of the noise categories.

In order to prevent destruction of the living environment by traffic noise, thoroughgoing measures, such as the erection of noiseproofing facilities along roadsides, restriction of driving routes and hours, and so forth, are necessary in addition to the reduction of noise emission by individual vehicles.

1. Control of Individual Vehicle Noise

To reduce the noise emitted by individual vehicles, maximum permissible levels are established by the director-general of the Environment Agency (Art. 16, Par. 1), and compliance with these levels is ensured by the Minister of Transport by orders pursuant to the Road Transportation Act (Art. 16, Par. 2).

However, an examination of the "Maximum Permissible Levels for Automotive Noise" shows that these are far less rigorous than the standards for factory and construction noise. For example, for large freight vehicles (of over 3.5 tons total weight and over 200 hp) the permissible levels are set at 80 phons at cruising speed and 92 phons during acceleration. Wherever there are roads, motor vehicles are able to approach close to dwellings, and accordingly the standards for their noise levels should rightly be high enough to meet the standards for special designated areas under the environmental standards for noise, if the tranquillity of the residential environment is to be ensured. The existing maximum permissible levels can be said to reflect the underdeveloped stage of vehicle noise control technology.

2. Necessity of Noiseproofing Facilities Along National Expressways

Granted that noise control of individual vehicles will for some time remain difficult for technical reasons, a greater concentration of effort on roadside noiseproofing facilities is called for. Particularly in the case of roads, such as the Tōmei (Tokyo-Nagoya) Expressway, which carry tens of thousands or cars by day and night, roadside residents will be increasingly seriously afflicted by noise unless measures are taken, such as completely covering with noise-insulating structures those sections which pass through residential areas. Tree-planting and wall-building intended as sound barriers are virtually useless. With the recent increase in suburban high-rise apartment buildings close to national expressways, the problem of how to exclude the traffic noise which rises from the highways has taken on great importance. Noiseproof walls, while effective in controlling noise in the horizontal plane, are powerless against noise rising vertically. Thus a roofed noiseproof structure becomes absolutely essential. The use for noise control of a tunnel-shaped structure, like that installed over the above-ground sections of the Sapporo City subway to keep the winter snows off the line, would surely go a long way toward restoring the living environment along such national highways as the Tōmei Expressway.

The noise problem along these routes can more rationally be seen as national expressway noise, rather than as automobile noise, and be dealt with accordingly by noise-control measures. This would involve regarding the national expressways themselves as noise sources similar to factories and construction works, and implementing measures to require their builders and managers to install noiseproofing facilities. Since, of course, the national expressways are included in the "public facilities" referred to in Article 2 of the State Liability for Compensation Act, parties affected may take civil action to seek damages or an injunction. Where a disturbance beyond tolerable limits exists, the installation or management of the national expressway would be judged to be defective.

3. Necessity of Measures to Restrict Driving Hours on National Expressways

If, as discussed above, national expressways were viewed as a noise source in the same way as factories and construction sites, and the necessary noise-prevention measures were instituted, there would be no reason why restrictions should not be imposed on late-night driving. In particular, the late-night operation of large freight vehicles on expressways will probably have to be prohibited in the future. In the case of the Shinkansen railway, trains are not normally scheduled to run late at night. At Tokyo and Osaka airports, also, as a rule late-night take-offs and landings are prohibited. Yet on the national expressways there is no restriction at all on the number and tonnage of trucks operating at night. We must apply the scalpel of the law to this unregulated situation to bring the noise under control before it becomes accepted as as a *fait accompli.* In this connection, it is noteworthy that the Metropolitan Police Board recently decided to exclude large freight vehicles from Central Tokyo from 10:00 P.M. every Saturday to 7:00 A.M. the following Sunday.

The necessary regulatory measures can be enforced under the existing Road Traffic Act. That is, the "Pollution Diet" of 1970 introduced the concept of "traffic pollution" to the Road Traffic Act (Art. 2, Item 23), and authorized the prefectural public safety commissions to regulate traffic where deemed necessary to prevent traffic pollution (Art. 4, Par. 1). (See also Article 17 of the Noise Regulation Act.) The problem now confronting us is how these provisions can best be applied.

4. The Concept of Special Legislation

The construction of national expressways involves a number of complex conditions such as the fact that their expansion is seen as a necessity from the standpoint of government policy, while at the same time traffic noise along such routes is a problem of special gravity when compared with other roads. Consideration should be given to enacting a special law such as, perhaps, a "Bill for Prevention of Harmful Effects Due to Motor Vehicle Noise around National Highways."[1] The same law could also cover prevention of damage due to automotive exhaust gases. This law should contain the following provisions concerning measures to prevent damage:

a. Specification of Driving Operations

The authorized minister may designate the hours, speed, and other matters permitted in the operation of a particular type of vehicle on a particular national expressway where this is deemed necessary in order to prevent or reduce harmful effects caused by motor vehicle noise in the vicinity of that expressway.

b. Installation or Improvement of Noise-Control Facilities

The prefectural governor may require the specified national expressway authorities to install or improve noise-control facilities where this is necessary in order to prevent or reduce the harm caused by motor vehicle noise in the vicinity of that expressway. (It is also necessary to prohibit, by zoning, the erection of dwellings and other buildings on land within the range most severely affected by noise.)

c. Compensation for Costs of Noiseproofing

The authorities of a specified national expressway shall render compensation for all or part of the expenses entailed for noiseproofing ordinary dwellings, schools, hospitals, and other structures in order to prevent or reduce the harmful effects produced by motor vehicle noise in the vicinity of that expressway.

d. Compensation for Costs of Relocation

The authorities of a specified national expressway shall, where losses are incurred by the owner of a structure in a designated area (that is, a roadside area designated as subject to noise in excess of a certain level) in removing said structure or in relocating it to an area outside of the designated area, compensate the owner and other parties concerned for said losses.

e. Obligatory Land Purchase

The owner of land within a designated area may claim the right to obligatory purchase of the land by the authorities of the specified national expressway.

f. Compensation for Loss

The authorities of a specified national expressway shall compensate losses incurred by any party adversely affected by noise caused by the frequent passage of motor vehicles.

IV. Superexpress Railway Noise

A second problem which, like national expressway noise, is expected to spread throughout the country is that of Shinkansen railway noise. Insofar as it consists of intermittent shock sound, this noise resembles aircraft noise more than that of expressway traffic. At present, however, Shinkansen noise has been left unregulated by the Noise Regulation Act and other legislation.

Civil litigation brought by affected residents seeking an injunction against Shinkansen noise is at present pending in Nagoya District Court.

V. Airport and Air Base Noise

Measures to deal with aircraft noise are based on the Act for Control of Aircraft Noise around Public Airports (Act No. 110, 1 August 1967) and the Act for the Adjustment of the Living Environment around Defense Facilities (Act No. 135, 2 July 1966).[2] Nevertheless, efforts are required both to extend and to improve the content of these measures and to develop low-noise aircraft and introduce them into commercial aviation.

1. Public Airport Noise

Under the Act for Control of Aircraft Noise around Public Airports, enacted in 1967, the following measures are now in force to regulate public airport noise.

a. Specification of Flight Operations

The Minister of Transport may, in order to ensure prevention or reduction of aircraft noise, designate by notice take-off and landing flight paths, hours, and other flight specifics at public airports and their vicinities to such an extent that the safety of air traffic is not impeded (Art. 3, Par. 1).

At such airports as Tokyo and Osaka International, a ban has been placed on jet take-offs and landings during the night hours (10:00 P.M. to 6:00 A.M.); since the Osaka High Court decision, however, take-offs and landings, in effect, cease at 9:00 P.M. Many problems remain for review, however, such as the exemption from the above measure of "take-offs and landings unintentionally delayed or of emergency nature or producing noise which is not of such a level that sleep or rest of the residents is disturbed."

Furthermore, since the penal provisions for infringements of the designated operational specifics apply only to the pilot and crew of the aircraft (Art. 18), provisions which authorize punishment of the airline company as well are necessary.

b. Assistance with Costs of Noiseproofing

The authorities of a specified airport are required to provide full or partial assistance toward meeting the costs entailed by local public bodies in carrying out noiseproofing of particular facilities, such as schools, hospitals, and child-care facilities (Art. 5).

In the first place, as of 31 August 1978, only fifteen airports—for example, Tokyo, Osaka, and Fukuoka International—have been designated as specified airports. No measures have been taken to protect the environs of the other airports that carry busy jet traffic.

The second problem is the extremely narrow restriction of the facilities subject to these measures. As to the dwellings of private citizens, those of only one room are included in the scope of assistance, but those of two rooms are included only if they house the aged or the sick, or if the number in the family exceeds five.

Third, the term "assistance," which gives the impression of granting a favor, is inappropriate and should be amended to read "compensation." The responsibility of the airport authorities to pay compensation should be clearly recognized by the law, and detailed measures established on that basis.

c. Compensation for Relocation

Compensation for relocation (Art. 9, Par. 2) is also granted only in the vicinity of the three specified airports. Not only must the number of airports to which this is applicable be increased in the future, but the designated areas around each airport (Art. 9, Par. 1; areas designated by the Minister of Transport) must be extended.

d. Purchase of Land

The authorities of a specified airport may purchase land within a designated area when the owner of said land so requests, within the extent of the budget (Art. 9, Par. 3). But the right of the landowner to file a claim for obligatory purchase by the authorities is not recognized. Further, as a rule the land subject to such purchase is limited to residential land. In addition, the authorities are favored by the qualification "within the extent of the budget."

e. Compensation for Loss

The authorities of a specified airport are required to compensate any party who, in the operation of an agricultural or other business stipulated by Cabinet Order, which was previously lawfully conducted, incurs loss due to the frequent take-off and landing of aircraft at said airport (Art. 10).

However, only those engaged in agriculture or fisheries may apply for such compensation; those engaged in other business, and ordinary citizens, may not do so.

Thus this law contains many points which still require improvement. The friction occasioned by aircraft noise will inevitably spread throughout the country with the increase in aircraft speed and size, and number of flights. Decisive legislative measures, such as prohibition of new residential building in areas severely affected by aircraft noise, are called for.

Accordingly, in April 1978, a new act was enacted, namely, the

Act of Special Countermeasure against Aircraft Noise around Specified Airports. (In its short form, the Land Use Control Act around Specified Airports.) This law was to be enforced in October 1978. An outline of this act follows:

(1) The government ordinance designates those airports as specified airports where it is necessary to prevent aircraft noise nuisance and to control land use in the surrounding area. (The first specification was made for Narita International Airport.)

(2) The owner of the specified airport should ask the prefectural governor to make a master plan for countermeasures for aircraft noise, showing the map of aircraft noise. In making the plan, the governor needs the consent of both the Minister of Transport and the Minister of Public Works.

(3) The governor can designate two kinds of areas (referred to herein as Zone A and Zone B) in which it is deemed necessary to control land use to prevent disturbance caused by aircraft noise. The standards for designating zones A and B shall be set by the government ordinance. The Ministry of Transport is now examining that standard, and it is expected that Zone A will be an area having over 75 WECPNL (Weighted Equivalent Continuous Perceived Noise Level) and Zone B will be an area having over 80 WECPNL.

(4) In Zone A, the law requires that dwellings, schools, and hospitals be noiseproof.

(5) In Zone B, no one can build dwellings, schools, or hospitals without permission of the governor. The owner of the specified airport must either pay compensation to the landowner who suffered losses from the land use control or buy that land upon an offer from the landowner.

This new law was enacted mainly for Narita International Airport, and will be effective before the surrounding area is urbanized. But it does not work for most of the existing airports around which urbanization has already taken place.

2. Air Base Noise

With regard to noise from the Self-Defense Force and other bases, the following measures are in force under the Act for the Adjustment of the Living Environment around Defense Facilities, which was enacted in 1966.

1. Assistance with Costs of Noiseproofing (Art. 3, Par. 2). In this connection, the second and third criticisms of the same problem in public airports are applicable (pp. 132–33).

2. Compensation for Relocation (Art. 5, Par. 2). As in the case of public airports, there is a need to extend the range of the designated areas (Art. 5, Par. 1).

3. Purchase of Land (Art. 5, Par. 3). The problems discussed with reference to public airports are also relevant here.

4. Compensation for Loss. The government is required to compensate any party who, in the operation of an agricultural, forestry, fisheries or domestic transportation business, which was previously lawfully conducted, incurs loss due to the frequent take-off and landing of Self-Defense Force aircraft (Art. 9, Par. 1). However, no provision is made for compensation for those engaged in other business or for private citizens.

In the case of loss due to the frequent take-off and landing of aircraft of the U.S. forces stationed in Japan, similar measures are in force under the Act for Compensation for Special Loss Due to Acts of the U.S. Forces Stationed in Japan (Act No. 246 of 25 August 1953).

VI. Civil Litigation

While civil litigation, especially that seeking injunctions, is effective in combating noise, its function is complementary to that of the legal controls. As long as the legal controls remain inadequate, however, the function served by injunction suits is of major importance.

1. Cases Concerning Airports

The best known case involving an airport in Japan is that of Osaka International Airport. This involved residents of Kawanishi City, Toyonaka City, and other areas in the vicinity of Osaka International Airport who sought compensation for damages and the enjoining of nighttime flying from the national government, as the airport authority. The ruling in the first instance was a ratification of the administrative measures already instituted to limit take-off and landing (i.e., prohibition from 10:00 P.M. to 7:00 A.M.), and thus constituted an injunction.[3] However, on appeal this decision was altered to commence restriction of take-off and landing by administrative measures as requested by the plaintiffs, and an injunction was thus imposed from 9:00 P.M. to 7:00 A.M.[4] There have been very few court cases in this country involving aircraft noise; the Osaka Airport case was only the third, following the Okayama helicopter noise case of 1970 and the Niigata Airport case of 1973.

In contrast, in the birthplace of aviation, the United States, beginning with the 1946 Causby case,[5] there have been numerous precedents set regarding aircraft noise, and the general trend therein has become predictable. Namely, in the United States claims for damages against military and civil airfields are relatively likely to succeed, whereas requests for injunctions are hardly ever granted. There is no precedent whatsoever for restriction of the direction or angle of approach, number of flights allowed to take off and land, noise level, take-off and landing hours, and so forth. As a general theory, there is a strong tendency toward the view that if the continued operation of an airport is indispensable from the viewpoint of the public interest, the court should limit its injunction orders to the minimum and compensate for any losses that cannot be eliminated by these orders by requiring the payment of damages. In actual practice, the traditional doctrine of weighing the conflicting legal interests is applied in granting an injunction and also in determining the details of such an injunction.[6]

This doctrine is also appropriate in the case of injunctions in Japan. However, we can expect to find considerable difference between the conclusions reached through the application of this doctrine in the two countries. In 1965, the author visited several airfields in the United States where there had been many lawsuits, but the neighboring dwellings were scattered. There seemed to be no situation which resembled that of Japan's airports and bases, where houses are packed densely together right up close to the end of the runway. Moreover, most Japanese houses are of an open wooden construction, which is ineffective in shutting out roaring sounds and vibrations. When the number of persons affected and the severity of the effects suffered were compared, it seemed strange that, at that time, there had been no lawsuits brought against aircraft noise in Japan.

However, the first real decision in Japanese aircraft noise litigation (although it was the third case) came with the Osaka Airport case. This first-instance judgment was delivered in February 1974, and the second-instance judgment in November 1975. Since then, this case has been appealed to the Supreme Court, where it is now pending.

The highlight of this case was whether or not the court would approve a stricter ban on take-off and landing than that of the administrative measures already imposed (which banned take-off and landing between 10:00 P.M. and 7:00 A.M.). The first-instance judgment merely ratified the take-off and landing restrictions of the adminstrative measures, making no changes at all. The second-instance judgment, however, amended the first and accepted the placing of an injunction on flights from 9:00 P.M. The basis of injunction has also been discussed. The second-instance judgment recognized injunction based on personal right.

2. Cases Concerning Expressways

A case which concerns expressway pollution is the Hanshin (Osaka-Kobe) Expressway case.[7] The thirty-six complainants were persons residing within 85 meters (except for one who operated a clinic, but did not reside, in this area) of general national highway Route 43, which runs from east to west through the southern part of Amagasaki City (near Osaka City). The defendant (Hanshin Expressway Public Corporation) is a special corporation under public law, which was engaged in new construction work on the Osaka-Nishinomiya route of the Hyōgo Prefectural Highway, and which would manage the road after its completion. Since the plan was to build most of that part of the expressway which was to pass through Amagasaki City above the existing Route 43, the complainants applied for a temporary disposition to prohibit construction of the expressway by the defendant, Hanshin Expressway Public Corporation. This action was taken because the additional traffic pollution resulting from the expressway in question, over and above that (exhaust gases, noise, vibration, dust, etc.) caused by Route 43, would seriously impair the residential life of the complainants.

The court rejected prohibition of the construction work, but it did order the restrictions necessary to prevent aggravation of the traffic pollution (noise and exhaust gases). It held that, in terms of common sense, there was an undeniable risk of increased noise after the opening of the elevated expressway, and approved the claims for necessary remedies. However, the court considered the following to be adequately effective as the necessary measures:

1. The defendant may proceed to complete the expressway, but the limit for multiple road noise shall be prescribed for the new Route 43 in accordance with the traffic volume, and the defendant shall be compelled to prevent the noise from exceeding this limit. The limit shall be effectively lower than or equal to the noise value of the existing Route 43.

2. Standards shall also be prescribed for the noise of the expressway only, compliance therewith shall be sought, and consideration shall be given to preventing any influence of the expressway noise on the Route 43 noise.

3. In the event of noise being generated in excess of the above noise

limit, the defendant shall immediately be required to take measures to reduce this excess noise, by means of improvements to the road, traffic controls, erection of noiseproofing walls, and so forth.

Further, the court approved the seeking of necessary measures with regard to exhaust gas, in view of the fact that if traffic volume increases, there is an appreciable risk of future increase of air pollution during prolonged windless weather, with the large volume of nitrogen oxides emitted by the expressway traffic descending within a range of 20 meters on either side of Route 43. However, the court deemed the following measures to be sufficiently effective:

(1) The defendant shall restrict the total flow of traffic on the expressway and Route 43 to not more than 150,000 vehicles daily (annual average), for the sake of the complainants residing within a range of 20 meters of Route 43.

(2) The right of the complainants to seek the above restriction shall lapse six months after the 1975–76 controls ("Japan's Muskie Act") come into force.

VII. Summary

Three types of legislative approach may be taken for the prevention of noise: (1) regulatory measures against the noise source; (2) noiseproofing measures between the noise source and the affected area; and (3) measures to prevent harmful effects in the affected area. In the case of factory and construction work noise, the principal approach under the Noise Regulation Act is that of (1), but there is still much room for improvement.

In the case of expressway traffic and Shinkansen railway noise, the proper course would be to apply the approach of (1) thoroughly to the motor vehicles and superexpress trains in use, i.e., to develop quiet automobiles and trains; but since at the present state this remains technically difficult, approaches (2) and (3) have had to be adopted. In actual practice, however, hardly any measures have been taken.

The same can be said of airport and air base noise. Until quiet aircraft can be developed, effort should be concentrated on approaches (2) and (3). In this case (3) has been put into practice to a limited extent by means of special legislation. In the future, however, the introduction of approach (2) is called for, e.g., by the establishment of spacious airport sites, tree-planting for sound protection, and restriction of land use in the vicinity of airports. Further, the role of litigation should be valued and active recourse should be made thereto.

Notes

1. Nomura Yoshihiro, *Kōgaihō no Kisochishiki* [Fundamental knowledge of environmental law], Tokyo: Teikoku Chihō Gyōsei Gakkai, 1973, p. 99.
2. Nomura Yoshihiro, "Kōkūki sōon" [Aircraft noise], *Kōgaihō no Seisei to Tenkai* [Japanese law of public nuisance], Tokyo: Iwanami Shoten, 1968, p. 230.
3. Osaka District Court, Shōwa 49 (1974). 2. 27, 729 *Hanrei Jiho* 3 (1974).
4. Osaka District Court, Shōwa 50 (1975). 11. 27, 797 *Hanrei Jihō* 37 (1976); Nomura Yoshihiro, *Kankyō mondai* [Environmental problems], Tokyo: Chikuma Shobō, 1978, p. 51.
5. United States v. Causby, 328 U.S. 256 (1946).
6. Nomura Yoshihiro, "Amerika ni okeru kōkūki-sōon" [Aircraft noise nuisance in the United States], *Gaikoku no Kōgaiho* (*Jō*) [Foreign laws of public nuisance] Tokyo: Iwanami Shoten, 1978, p. 137.
7. Kobe District Court, Shōwa 48 (1973). 5. 11, 702 *Hanrei Jihō* 18 (1973).

Community Strategies for Improving Our Quality of Life

From Pollution Control toward "Amenity" Development and Enhancement

Fukashi Utsunomiya

A problem which is close to us is the question of how to improve or how to create our living environment. In other words, our concern is about the enhancement of amenities in our living place. Everybody feels that in Sapporo people are enjoying a good and pleasant life. On the other hand, in other major cities like Tokyo, Yokohama, Osaka, and so on, people are suffering from the gradual degradation of their living places. Environmental discontents grow intense. But the present legal and administrative arrangements are not only ineffective but also inadequate in coping with the issue of amenities. During the decade since the Basic Law for Environmental Pollution Control was enacted in 1967, environmental administration concentrated upon the control or abatement of seven types of pollution: air pollution, water pollution, noise, vibration, ground subsidence, soil pollution, and offensive odors.

The problem of quality of life was not the target of environmental policies in Japan. First, an examination of the evolution of these policies is in order. Through this analysis, the need for new environmental policies embodying the issue of amenity will be emphasized. Second, what is meant by "amenity"? It is an elusive and subjective concept. To clarify and to conceptualize the meaning of amenity in a practical way will be a most difficult task. Finally, it will be suggested that the community in which we live be reinstituted as the center for social change, and there will be a proposal for community strategies to improve our quality of life and to preserve the interests of amenities within our community boundaries.

I. Evolutionary Development of Environmental Policy

The evolution of environmental policy may be divided largely into four periods.[1] The first period covers the years from 1955 to 1965. This was the age of a sustained and rapid economic growth fueled by the proliferation of heavy and chemical industrial complexes across the country under the government's Doubling National Income Plan. The government promoted further economic growth by relocating population and industries into the local areas through enactment of the Act for Promoting the Establishment of New Industrial Cities (1962) and the Act for Promoting the Development of Special Areas for Industrial Consolidation (1964). In this period, this developmental planning was being implemented with little or no attention to ecological impacts upon people and society as a whole. Moreover, local leaders were enthusiastic in inviting industries in their area, by means of a Kōjō Yūchi Jōrei (a muncipal ordinance for enticing a manufacturing company to set up a plant). However, the industrial businesses did not make investments in pollution control.

On the other hand, this period witnessed the occurrence of a number of pollution-caused incidents, such as the Minamata disease in Kumamoto Prefecture (1956), the Itai-itai disease in Toyama Prefecture (1955), the bronchial asthma in Yokkaichi (1961), and the typhoon-caused flooding of a residential area due to the ground subsidence (1964 and 1966). But the administration reacted to these problems only in fragmented ways; for example, the enactment of piecemeal laws in the early part of the 1960s, which were designed to regulate the discharge of factory effluents, the pumping of underground water, and the emission of stack smoke.

The second period covers the years from 1965 to 1969, during which the administration adopted a policy to maintain increasing economic growth through the New National Comprehensive Development Plan (1969) and at the same time to control environmental pollution. In 1967, to provide preventive measures against pollution, the Basic Law for Environmental Pollution Control was enacted. The Basic Law narrowly defines the issues of environmental pollution in only seven categories, as we have mentioned. The abatement of these seven pollution problems was the target of environmental policies. But these contradictory approaches to the issues of growth and environment proved ineffective in the control of pollution, and industrial pollution had spread throughout the entire industrialized Pacific seaboard. For example, the bronchial disease caused by sulfur dioxide, the so-called Yokkaichi asthma, has afflicted victims throughout the entire industrial belt along the Pacific shore from the Kashima industrial district in the east to Mizushima on the Seto Inland Sea in the west.[2] Thus in the late 1960s, Japan's environmental pollution spread horizontally as well as vertically. Residents suffering damage from pollution organized anti-pollution movements, which erupted and spread all over the country.

The third period covers the years from 1969 to 1973. The government's environmental policy took a turn in 1970. Toward the end of that year, the Diet enacted a sweeping change in the system of pollution control laws, involving an amendment to the Basic Law for Environmental Pollution Control and enactment or amendment of a total of fourteen pollution laws. As a result, the regulation standards and other control measures were definitely stiffened, and under the new and amended laws, provisions designed to balance pollution control measures against economic development were deleted. After the promulgation of the 1970 amendment to the Basic Law, the number of organizations and personnel charged with the administration of pollution control measures increased rapidly. In 1971, the Environment Agency was instituted for the purpose of formulating and administering environmental policy from an integrated point of view, and coordinating the environment-related functions of the various agencies. Local governments established pollution or environment departments and sections, the roles of which were to survey, monitor and inspect activities. Despite the fact that pollution laws and administration were well organized, there is no end to the spread of pollution. In this period anti-pollution campaigns by local citizens intensified; the demands are diversified, ranging from opposition to the construction of expressways and power plants to opposition to air, water, and noise pollution, and environmental destruction.

The final period covers the years from 1973 to the present. Since the oil crisis of October 1973, the Japanese economy has suffered a low rate of growth and a recession. At the same time, there has been some noticeable effect in preventing and abating pollution by means of a severe pollution regulation, and an enormous pollution-related investment by the private sector.[3] It might be said that since the end of 1973, pollution problems have been in some degree abated and the critical point has been passed. Indeed, as a report by the Organization for Economic Cooperation and Development (OECD) notes, Japan has been successful in pollution control.[4] On this point the government clearly emphasizes that the state of the environment is on the whole tending toward improvement.[5] Table 1 shows the changes in the major indices of pollution. It is fairly obvious that environmental pollution (which had been increasing up to 1971) took a turn for the better in 1972 and improved markedly in 1974 and 1975.[6] But at this stage, not only environmental administra-

Table 1. Index of Changes in Environmental Pollution

Elements	Year	1970	1971	1972	1973	1974	1975
Air Pollution	Sulfur oxides	+	+	+	+	+	+
	Nitrogen oxides	−	0	0	−	0	0
	Carbon monoxide	+	−	+	+	+	+
	Number of oxidant alerts issued	(−)	−	−	−	+	+
Water Pollution	City-bound rivers (BOD)	−	+	+	−	+	+
	Rural rivers (BOD)	−	−	+	−	+	+
	Lakes (COD)	−	+	+	−	+	−
	Coastal water bodies (COD)	+	+	+	+	+	0
	Number of occurrences of red tide in the Seto Inland Sea	−	−	−	−	−	0
Ratio of Improvement		−33	0	44	−33	67	44

Remarks: 1. The changes in the level of environmental pollution shown above are determined by comparing the yearly average values calculated from data reported by comparable monitoring stations. The symbol "+" stands for an improvement over the preceding year, "−" for deterioration and "0" for no appreciable change.

2. The ratio of improvement

$$= \frac{\text{No. of improved elements}}{\text{Total No. of elements}} \times 100$$

where improvement is represented by 1, no changes by 0 and deterioration by −1. Accordingly, if all elements have improved, the ratio is 100, while if all deteriorated, the ratio is −100.

3. The changes in air pollution are measured in terms of fiscal years, while those in water pollution are measured in terms of calendar years.

4. The marks given in parentheses are based on estimates.

5. The year 1973 was a water shortage year, and the minus marks given for rivers and lakes may be largely attributable to the relatively small precipitation during the year.

6. The number of occurrences of red tide in the Seto Inland Sea is based on the survey conducted by the Fishery Agency.

Source: Environment Agency, *Quality of the Environment in Japan*, p. 3.

tion but also anti-pollution movements seem to be thrown into confusion. Environmental administration has lost its own direction toward where it is going or should go. And the movements which displayed an enormous energy in anti-pollution campaigns seem to be losing their effectiveness.

There are several reasons for this lost direction. First, the main concern of both environmental administration and citizen's movements was to control pollution, but this target was accomplished. Second, at present pollution is not the primary issue but economic and social problems, such as price stability, unemployment, and welfare, are more pressing. Third, there may be a return to a conservative tendency in the political field. Environmental problems are not a point at issue, and the Liberal Democratic party and opposition parties do not consider environmental problems one of the important policies. It is true that both environmental administration and anti-pollution movements have begun to grope for a new road or a new vision. The issue of amenities may be one of the focal goals in the coming decade for both environmental policy and popular movements.

II. Multi-Dimensional Approach to the Concept of Amenity

One of the important conclusions to note in the OECD Report is that "although Japanese environmental policies largely succeeded in abating pollution, they did not succeed in eliminating environmental discontent, and that the real cause of environmental discontent was not—and is not—increasing pollution, but decreasing environmental quality."[7] Such discontent has been mainly caused by the consequences of developmental activities which had destroyed the amenities of the countryside, had reclaimed land from the shoreline, and felled trees carelessly. According to the Natural Environmental Conservation survey, of a total of 26,540 kilometers of shoreline, 5,650 kilometers (21.2 percent) have been reclaimed and as a result the shoreline has become an artificial one, and 5,060 kilometers (19.2 percent) have been worked upon to some considerable degree.[8] The percentages of land remaining as pure natural coast are: Tokyo, 0 percent, Osaka, 2.1 percent, Hiroshima, 6.6 percent, and Aichi, 14.7 percent. The survey also notes that about 90 percent of the Tokyo and Osaka metropolitan areas has become an urban desert where there is no vegetation.

The issue of environmental discontent is the one that has been neglected by Japanese environmental policies. This new issue is concerned with the problem of amenity, which cannot be dealt with by the techniques of pollution control and the enforcement of ppm standards. "Amenity" would be one of the key concepts in a new environmental policy in Japan. However, pollution problems are fairly well defined, while, like the term "public interest," "amenity" is an elusive concept which is difficult to define. In England, the concept of amenity has been recognized, used, and developed for a long time. It has been not only one of the guiding principles in executing planning administration at the local and national levels, but also it is one of the factors that needs to be taken into account in land-use planning, urban design, and advertisement control. Indeed, the phrase "injurious to the interests of amenity" has become part of the jargon of the planning world.[9] The Oxford English Dictionary defines "amenity" as "the quality of being pleasant; of places, their situation, aspect, climate, etc." And amenity is derived from the Latin *amoenitas* (meaning pleasantness), from the root *amare* (to love).[10] According to Sir William Holford, "—amenity is not a single quality, it is a whole catalogue of values. It includes the beauty that an artist sees and an architect designs for; it is the pleasant and familiar scene that history has evolved; in certain circumstances it is even utility —the right thing in the right place—shelter, warmth, light, clean air, domestic service . . . and comfort stations."[11]

Holford demonstrates that the amenity concept involves not a one-dimensional aspect, but multi-dimensional or complex ones of environmental quality. It is concerned not only with clean air and water, but also with art and beauty. On this point, David L. Smith argues that there are three different parts of the amenity concept: the first is a concern for public health, pollution, and urban efficiency; second, the pursuit of pleasantness—something more than the minimum requirements for health and safety; and finally, the cultural cause of the preservation, directed at first toward the protection of medieval architecture.[12] These three aspects of the amenity concept are similar to three categories of environmental policies, such as pollution control, environmental improvement, and conservation. Therefore, pollution control or abatement should be regarded as only one aspect of environmental policies. This suggests that there is a need to change environmental policies in Japan from pollution control toward "amenity" enhancement and development, and to expand our conceptual scope of the environment to deal with the issue of pleasantness and preservation and beauty.

In addition, environmental policies must take into account "the total environmental needs of man— ethical, aesthetic, physical, and intellectual, as well as economic."[13] Man's total environmental (amenity) needs may be classified into four elements: physiological, economic and safety, social, and psychological and emotional. In developed countries most people have been content to satisfy the basic needs of food, shelter, clothing, safety, and in many cases, security. It is said that those who have satisfied such basic needs try to seek the satisfaction of such higher needs as social and emotional or cultural needs. There is ample evidence that human needs are being shifted in emphasis from the basic needs to needs for pleasantness, quietness, and privacy. Even if people were satisfied with food, safe water, and freedom from illness, but dissatisfied with such higher needs as social and psychological ones, environmental discontent would not be eliminated. In Japan, psychological dissatisfaction has become more intense. For example, since 1973 complaints against pollution-caused damage have been decreasing, but in 1976, complaints about sensory or psychological damage like noise, vibration, and offensive odors have continued to increase.[14]

It is necessary to set up a new environmental policy which will meet such higher human needs, and to create a physical environment that will satisfy not only the basic needs but social and psychological needs. In this sense, amenity functions as a dependent variable and the physical living environment as an independent variable. The extent to which these needs are satisfied may depend upon how interested people are in improving, creating, enhancing, developing, maintaining, and controlling their living environment. The community strategies proposed herein may be one of the most effective ways to improve our quality of life.

III. Community Strategies for "Amenity" Enhancement

Our first important task would be to establish our living place as the basic strategic unit for improving our quality of life. However, in the past our living place has not been the chief concern of the political system. It has been neglected by the people in the community themselves. The centralized political administrative system has played a significant role in accomplishing national development policies. This is a social monocentric system; that is to say, the more power is consolidated and directed from a single center the more responsible and efficient it will become. The heart of this system is a large-scale bureaucratic organization relying on a pyramidal authority structure, whose principles are efficiency, functional rationality, and competition. In this system policies are usually made by the central government, the orders of which flow down from the top through vertical chains (from central government—prefectural government—local government—residents). Although this centralized system proved effective in pollution control to some degree, it would be ineffective in dealing with such unmeasurable or subjective concerns as amenity or quality of life.

There is a need for reorganizing our political system toward a decentralized one in which policies concerning local matters are made at the local level, not at the center. And the people of the community should participate fully in the decisions that affect their lives. These are things that happen where people live. Whether the community should construct a highway or an industrial center within its own boundaries must be decided by public participation as long as it directly affects the interest of the local amenity. Of course, institutionalization of the environmental impact assessment system may prevent environmentally dangerous development, but it may be ineffective in promoting environmentally desirable developments. There is no available method to cope with such an intangible subject as amenity but the systemization of public participation at the grass roots. The definition of "community" would be the small unit in which people interact together in their living place—the community area would be 5 to 13 square kilometers, and the size of the population would be around 3,000 to 50,000. These people would be fully responsible for the protection, preservation, and enhancement of their living environment within their boundaries. A return to a sense of community would make it possible for people to satisfy their social and psychological needs by living together peacefully.

Second, public access to governmental information is a precondition for public participation. The United States has the Administrative Procedure Act of 1945, the Freedom of Information Act of 1966, and the Government in Sunshine Act of 1976. But in Japan there are no such laws. People have been deprived of the so-called right of access to the government. Moreover, in accordance with Article 100 of the National Public Servants Act, a government official must not disclose any secrets in his office. Our society should be oriented toward an open society and for this purpose should institutionalize freedom of information, the right to know.

Third, to deal with the issue of amenity, local administration must be reorganized from a passive one to an active one. Through this, administrative reform power would be decentralized and returned to the community close to the people. Restructuring the local planning section would be the most important job, because planners must decide upon the degree and importance of amenities, and which amenities should be preserved. In England, local planning authorities have the power not only to prevent developments that would clash with amenity, but also to reject developments that are not intrinsically harmful but are badly designed.[15] In this sense planners must be retrained and reoriented toward an awareness of artistic values. They must take into consideration total urban design (urban layout), ranging from green areas, open space, and parks to water and air quality, preservation of historical heritages, and cultural facilities for the satisfaction of human psychological and aesthetic needs. This new planning organization would be charged with land-use planning and zoning, which have an important role to play; ecological planning dealing with noise level, light, green areas, good design; control of advertisements, building height control and development control as a whole.

The fourth strategy would be to enact a new law or to amend the existing laws recognizing amenity rights, which are more specific and comprehensive than environmental rights. The legal right to a healthy environment is based on Article 25, Section 1, of the constitution of Japan which states, "All people shall have the right to maintain the minimum standards of wholesome and cultural living." It is said that people have a legal right to enjoy a healthy environment. The amenity rights recognize privacy, quiet, and clean air as scarce resources which are indispensable to the enjoyment of the good and happy life. E. J. Mishan, a British economist, regards amenity legislation as an alteration of the present legal framework within which the recognition of amenity rights would provide industry with the incentive necessary to undertake research into methods of removing the potential and existing amenity-destroying features of so many of today's products and services. This would also have favorable distributive effects on the welfare of society.[16] Mishan proposes an amenity rights doctrine in which people have a legal right to enjoy a good, quiet, and pleasant life.

The proposal requires further examination but may have some significant implications for new environmental administration in Japan. The Revised Pollution Control Ordinance (1978) in Kanagawa Prefecture may be the beginning of amentiy legislation, although it is inadequate. It has shifted its emphasis from pollution control toward creation of a better living environment. According to the new provisions, any person is prohibited from burning tires, hides, and so forth, except in an incinerator. Also, the manufacturers of noise-producing instruments like pianos or air conditioners are requested to indicate the noise level, with noise control instructions attached, and the users of these devices must be careful not to disturb the quiet of others.

The Beautification of Roadside Scenery Ordinance (1969) in Miyazaki Prefecture designated the beautiful sites along the national road within the prefecture as roadside natural scenic view districts, within which new construction and remodeling of buildings, and their design, color, and advertisements are to be regulated.

The Building Standard Act controls the upper limit of building height and building use in the Low-Rise Exclusive Residential Area where the limit of building height is 10 meters maximum. Houses, apartments, boarding houses, houses with shops compatible with a residential area, shrines, temples, churches, police boxes, clinics, and libraries are permitted to be built in the Low-Rise Exclusive Residential Area. Residents who live in Tsukushino and Minami Tsukushino districts in

Machida City, Tokyo, concluded a "Building Agreement" which is more strict than the Act. According to the Agreement, buildings should be limited as follows: (1) only detached single-family houses may be built; (2) the number of floors is to be less than two except the basements; (3) the limit of building height is 9 meters maximum; (4) walls must be set back from the lot boundary at least 1.5 meters; (5) existing walls are not to be made higher; and so forth. The Machida City government suggests to a builder who applies for a permit that there is a Building Agreement in the area and it is good to consult with area residents.[17]

Ordinances concerning the control of signboard advertisements, noise at the neighborhood level, and coastal zoning are to be considered as the objects of amenity legislation. In Honolulu, Hawaii, all billboards are gone because they are prohibited by ordinance (1927). Moreover, a state law requires that 1 percent of the total construction cost of new public schools and public buildings be set aside for works of art, such as paintings or sculptures. In many other American cities, ordinances regulate power tools, air conditioners, and other mechanical equipment. Memphis, Tennessee, for example, prohibits playing radios, phonographs, and other devices when they "annoy or disturb the quiet, comfort or repose of persons" in or near the vicinity.[18]

The final strategy is concerned with the positive role of citizens' movements in protecting, preserving, and enhancing their own living environment within the community boundaries. Organizing people for these new causes like the amenity movement may be the effective way to activate the political and administrative process in the direction of new environmental policies and the enactment of new amenity ordinances to create and enhance "community environment." In England, by 1968, over 600 local organizations were in existence, the objective of which was to preserve or enhance the amenities of their own localities.[19] These new amenity movements in Japan may be universal and permanent movements, whose purposes are to promote the interests of local amenities, rather than merely to oppose pollution. The positive and creative role of citizens' movements may be highly evaluated.

The Movement Against the Development of a Hill at the Back of Tsurugaoka Hachiman Shrine in Kamakura City symbolizes such a new type of citizens' movement. This project was stopped by a group of citizens in 1964, and as a result the beautiful natural features of the old capital were preserved. This movement also led to the Act for Special Measures for the Preservation of Historical and Natural Features of Ancient Cities (1966). Another case is the Movement to Buy Back the Tenjinsaki Shoreline in Tanabe City in Wakayama Prefecture.

Tanabe City is situated at a distance of two-and-a-half hours by train from Wakayama City. In this city there is a Tenjinsaki cape of 200,000 square meters. A developer bought 50,000 square meters for a high-class residential project. Against this development a group of citizens formed the Association to Value the Nature of Tenjinsaki in 1974 and collected 16,000 signatures. In 1978, this group applied to the Juridical Foundation in the name of the Tenjinsaki Preservation Association, and by October 1978 had collected around $630,000 for purchasing back the shoreline.[20]

It is time that everybody should act and participate in the enhancement of his or her living environment. Through these community strategies our future could be reconstructed toward enjoying a good and pleasant life.

IV. Conclusion

It has been suggested above that the issue of amenity may be one of the focal goals in the coming decade for both environmental policy and citizens' movements in Japan. But in my opinion such an intangible subject as amenity cannot be dealt with by the techniques of pollution control or the enforcement of ppm standards. New approaches to this new issue must be developed. Community strategies are proposed for coping with the problem of amenity. First, we should move toward an open society, and for this purpose public participation and freedom of information should be institutionalized at the national and local levels. Second, there is a need for reorganizing our political system toward a decentralized one in which environmental policies concerning local matters are made at the local level, not at the center. Third, planners must be retrained and reoriented to have a wider sense of art and beauty.

The three aspects of the concept of amenity developed by David Smith may have some important implications for both developed and developing nations.[21] But the meaning of amenity may have different connotations in different cultures. Therefore, it is very difficult to generalize the concept of amenity applicable to all nations. I strongly suggest that cross-cultural empirical research should be undertaken on this new issue.

Notes

1. For a discussion and an analysis of the evolution of environmental policy, see The Government of Japan, *Environmental Policy of Japan* (1976), pp. 11–17.

2. There are over 53,400 official victims of air pollution diseases (e.g., chronic bronchitis, bronchial asthma, pulmonary ailments, emphysema). See Environment Agency, *Quality of the Environment in Japan* (1977), p. 187.
3. The ratio of pollution-relating investment in the private sector to GNP reached 1.5 percent in 1975. See The Government of Japan, *Environmental Policy of Japan*, p. 18.
4. See Organization for Economic Co-operation and Development, *Environmental Policies in Japan* (Paris, 1977).
5. Environment Agency, *Quality of the Environment in Japan*, p. 4.
6. Ibid., p. 3.
7. OECD, *Environmental Policies in Japan*, p. 87.
8. Environment Agency, *Survey on the Natural Environmental Conservation* (1973).
9. J. B. Cullingworth, *Town and Country Planning in England and Wales* (London: Allen and Unwin, 1964), p. 132.
10. David L. Smith, *Amenity and Urban Planning* (London: Crosby Lockwood Staples, 1974), p. 5.
11. Sir William Holford, *Preserving Amenities* (London: Central Electricity Generating Board, 1959).
12. Smith, *Amenity and Urban Planning*, p. 177.
13. Lynton Keith Caldwell, *A National Policy for the Environment* (Washington: U.S. Government Printing Office, 1968), p. 16.
14. *Asahi Shimbun*, 25 July 1978.
15. Cullingworth, *Town and Country Planning*, p. 133.
16. E. J. Mishan, "Property Rights and Amenity Rights," in *Economics of the Environment*, ed. Robert Dorman and Nancy S. Dorman (New York: W. W. Norton & Company, 1977), pp. 249–50.
17. *Asahi Shimbun*, 7 January 1977.
18. U.S. Council on Environmental Quality, *Environmental Quality, The Third Annual Report* (August 1972), pp. 214–15.
19. Roy Gregory, *The Price of Amenity: Five Studies in Conservation & Government* (London: Macmillian & Company, 1971), p. 4.
20. Toyama Hachirō, "Tenjinsaki o Taisetsu ni Suru Undō," [The movement to value Tenjinsaki], 9 *Kankyō hakai* [The Journal of Environmental Disruption] 20–28 (1978).
21. Smith, *Amenity and Urban Planning*, p. 177.

Environmental Assessment in Japan
With Reference to the U. S. Experience

Ichirō Katō

I. Necessity of Environmental Assessment in Japan

The Japanese government has failed to present a bill for environmental assessment to the Diet three times in three years so far.[1] The Environment Agency prepared a draft law for environmental assessment,[2] but other ministries, especially the Ministry of International Trade and Industry (MITI), the Ministry of Construction, and the Ministry of Transport strongly opposed it. The Environment Agency could not reach agreement in its negotiation with other ministries. The Environment Agency has no authority to present a bill to the Diet without consent of other ministries.

The reasons for opposition or objection of such ministries are various. First, they point out that scientific techniques of environmental assessment are not fully developed or established, and to make environmental assessment mandatory by law is not adequate at this stage. This argument will be easily rebutted by responding that we should use feasible techniques at present and that we have a good precedent in the United States. If we wait for the development of such scientific techniques, we can never establish a law.

The second argument of the opposition is that environmental assessment is time-consuming and money-consuming, and delays development projects. However, environmental assessment is necessary in order to advance development projects, even if it is time- and money-consuming, because citizens' movements in Japan for protecting the environment and against development are becoming stronger. We therefore need a device to make development planning reasonable and conscious of the environment as well as to persuade concerned citizens.

Third, the opposition probably fears that environmental assessment would stimulate citizens' movements. For example, if the law makes a public hearing mandatory, radicals opposing development may try to block it with violence and to destroy the whole procedure. At any rate, environmental assessment may cause trouble, stimulate lawsuits, and stop or unreasonably delay development projects. In my opinion, such considerations would be the real reason for opposition.

However, as mentioned above, nowadays we cannot implement development plans or projects without environmental assessment. Reasonable planning is needed in facing strong citizens' movements, even if environmental assessment may cause trouble on the other hand. Actually the government requires environmental assessment in many significant cases, such as power plant planning and bridge construction between Honshū (the main island) and Shikoku Island, by means of specific laws or administrative guidance.

Therefore, our problem is not whether environmental assessment is necessary or not, but what sort of environmental assessment is needed and how to execute it. We certainly need environmental assessment for better planning.

II. Viable Method of Environmental Assessment

There are criticisms in Japan as well as in the United States of methods of environmental assessment. First, in Japan environmental assessment is usually performed after a plan has already been decided upon. For example, in the case of the bridge construction between Honshū and Shikoku Island, its location had already been determined and thereafter environmental assessment was performed and published. It is almost impossible to change the basic plan at this stage. In such a case environmental assessment seems to be a device only to persuade residents or to further a plan against residents. At best environmental assessment is only able to diminish adverse environmental effects to some extent under a predetermined plan. Environmental assessment is meaningless if it is only utilized in order to ratify or to justify a predetermined plan.

The second criticism is that the present method of environmental assessment, or the present form of environmental impact statement, which is a statement of the result of environmental assessment, is not adequate. An environmental impact statement often results in one thick volume or several volumes. It is difficult for ordinary citizens or laymen to understand real issues through an environmental impact assessment.

Environmental assessment should be concentrated on real issues and be readable by ordinary citizens.

There are major criticisms against the present method of environmental assessment in Japan, but there are similar criticisms in the United States. A visit in 1978 with an official of the Council on Environmental Quality disclosed the fact that the Council was preparing a new regulation under the National Environmental Protection Agency (NEPA), which would supplant present guidelines under NEPA. This regulation was expected to be binding on governmental agencies, whereas the guidelines are not binding. However, the contents or substance of this regulation are more important than the legal force of binding.

First, the environmental assessment should be done at the earliest state of planning in order to integrate it into the comprehensive planning process. This means that the environmental assessment should be referred to and considered in the original decision-making process, not after the plan has been decided upon.

Second, the environmental assessment should examine all feasible alternatives, and in the decision making the reason for selecting one of them should be clearly defined and stated. For example, if a decision-maker in a governmental agency abandons the most environmentally desirable alternative and selects another one, he has to state the reason clearly.

Third, the environmental impact statement should be more efficiently devised. It should be readable and concentrated on real issues. The volume of an environmental impact statement will be limited to 150 pages in ordinary cases, and even in special cases to 300 pages. In addition, other similar procedures should be utilized in order to avoid duplication and to shorten a time-consuming process.

These are the main features of the NEPA regulation, which should respond to criticisms against NEPA in the United States. It will also respond to such criticism against environmental assessment in Japan.

III. Purpose and Objective of Environmental Assessment

The purpose and objective of environmental assessment may be summarized as follows: in Japan environmental assessment is often regarded as a means to persuade residents and to facilitate implementation of a development plan. This is surely one phase of environmental assessment, but the original and essential objective of environmental assessment is to integrate environmental aspects into development planning for better decision making, in order to brake or stop thoughtless development and to preserve a desirable environment.

In the United States, the Council on Environmental Quality, after various experiences under NEPA, is endeavoring to make environmental assessment more effective for its original objective. It indicates a right course. If we adopt environmental assessment as a legal requisite in Japan—as in my opinion we must—we should prepare a procedure similar to the NEPA regulation described above, even if some modifications will be necessary in order to meet actual conditions in Japan.

Notes

1. The NEPA uses the words "environmental impact statement," but I have used the words "environmental assessment" in order to make it brief. At the same time, "environmental assessment" will involve a positive meaning, whereas "environmental impact statement" gives a negative impression to indicate only adverse effects. In Japanese we usually use the words "kankyō asesumento," that is, "environmental assessment."
2. The Environment Agency was established in 1973. Formally it belonged to the Prime Minister's Office, but actually it is a kind of ministry. Its director is a minister, that is, a cabinet member.

The United States and International Cooperation

The Growing International Implications of the U.S. Requirements for Environmental Impact Assessments

William H. Matthews and Richard A. Carpenter

I. Recent Developments in the United States

The U.S. National Environmental Policy Act (NEPA) of 1969 requires that all federal agencies prepare an environmental impact statement (EIS) on "major actions significantly affecting the quality of the human environment." As a result of the implementation of this act and numerous court cases involving it, a complex set of procedures and expectations has developed with respect to the EISs.

From the time of passage, there has been a great deal of confusion and debate about the application of NEPA to activities in territories outside U.S. legal jurisdiction. In 1975, the U.S. Agency for International Development (AID) was sued by a public-interest group to force the preparation of EISs on its grants and loans to other countries. As a result of this court case, USAID instituted, in June 1976, a process of environmental impact assessments on many of the projects with which it is involved.

During this past year, the intensity of the debate on the foreign extension of NEPA has escalated. The U.S. Export-Import Bank is now in suit for non-compliance with NEPA in the matter of loan guarantees for nuclear fuel exports. The State Department was sued and in response decided to prepare an assessment concerning the furnishing of a herbicide to Mexico for spraying marijuana. The Congress of the United States has become directly involved in resolving this issue. The President of the United States has taken a direct role in formulating guidelines for the extraterritorial extension of NEPA. These activities suggest that although other countries have the right to set their own priorities for development of their natural resources, to make their own trade-offs between short- and long-term gains, and to establish their own environmental quality standards, this does not excuse involved agencies of the U.S. Government from the responsiblility of informing the other countries about risks, consequences, and external costs accompanying projects.

Early in 1978, the Council on Environmental Quality (CEQ), which reports directly to the President, circulated draft regulations on the foreign extension of NEPA, but they were not well received by all the federal agencies. The President's Counsel then asked CEQ and the Department of State to map out an acceptable approach for consideration by the President. These deliberations led to the promulgation in January 1979 of an executive order (a statement by the President with the force of law) on reviewing environmental effects of major federal actions abroad. The text is in the Appendix to this paper.

Provisions of Executive Order: "Environmental Effects Abroad of Major Federal Actions"

Some points in the executive order that are particularly significant include the following (quotes are from the executive order; italics are added for emphasis):

1. The intention is "to further environmental objectives *consistent with* the foreign policy and national security policy of the United States."
2. The " 'Environment' means the natural and physical environment and *excludes* social, economic, and other environments."
3. The U.S. Department of State is given the authority to "coordinate all communications by agencies with foreign governments concerning environmental agreements and other arrangements in implementation of this Order."
4. Federal agencies will be given eight months to develop procedures to implement the executive order and must consult with CEQ and the State Department prior to placing them into effect.
5. The order would require that environmental impact statements, multilateral studies, or concise reviews of environmental issues be prepared and taken "into consideration in making decisions" for actions "*significantly* affecting":

(a) The environment of the global commons;
(b) The environment of a foreign nation not participating with the United States and not otherwise involved in the action;
(c) The environment of a foreign nation when the activity involves radioactive substances or an emission of effluent prohibited or strictly regulated by U.S. Law;

(d) Natural or ecological resources in the participating nation that are designated to be of global importance by the President or by international agreement.

For action (a) an environmental impact statement is required. For actions (b) and (c) the agency may determine whether to undertake a bilateral or mutilateral study or merely to perform a concise review of available information. For action (d) the agency may use any one of the three assessment formats, i.e., EIS, multilateral study, or concise review.

1. Exemptions to the order include actions taken by the President, those involving national security or arising in the course of armed conflict, intelligence activities and arms transfers, and certain export licenses, permits, and approvals involving radioactive substances (but not nuclear reactors or nuclear waste management facilities).

2. Each agency can (and must) make its own "appropriate provision for determining *when* an affected nation shall be informed . . . of the *availability* of environmental documents prepared pursuant to these procedures."

II. Trends in Asian Countries

The promulgation and implementation of this executive order involves the United States much more directly in many societal and political processes in other countries than has been the case in the past. In many of those countries, particularly in Asia, there are also emerging pressures and initiatives in the environmental area. If these converging interests are coordinated sensitively and with diplomacy, they can be mutually supportive and result in important advances in resource and environmental management and in a new type of international partnership in the development process. If handled poorly, they could result in actions and procedures that are detrimental to sound environmental planning and to good relations.

The new area with this potential for tension or partnership is related to a broad set of activities that comprise "natural resource and environmental assessment"—the continuing process of acquiring, analyzing, understanding, interpreting, and transferring information about ecosystems as they are related to development projects. In the countries of Asia and in international and U.S. institutions that deal with them, there is a growing receptivity for environmental assessment as a useful, constructive tool for managing development.

Developing countries are experimenting with new assessment activities with a mixture of hope that they will benefit development and suspicion that they will retard growth projects. Developed countries, and particularly the United States, are urging Third World countries to incorporate natural resource and environmental assessment into their planning in order to obtain optimum and sustained benefits from their resource base and to avoid costly and even disastrous consequences in the future. In some cases, institutions dominated by industrialized countries have taken the responsibility for conducting assessments on projects supported in developing countries. This is being done with an often disconcerting blend of management concern, missionary zeal, skepticism, and reluctance. Even some multinational corporations are encouraging better environmental assessment and decision making in developing countries, partially to avoid later problems caused by a shift in ground rules when public concern ultimately increases.

Some of the recent developments in this direction in Asian countries include the following:

1. Japan has taken major steps in understanding, monitoring, and ameliorating a broad range of environmental problems through extensive legislative and institutional initiatives. The Japanese law that provides compensation to victims of pollution is unique and may serve as an example to other nations as an innovative instrument for dealing equitably with this difficult problem.
2. A new Ministry of State for Development Supervision and Environment has been created in Indonesia.
3. In the Philippines, several agencies including the newly created national Environmental Protection Council have been combined in a new Ministry of Human Settlements.
4. Legislation in Thailand has given the National Environmental Board far-reaching powers.
5. Malaysia is beginning to implement the Environmental Assessment Policy of its Third Malaysian Plan.
6. There is a growing governmental commitment in South Korea to rectify some of the adverse effects of rapid industrialization.
7. ESCAP (Economic and Social Commission of Asia and the Pacific) and UNEP (United Nations Environment Program) are planning to create regional capability for environmental management.

These developments indicate that the value of environmental analysis and assessment in setting policies for the wise use of resources and environmental carrying capacity to meet human needs is being recognized. However, this acceptance is at a critical stage. The experiences, whether good or bad, with this relatively new approach over the next few years may well determine the long-term pattern of acceptance and implementation in most countries. Any misunderstandings or tensions introduced by the action of other countries, directly or through multinational institutions, could prematurely restrict the full potential of environmental assessment in the development process.

III. Potential Asian Concerns of the Extension of NEPA

Although the trends noted above in Asia and the United States appear to be in the same direction, they are not necessarily mutually supportive. The goals may sound similar in the abstract, but the approaches at an operational level may be so fundamentally different that countries may clash rather than cooperate in trying to reach them. In addition, there are also many trends in all these countries that run counter to the goals of incorporating environmental considerations into development planning. Often these trends are the dominant ones.

The reactions of other countries to a U.S. requirement for foreign environmental assessments, particularly as a part of the development assistance process will be of paramount importance in determining whether it will be a new source of tension or of partnership. Those reactions are understandably based on issues of sovereignty, previous experience and practice, and emotion. The practical implementation of this requirement is not yet clear, and uncertainty is generating concerns such as the six outlined below.

1. The U.S. preoccupation with process and procedure creates the impression of a stumbling block rather than an aid to progress. Delay in development is a genuine concern because of the urgency to increase food supplies, create jobs, secure foreign exchange, and achieve a greater measure of self-reliance. The U.S. NEPA is regarded by other countries (developed and developing) as a means for intervenors to delay projects on trivial environmental and procedural points even though their real motivations may include unrelated issues of social or political philosophy.

2. The political use of environmental assessment information is a major concern. While informal U.S. public comment on international trade and development projects in other countries is expected (if not always welcome), the possibility of formal intervention raises problems. If the intervention is at a professional level of environmental experts consulting about scientific information, the reaction may be favorable. If a U.S. or donor agency environmental statement deals with the fundamental strategy or policy of the recipient country, the interven-

tion may be resisted. If the U.S. public access to the decision-making process involving a foreign government includes attempts by environmental groups and the press (in the United States or the recipient country) to influence public opinion in the recipient country, the government could regard such intervention as inappropriate.

3. While environmental assessment information is welcome, the final balancing decision of what is appropriate for another country is generally expected to be left to the government of that country. A veto of development assistance, for example, by U.S. agencies on controversial procedural or substantive grounds might result in the recipient country turning to other donors or proceeding with other sources of funds where possible. Such an explicit and visible difference in values and priorities could cause strains in international relations.

4. An environmental assessment requires the acquisition and analysis of a great deal of information to which some countries may not wish the United States to have access (e.g., resource inventories). Even in cases where the United States already has the data, the country may not wish it to be made publicly available to other countries or to the private sector.

5. There is concern in other countries that factions in recipient countries that are opposed to U.S. trade and aid may use foreign environmental statements to generate antagonism against further cooperation.

6. The United States, as a result of the foreign environmental statement, might become awkwardly involved in a dispute to which it was not a direct party. For example, some development projects may cause transnational pollution resulting in disagreements between two or more foreign governments.

IV. Steps that Should Be Taken

In order to respond to the range of concerns outlined above, the United States and affected nations should begin exploring ways to take the following steps.

1. It is very important that the precise nature of U.S. concerns be made reasonably explicit in the early stages of implementing a policy for foreign environmental assessment. The reaction of other countries will vary markedly depending on whether the assessment is to reflect U.S. concerns about U.S. interests or, on the contrary, concerns of the United States about what it thinks should be the interests of others. There are different perceptions of the legitimacy of various U.S. in-

terests that could further complicate the implementation of policy. The assessment process will not be favorably received if it becomes a device for imposing on other countries U.S. environmental values and priorities rather than simply integrating them into the process of internal U.S. decision making.

2. Affected countries, especially those eligible for technical and financial assistance, should be given the opportunity to collaborate now in the process of implementing the foreign environmental statement. Potential misunderstandings can arise from differences in needs, values, priorities, traditions, styles, processes, and capabilities. Some of the sensitive areas are:

(a) Access to the assessment documents;
(b) Selection of the performer of assessment, with special emphasis on strengthening local capabilities;
(c) The role of public participation, in the United States and in the other country;
(d) The stage in the development sequence (from prefeasibility analysis to operation) where assessment is required;
(e) Who decides on trade-offs among alternatives;
(f) Scope of assessment (e.g., inclusion of socio-cultural impacts).

If environmental assessment in the form of the foreign environmental statement, study, or review is going to accomplish the intent of the NEPA, these questions may have to be discussed and negotiated on a country-by-country and even case-by-case basis. This would require a flexible policy framework.

3. Other developed nations, such as Japan and Australia, that are also involved in financial and technical assistance programs should be consulted and fully informed as the implementation by the United States of foreign environmental assessment goes forward. Projects of different donors may depend upon and have an impact on the same natural systems so that coordination of assessment information is desirable.

4. When required as part of a development assistance project, assessment procedures and content must be adapted and simplified to the needs, capabilities, timetables and sociocultural systems of the host countries. Money and manpower to perform assessments will always be limited and the priorities for gathering and analyzing information should reflect local values and criteria.

5. Special care and attention must be devoted at the earliest possible time to the process that the United States and others will adopt for exploring the types of issues, sensitivities, and suggestions outlined here. Some of these issues are so deeply enmeshed in the internal affairs and practices of sovereign states that the potential for strained relations

is very great, often in areas that might be considered ancillary to the assessment process as envisioned by U.S. officials. As with most issues in the realm of international relations, these will require negotiations based on respect, cordiality, and diplomacy. These negotiations should also be viewed as an opportunity to strengthen international relations and understanding in development planning and financial assistance in general.

V. Conclusion

When the Congress of the United States passed the National Environmental Policy Act of 1969, there was little appreciation for the potential impact of the provision requiring EISs for major federal activities. The effects on decision making by federal agencies have been profound and wide-ranging. Some political scientists and environmental managers speculate that if NEPA were to be considered by Congress now, with benefit of hindsight, the "action forcing" mandate for environmental impact assessment would not be included.

The United States is about to initiate another set of activities and procedures in the short but full history of the application of NEPA, this time in the international arena. Whether policy-makers will some day regret those steps may depend to a large extent on the forethought and care given to dealing with the types of issues raised in this paper. The challenge is enormous and the stakes, both environmentally and politically, are high enough to demand attention by government officials and scholars in the United States and throughout Asia.

Appendix

Text of Executive Order on Reviewing Environmental Effects Abroad of Major Federal Actions
Issued by President Jimmy Carter
January 4, 1979

By virtue of the authority vested in me by the Constitution and the laws of the United States, and as President of the United States, in order to further environmental objectives consistent with the foreign policy and national security policy of the United States, it is ordered as follows:

Section 1.

1–1. Purpose and Scope. The purpose of this Executive Order is to enable responsible officials of Federal agencies having ultimate responsibility for authorizing and approving actions encompassed by this Order to be informed of pertinent environmental considerations and to take such considerations into account, with other pertinent considerations of national policy, in making decisions regarding such actions. While based on independent authority, this Order furthers the purpose of the National Environmental Policy Act and the Marine Protection Research and Sanctuaries Act and the Deepwater Port Act consistent with the foreign policy and national security policy of the United States, and represents the United States government's exclusive and complete determination of the procedural and other actions to be taken by Federal agencies to further the purpose of the National Environmental Policy Act, with respect to the environment outside the United States, its territories and possessions.

Sec. 2.

2–1. Agency Procedures. Every Federal agency taking major Federal actions encompassed hereby and not exempted herefrom having significant effects on the environment outside the geographical borders of the United States and its territories and possessions shall within eight months after the effective date of this Order have in effect procedures to implement this Order. Agencies shall consult with the Department of State and the Council on Environmental Quality concerning such procedures prior to placing them in effect.

2–2. Information Exchange. To assist in effectuating the foregoing purpose, the Department of State and the Council on Environmental Quality in collaboration with other interested Federal agencies and other nations shall conduct a program for exchange on a continuing basis of information concerning the environment. The objectives of this program shall be to provide information for use by decisionmakers, to heighten awareness of and interest in environmental concerns and, as appropriate, to facilitate environmental cooperation with foreign nations.

2–3. Actions Included. Agencies in their procedures under Section 2–1 shall establish procedures by which their officers having ultimate responsiblity for authorizing and approving actions in one of the following categories encompassed by this Order, take into consideration in making decisions concerning such actions, a document described in Section 2–4 (a):

(a) major Federal actions significantly affecting the environment of the global commons outside the jurisdiction of any nation (e.g., the oceans or Antarctica);

(b) major Federal actions significantly affecting the environment of a foreign nation not participating with the United States and not otherwise involved in the action;

(c) major Federal actions significantly affecting the environment of a foreign nation which provide to that nation:

(1) a product, or physical project producing a principal product or an emission or effluent, which is prohibited or strictly regulated by Federal law in the United States because its toxic effects on the environment create a serious public health risk; or

(2) a physical project which in the United States is prohibited or strictly regulated by Federal law to protect the environment against radioactive substances.

(d) major Federal actions outside the United States, its territories and possessions which significantly affect natural or ecological resources of global importance designated for protection under this subsection by the President, or, in the case of such a resource protected by international agreement binding on the United States, by the Secretary of State. Recommendations to the President under this subsection shall be accompanied by the views of the Council on Environmental Quality and the Secretary of State.

2–4. Applicable Procedures. (a) There are the following types of documents to be used in connection with actions described in Section 2–3:

(i) environmental impact statements (including generic, program and specific statements);

(ii) bilateral or multilateral environmental studies, relevant or related to the proposed action, by the United States and one or more foreign nations, or by an international body or organization in which the United States is a member or participant; or

(iii) concise reviews of the environmental issues involved, including environmental assessments, summary environmental analyses or other appropriate documents.

(b) Agencies shall in their procedures provide for preparation of documents described in Section 2–4(a), with respect to actions described in Section 2–3, as follows:

(i) for effects described in Section 2–3(a), an environmental impact statement described in Section 2–4(a) (i);

(ii) for effects described in Section 2–3(b), a document described in Section 2–4 (a) (ii) or (iii), as determined by the agency;

(iii) for effects described in Section 2–3(c), a document described in Section 2–4(a) (ii) or (iii). as determined by the agency;

(iv) for effects described in Section 2–3(d), a document described in Section 2–4(a) (i), (ii) or (iii), as determined by the agency.

Such procedures may provide that an agency need not prepare a new document when a document described in Section 2–4(a) already exists.

(c) Nothing in this Order shall serve to invalidate any existing regulations of any agency which have just been adopted pursuant to court order or pursuant to judical settlement of any case or to prevent any agency from providing in its procedures for measures in addition to those provided for herein to further the purpose of the National Environmental Policy Act and other environmental laws, including the Marine Protection Research and Sanctuaries Act and the Deepwater Port Act, consistent with the foreign and national security policies of the United States.

(d) Except as provided in Section 2–4(b), agencies taking action encompassed by this Order shall, as soon as feasible, inform other Federal agencies with relevant expertise of the availability of environmental documents prepared under this Order.

Agencies in their procedures under Section 2–1 shall make appropriate provision for determining when an affected nation shall be informed in accordance with Section 3–2 of this Order of the availability of environmental documents prepared pursuant to those procedures.

In order to avoid duplication of resources, agencies in their procedures shall provide for appropriate utilization of the resources of other Federal agencies with relevant environmental jurisdiction or expertise.

2–5. Exemptions and Considerations. (a) Notwithstanding Section 2–3, the following actions are exempt from this Order:

(i) actions not having a significant effect on the environment outside the United States as determined by the agency;

(ii) actions taken by the President;

(iii) actions taken by or pursuant to the direction of the President or Cabinet officer when the national security or interest is involved or when the action occurs in the course of an armed conflict;

(iv) intelligence activities and arms transfers;

(v) export licenses or permits or export approvals, and actions relating to nuclear activities except actions providing to a foreign nation a nuclear production or utilization facility as defined in the Atomic Energy Act of 1954, as amended, or a nuclear waste management facility;

(vi) votes and other actions in international conferences and organizations;

(vii) disaster and emergency relief action.

(b) Agency procedures under Section 2–1 implementing Section 2–4 may provide for appropriate modifications in the contents, timing and availability of documents to other affected nations, where necessary to:

(i) enable the agency to decide and act promptly as and when required;

(ii) avoid adverse impacts on foreign relations or infringement in fact or appearance of other nations' sovereign responsibilities; or

(iii) ensure appropriate reflection of:

(1) diplomatic factors;

(2) international commercial, competitive and export promotion factors;

(3) needs for governmental or commercial confidentiality;
(4) national security considerations;
(5) difficulties of obtaining information and agency ability to analyze meaningfully environmental effects of a proposed action; and
(6) the degree to which the agency is involved in or able to affect a decision to be made.

(c) Agency procedures under Section 2–1 may provide for categorical exclusions and for such exemptions in addition to those specified in subsection (a) of this Section as may be necessary to meet emergency circumstances, situations involving exceptional foreign policy and national security sensitivities and other such special circumstances. In utilizing such additional exemptions agencies shall, as soon as feasible, consult with the Department of State and the Council on Environmental Quality.

(d) The provisions of Section 2–5 do not apply to actions described in Section 2–3 (a) unless permitted by law.

Sec. 3.

3–1. Rights of Action. This Order is solely for the purpose of establishing internal procedures for Federal agencies to consider the significant effects of their actions on the environment outside the United States, its territories and possessions, and nothing in this Order shall be construed to create a cause of action.

3–2. Foreign Relations. The Department of State shall coordinate all communications by agencies with foreign governments concerning environmental agreements and other arrangements in implementation of this Order.

3–3. Multi-Agency Actions. Where more than one Federal agency is involved in an action or program, a lead agency, as determined by the agencies involved, shall have responsibility for implementation of this Order.

3–4. Certain Terms. For purposes of this Order, "environment" means the natural and physical environment and excludes social, economic and other environments; and an action significantly affects the environment if it does significant harm to the environment even though on balance the agency believes the action to be beneficial to the environment. The term "export approvals" in Section 2–5(a) (b) does not mean or include direct loans to finance exports.

3–5. Multiple Impacts. If a major Federal action having effects on the environment of the United States or the global commons requires preparation of an environmental impact statement, and if the action also has effects on the environment of a foreign nation, an environmental impact statement need not be prepared with respect to the effects on the environment of the foreign nation.

Relations Between Levels of Government in Preservation of the Natural Environment

Fred P. Bosselman

As people in the United States are increasingly recognizing the complexity of the natural environment, they are also recognizing the inadequacy of the traditional roles of various levels of government in the environment's preservation. Out of this recognition has come a growing tendency for various levels of government to cooperate in new methods of preserving the quality of particular places.

Before explaining and commenting on this new trend, it is important to explain the traditional roles of various levels of government in the United States in the preservation of natural areas.

I. Traditional Roles of Levels of Government

Government in the United States consists of three levels: federal, state, and local. Each level is elected independently, and each has grown to play a significant role in the preservation of natural areas.

1. Federal

The role of the United States federal government in the preservation of the natural environment has been influenced by the unique history of the United States government in relation to the public lands. When the United States of America was created by the union of the states in 1789, the founders debated what sources of revenue to give to the newly formed federal government. They decided to give it all of the lands westward of the existing colonies so that the federal government could raise revenue by selling those lands to new settlers.[1] Thus began a long process by which the federal government opened up the West through the sale of public land to railroads, mining companies, homesteaders, and other settlers.[2]

This process still continues but on a much reduced scale. Over a century ago perceptive observers began to realize that the American land was not as inexhaustible as it had originally appeared. With the settlement of the Pacific coast and the coming of the transcontinental railroads, Americans were no longer explorers pushing an ever-moving frontier into unbounded wilderness, but settlers filling in the gaps of a fully mapped continent.

Americans began to realize that unless portions of the wilderness were consciously preserved, future generations would have no idea of the majestic attributes of the western United States as perceived by their explorer ancestors.[3]

In 1872 Congress set aside a tract of land near the headwaters of the Yellowstone River "as a public park or pleasuring-ground for the benefit and enjoyment of the people. . . ."[4] In 1880 Yosemite and Sequoia National Parks were established, to be followed early in the twentieth century by such parks as Crater Lake, Glacier, and Rocky Mountain.[5] Each of these parks was a large tract of land in its primeval condition. More by example than by conscious policy, the federal role in the preservation of the natural environment came to be seen as the preservation of primeval landscapes.[6]

Most of the early national parks were located on land that had already been owned by the federal government and was far removed from major urban habitation. Thus, the federal government obtained little experience in dealing with private landowners, either as sellers or neighbors. Isolated from the increasingly urbanized society, the National Park Service emphasized the values of the wilderness.

2. State

The states were slow to take a major role in the preservation of natural areas. With a few exceptions, the states entering the union after 1789 owned only small amounts of their own land. Prior to the 1920s, only a few states had seen the need to acquire land for the purpose of preserving the natural environment.[7] The rapid development of the automobile in the 1920s, however, stimulated many states to acquire land to serve the needs of automobile-oriented recreation.

New York's Robert Moses was the prototypical leader of the state parks movement. He emphasized the need for major recreation areas such as beaches located outside urban areas but connected to them by systems of parkways, allowing the city dweller to escape the urban atmosphere and to drive through a rural environment to these spacious places for active outdoor recreation.[8]

Consequently, the role of the state governments was closely tied in with their major role in the development of the nation's highway system. The states sought to acquire and maintain large areas designed for active recreation outside of major urban areas. Few states made an effort to preserve large tracts of primeval wilderness.[9]

3. Local

Within the urban areas themselves, the local governments have exercised the primary responsibility for the maintenance of isolated segments of a natural environment that had largely been replaced by urbanization.

The history of American local governments' efforts to preserve the natural environment can be divided into two phases. The first phase began in the latter half of the nineteenth century with the development of New York's Central Park. This inspired other major cities to acquire large natural areas as civic showpieces. This coincided with the "city beautiful movement" through which architects and planners, such as Daniel Burnham, emphasized the importance of large open spaces to set off the grand buildings in the beaux arts style that were seen as the future focal points of the city. In the late nineteenth century the large urban parks were also seen as having an inspirational influence on the vast numbers of new immigrants who were crowding into the nation's cities.[10]

By the middle of the twentieth century, however, this inspirational approach had largely been replaced by a statistical one. The need for recreation was seen as equivalent to the need for calories of food or hours of sleep. With quasi-scientific precision, urban recreation specialists produced tables showing the quantities of various categories of open space necessary to meet the recreation needs of the average person.

This statistical approach has dominated the preservation of the natural environment in American suburban areas—the areas in which growth was concentrated during the 1950s and 1960s. Local governments paid less attention to preserving specific tracts of land than to meeting certain statistical requirements for the amount of open space. This open space was usually obtained by inducing private land developers to contribute land to the community as a condition for obtaining approval for a new development. The developer typically chose to contribute the land least susceptible to development, rather than choosing the land on the basis of its particular environmental qualities.

4. Lack of Flexibility

In summary, therefore, until recently the roles of the federal, state, and local governments were quite stereotyped. The federal government was seen as the manager of large tracts of primeval wilderness. The state government provided active recreation land for automobile-oriented tourists outside of urban areas. The local governments, though originally interested in providing large showpiece parks as sources of esthetic beauty and spiritual inspiration, had, by mid-twentieth century, switched to the acquisition of numerous isolated parcels of open space designed to meet daily recreational needs.

If land did not fall into one of these stereotyped categories (or "pigeonholes," to use the American idiom), there was often no way to preserve it. The levels of government rarely cooperated with each other, and little attention was given to creation of special systems to preserve the natural environment of special places. On the national level, in particular, strong objections were posed by park enthusiasts against any effort to "dilute" the national park system by adding parks that lacked the primeval quality of the orginal parks.[11]

II. New Attitudes toward Places

Americans are now beginning to rethink the idea that the natural environment should be preserved only where it fits into one of a few stereotyped categories. A more flexible approach is now forthcoming.

The search for a new approach is heavily influenced by a growing recognition of the complexity of places. This recognition is partly attributable to the contributions of individual thinkers or groups of thinkers who viewed places from a new perspective. Some of the more important of these are as follows.

1. The Land Ethic

Aldo Leopold lamented the tendency to see man's relation to land as "strictly economic, entailing privileges but not obligations." Leopold called for a new land ethic that would recognize that human beings are members of a community of interdependent parts and that that community includes "soils, waters, plants, and animals, or collectively: the land."[12] Leopold's thinking became increasingly influential in the 1960s and 1970s because of two factors: (a) sprawling suburban development patterns ate up vast quantities of land and forced a realization that American land was growing scarce, and (b) wide dissemination of information about the science of ecology brought a realization that land is part of a network of interrelationships that affect our lives in ways only dimly perceived.[13]

2. Valueless Places

Jane Jacobs was the most prominent of a number of social critics who pointed out that much urban open space was not being effectively used. She criticized vast urban parks through which no one walked and urged that open space be designed to facilitate interaction between people.[14] Jacob's criticism stimulated interest in the growing field of environmental psychology, whose practitioners study how the nature and layout of places influence the ways people use them.[15]

3. Spiritual Places

René Dubos criticized mechanistic ways of looking at places as if they were interchangeable. He pointed out that places derive special qualities from a complex interplay of nature and culture, often determined by "forces and structures hidden beneath the surface of things." By trying to be too analytical in ascertaining the qualities of a place, one can often lose sight of a place's distinctive character.[16] Dubos' thinking is beginning to influence people to re-examine the special qualities of places in which they live.

4. Undesigned Places

Architect Robert Venturi has been in the forefront of a movement to recognize that places often thought of as ugly may have certain values not previously recognized. Venturi points out that the typical strips of commercial land uses on both sides of a highway often have attractive and useful qualities that have been ignored. He suggests that we could learn useful information about the design of open spaces if we would pay more attention to the ways in which places like Las Vegas have been developed.[17]

III. Management of Open Space

These and other new ways of looking at places have tended to open up American thinking about open space and the way it is used. This has led to a recognition that traditional ways of managing open space might need to be re-examined. This recognition has also been stimulated by certain apparent breakdowns in the way in which federal, state, and local governments are managing open space. For example:

The great primeval parks are becoming increasingly crowded. Yosemite National Park, once thought a classic example of primeval wilderness, is becoming so crowded with automobiles and campers that it seems more like New York's Central Park.

State governments are unable to keep up with the rapidly growing demand for recreation space near major urban centers. With shorter work weeks, more vacations, and more automobiles, urban residents are seeking more and more recreational opportunities. Only the federal government has the resources to meet this need, but the federal government lacks an effective program designed for this purpose.

Cities increasingly recognize that many urban parks and open spaces are serving no useful function because they are located or designed in a manner that serves neither environmental nor sociological needs.

As a result, Americans in recent years have been looking to other countries for examples of new techniques for managing open space.

1. Studying Experiences of Other Countries

Because of the common language, Americans often look to Britain when searching for models of different ways of doing things. In recent years the British national park system has attracted increasing interest in the United States.

The British national park system is relatively recent in origin. In 1945 a study undertaken by John Dower recommended the creation of a system of national parks. In Dower's words, these parks ought to consist of "beautiful and relatively wild county" in which (a) the characteristic landscape beauty is strictly preserved, (b) access and facilities for public open-air enjoyment are amply provided, (c) wildlife and buildings and places of architectural and historic interest are suitably protected, while (d) established farming use is effectively maintained.[18] In 1949 Parliament created a National Parks Commission (now called the Countryside Commission) and authorized it to designate national parks. In 1951 the Commission designated Britain's ten national parks.[19]

In Britain, designation of a national park does not require government acquisition of land within the park. In fact, Dower's report suggested that such acquisition was undesirable: "The available funds, whatever their scale, would go many times further on a procedure that relies mainly on control, reinforced when necessary by assistance, compensation or purchase, than on a procedure that takes outright purchases as its normal rule. For the broad purposes of planning and agriculture, public ownership is no more and no less desirable in National Parks than in the rest of the country."[20]

Thus most land in the British national parks is in private ownership. Development is controlled through a special system of planning controls, distinct from but integrated with the overall system of British planning. The administration of the national park system puts strong emphasis on local control, and the local people are usually strongly oriented toward conservation.[21] The Lake District National Park, for example, is managed by a park planning board having two-thirds of its members appointed by the local government and one-third by the national Department of the Environment. The national government pays 75 percent of the board's administrative costs.

The planning board adopts an overall plan establishing guidelines for park management and exercises control through the power to grant or deny planning permission for any development within the parks. The board often attaches conditions designed to avoid "intrusiveness." The goal is to give the appearance that the landscape is "the joint product of nature and of human use over many generations."[22]

Traditional agricultural practices are encouraged in the national parks. Since the English concept of scenic beauty ranks pastureland as high as wilderness, the English see no anomaly in traditional farming in the national parks. To at least one American observer, these parks have "a human element" often lacking in American parks—"a harmony in the way that the natural environment is infused with the works of man, especially in the way that the old villages and farms fit into the landscape."[23]

Preserving traditional agriculture has not proved to be easy. In England, as in many other parts of the world, the operation of small farms has become less economical.[24] Substantial government subsidies are needed to permit sheep farmers to continue in the traditional manner.

Variations on the British concept of national parks include Areas of Outstanding Natural Beauty, which are smaller than national parks but eligible for grants for the protection of amenities and the construction of recreational facilities. Development in these areas requires prior consultation with the Countryside Commission, but unlike the national parks no special local planning mechanism is required. As of the end of 1976, Britain had thirty-three Areas of Outstanding Beauty covering over 5,000 square miles. Since 1973 the Commission has also been authorized to designate Heritage Coasts, segments of the coastline having particular scenic or historic value. The Commission pays local authorities to employ heritage coast officers and rangers, who develop plans and enforce regulations to maintain the amenities in these coastal areas.[25]

In addition to England, other countries' park systems have been receiving American attention. The United States National Park Service has established a program of regular meetings and exchange of information with the Japanese Environment Agency to follow developments in the Japanese national park system. (However, the American public still has little knowledge about the Japanese system, and additional publications in English describing the system would be most gratefully welcomed.)

2. New Categories of Open Space

Within the last few years, the United States government has shown interest in parks consisting of a mixture of public land and publicly regulated private land of the type established in England and Japan. This interest is gathering momentum.

The first step in this direction was the creation of National Seashores, beginning in the early 1960s during the Kennedy administration.[26] In places like Cape Cod in Massachusetts and Fire Island, near New York City, Congress recognized that it was not feasible to acquire every privately owned home in an area proposed for federal acquisition. It agreed not to acquire these properties as long as they complied with federally approved local regulatory standards. However, most people viewed this as a compromise necessary to obtain the legislation's passage rather than a policy to be emulated elsewhere.[27]

As the 1970s began, two significant developments took place: the State of New York created the Adirondack Park Agency, authorized to prepare plans and regulations for the region of mixed public (state) and private land that is known as Adirondack Park;[28] and the states of California and Nevada, with federal cooperation, adopted an interstate compact creating the Tahoe Regional Planning Agency.[29] The agency was directed to prepare plans and regulations for the private lands in the Lake Tahoe watershed, which contains a mixture of private and public (mostly National Forest) lands.

Charles E. Little of the Library of Congress saw the opportunity to go beyond these isolated incidents toward a new policy that encouraged federally sponsored parks and recreation areas incorporating both public and private lands. Although other American scholars had called attention to the English model,[30] it was a 1975 legislative report by Little that stimulated federal interest in establishing public parks with an intentional mixture of public and private ownership.[31]

Many local groups had persuaded their congressmen to introduce legislation that would create a new park or recreation area in their district. Interior Department officials saw mixed ownership as a way of responding to strong local interest in finding new ways to preserve a wide variety of different types of these special places.

In 1978, President Carter and Interior Secretary Andrus decided to propose designation of a new category of places to be known as "areas of national concern." The first such area was to be the Santa Monica mountains. The proposed legislation would provide unified federal-state-local management for a large recreation area near Los Angeles. Much of the land would remain private.[32]

The administration's interest coincided with strong congressional support for more innovative approaches toward parks. Under the leadership of Congressman Phil Burton of California, the administration proposal for the Santa Monica mountains became part of the first omnibus "park barrel" bill—a bill that would authorize numerous new parks and recreational areas scattered among various congressional districts.[33]

The legislation passed in the final days of the 1978 session of Congress and became known as the National Parks and Recreation Act of 1978.[34] It authorized creation of a number of new areas of mixed public-private ownership, including:

Santa Monica Mountains National Recreation Area,
Pinelands National Reserve,
Jean Laffite National Historical Park,
New River Gorge National River,
San Antonio Missions National Historical Park.

The diversity of the names illustrates the innovative nature of the thinking that has gone into these proposals. Perhaps the most important point about them is that Americans realize each of these places is special. There is no need to force them all into the same mold, to hold them up against the Yosemite model and either cut them to fit or reject them. Diversity can be seen as a virtue rather than a vice.

A number of states are using "critical area" legislation to accomplish similar objectives. Of even greater significance are the efforts of local communities all over the United States to try to protect their unique qualities. Without waiting for aid from higher levels of government, hundreds of communities are putting into effect local programs to identify special local qualities and to direct growth in ways that will complement those qualities.

Efforts to emphasize the special qualities of places should be encouraged, and new techniques are undoubtedly needed. It must be stressed, however, that any new legislation devising a *uniform* system for recognizing the special qualities of places might merely create a new stereotype.[35] It is hoped that Americans will now retain the habit of looking at each special place individually and trying to design a system for managing the place that is tailored to its particular qualities.

Notes

Many of the ideas and material in this paper were derived from the author's participation in the International Land Use Project of The Conservation Foundation, Washington, D.C., funded by the German Marshall Fund of the United States.

1. Payson Jackson Treat, "Origins of the National Land System under the Confederation," in *The Public Lands: Studies in the History of the Public Domain*, ed. Vernon Carstensen (Madison, Wisconsin: University of Wisconsin Press, 1968), p. 7.
2. Marison Clawson and Burnell Held, *The Federal Lands: Their Use and Management* (Lincoln, Nebraska: University of Nebraska Press, 1957), p. 23.
3. Ibid., pp. 27–29. See also T. H. Watkins and Charles S. Watson, Jr., *The Lands No One Knows: America and the Public Domain* (San Francisco: Sierra Club Books, 1975), pp. 88–115.
4. "An Act to Set Apart a Certain Tract of Land Lying near the Headwaters of the Yellow Stone River as a Public Park," Vol. XVII *Statutes at Large* (1872) pp. 32–33.
5. See, generally, Devereux Butcher, *Exploring Our National Parks and Monuments* (New York: Oxford University Press, 1947).
6. Ibid., pp. 150–54.
7. See Freeman Tilden, *The State Parks: Their Meaning in American Life* (New York: Alfred A. Knopf, 1962), p. v.
8. Robert Caro, *The Power Broker: Robert Moses and the Fall of New York* (New York: Alfred A. Knopf, 1974), pp. 237–38.
9. There are a few exceptions, such as California's preservation of the redwoods and the Anza-Borrego desert as part of the state parks system, and the 72,000-acre Custer State Park in South Dakota. See Tilden, *State Parks*, p. 41.
10. August Heckscher, *Open Spaces: The Life of American Cities* (New York: Harper & Row, 1977), p. 164. Some county governments acquired large tracts of natural land on the fringes of urban areas. Classic examples are the forest preserves of Cook County, surrounding Chicago, and the Maryland-National Capital park system north and east of Washington.
11. Butcher, *Exploring Our National Parks*, p. 8.
12. Aldo Leopold, *A Sand County Almanac* (New York: Oxford University Press, 1949).
13. See, e.g., Lynton Keith Caldwell, *Environment: A Challenge for Modern Society* (Garden City, N.Y.: The Natural History Press, 1970); Barry Commoner, *The Closing Circle: Nature, Man, and Technology* (New York: Alfred A. Knopf, 1971).

14. Jane Jacobs, *The Death and Life of Great American Cities* (New York: Random House, 1961), pp. 89–111.
15. See, e.g., Harold M. Proshansky, William H. Ittelson, and Leanne G. Rivlin, *Environmental Psychology: Man and His Physical Setting* (New York: Holt, Rinehart & Winston, 1970).
16. René Dubos, *A God Within* (New York: Charles Scribner's Sons, 1972), pp. 22–23; see René Dubos, *Beast or Angel: Choices That Make Us Human* (New York: Charles Scribner's Sons, 1974).
17. Robert Venturi, Denise Scott Brown, and Steven Izenour, *Learning from Las Vegas* (Cambridge, Mass.: MIT Press, 1972).
18. John Dower, *National Parks in England and Wales* (London: Her Majesty's Stationery Office, 1945), p. 6.
19. See Mervyn Bell, ed., *Britain's National Parks* (London: David & Charles, 1975), pp. 8–10; Roger Bush, *The National Parks of England and Wales* (London: J. M. Dent, 1973), pp. 55–67. See Christopher Hall, "Is Compromise the Cure-all for Britain's Park System," *Planning* (U.S.) (March, 1978): 27.
20. Dower, *National Parks*, p. 45.
21. Peter Hall, Harry Gracey, Roy Drewett, and Ray Thomas, *The Containment of Urban England* (London: George Allen & Unwin, 1973), Vol. 2, p. 374.
22. Dower, *National Parks*, p. 19.
23. Stanley Johnson, *The Politics of Environment: The British Experience* (London: Tom Stacey, 1973), p. 102. See also John T. Starr, "The Green and Pleasant Land," *American Forests* (January, 1978): 38, 52.
24. See Exmoor National Park Committee, *Exmoor National Park Plan* (Somerset: Exmoor House, 1977), Ch. 3.
25. Countryside Commission, *Ninth Report of the Countryside Commission, 1975–76* (London: Her Majesty's Stationery Office, 1977).
26. See Jon A. Kusler and William Duddleson, "Alternative Federal Strategies for Strengthening State and Local Urban Outdoor Recreation and Open Space Programs Including the Establishment of Greenline Parks," National Urban Recreation Study Technical Reports, Volume I, Part B (Washington, D.C.: U.S. Department of the Interior, 1978), p. 62.
27. Jon A. Kusler, *Public/Private Parks and Management of Private Lands for Park Protection* (Madison, Wisconsin: University of Wisconsin Institute of Environmental Studies, 1974), p. 68. In addition, 1968 saw the inauguration of the Wild and Scenic River system, some of which also combine fee acquisition and regulatory techniques. See 16 U.S.C.A. Ch. 28 (1974).
28. Article 27, §§800–810, McKinney's Revised Statutes of New York (1971).
29. Public Law 91–148, 83 Stat. 360 (1969).
30. See Warren A. Johnson, *Public Parks on Private Land in England and Wales* (Baltimore: Johns Hopkins Press, 1971); Kusler, *Public/Private Parks.*
31. Charles E. Little, *Green-line Parks: An Approach to Preserving Recreational Landscapes in Urban Areas* (Washington, D.C.: Congressional Research Service, Library of Congress, 1975). See also J. William Futrell, "Parks to the People: New Directions for the National Park System," 25 *Emory Law Journal* 255 (1976).
32. U.S. Department of the Interior, News Release, May 5, 1978.
33. H.R. 12536, 95th Congress, 2d Session (1978). The term "park barrel" is copied from the term "pork barrel" traditionally used to designate legislation authorizing dams, canals, and other public works projects scattered among many member's districts.
34. S. 791, 95th Congress, 2d Session (1978).
35. See F. Fraser Darling and Noel D. Eichhorn, *Man & Nature in the National Parks: Reflections on Policy* (Washington, D.C.: The Conservation Foundation, 1967), p. 31.

Regional Cooperation for the Protection of the Environment in the East Asian Seas and the Pacific

Tsutomu Fuse and Tōru Iwama

I. Basis for Regional Cooperation: UN Efforts

The 1972 United Nations Conference on the Human Environment adopted the Action Plan which included a number of recommendations on the condition of the marine environment.[1] Annex III of the Report of the Conference, "General Principles for Assessment and Control of Marine Pollution," emphasized the regional approach toward combating marine pollution. Principle 9 in particular provides that states should join together regionally to concert their policies and adopt measures in common, to prevent the pollution of the areas which for geographical or ecological reasons form a natural entity and an integrated whole.[2]

Accordingly, the Governing Council of the United Nations Environment Programme (UNEP), which was established after the conference, decided in 1974 that priority should be given to regional activities in dealing with marine environmental problems.[3] It endorsed the following objective and strategies for the regional seas program at its third session,[4] and noted them with approval in its fourth session:[5]

> Objective
>
> To work out and support the implementation of plans for arresting pollution of the oceans and closed or semi-closed seas, and for managing aquatic living resources to ensure that the best use is made of them, and to make efforts to ensure that environmental considerations are taken into account at the Law of the Sea Conference.
>
> Strategies
>
> To assess the state of marine pollution, the sources and trends of the pollution, and the impact of the pollution on human health, marine

ecosystems and amenities; to monitor marine pollution and aquatic living resources; to promote international and regional conventions, guidelines and action for the control of marine pollution and for the protection and management of aquatic marine resources; to exchange information on subjects relevant to the protection, development and management of marine and coastal resources; to support education and training efforts that should enhance the participation of developing countries in the protection, development and management of marine and coastal resources.

According to these strategies, the governing council identified at first six regional seas as priority areas: the Mediterranean, the Caribbean, the Persian Gulf, the Gulf of Guinea, the Red Sea, and the East Asian Seas; and then added the Pacific (Southeast Pacific and Southwest Pacific). See Figure 1, a map of areas covered by the UNEP regional seas program.

Fig. 1. Areas covered by UNEP regional seas program. The land and seaward limits to the regional seas indicated on this map are merely illustrative. The definition of the boundaries is the responsibility of the governments concerned. Action plans approved or awaiting approval: 1. Mediterranean; 2. Red Sea; 3. Persian Gulf. Action plans in preparation: 4. Caribbean; 5. Gulf of Guinea; 6. East Asian Seas; 7. Southeast Pacific; 8. Southwest Pacific.
SOURCE: Report of the Executive Director, UNEP/GC. 6/7, 20 February 1978, p. 143.

With regard to the approach taken to achieve the stated objective, UNEP has adopted the same approach in all regional seas, though with appropriate adaptations to take into account each region's ecological, social, economic, cultural, and political characteristics. The said approach is to take the following activities step by step:

Activity A—In consultation with the Governments and other organizations concerned, the development of draft action plans for a number of the regional seas identified as priority areas within a framework agreed to at an interagency meeting on regional seas convened by UNEP in Paris in June 1976.

Activity B—Securing the approval of Governments for such plans.

Activity C—Implementation of the action plan with the cooperation of the Governments concerned. Where appropriate, pilot projects will be initiated with catalytic and financial support from UNEP, the costs being gradually transferred to the Governments concerned.

Activity D—Encouragement to Governments of the area to assume full responsibility for continued action for the protection of the marine environment.[6]

The timetable for achieving the objective and fulfilling the activities of the regional seas program, however, varies from one sea to another. Compared with other regional seas, the East Asian Seas and the Pacific have been slow in developing action plans and legal and institutional frameworks because of the complicated economic, social, and political situations of these regions.[7]

This paper intends to review the recent and current developments in these two regions, the East Asian Seas and the Southwest Pacific, and to give an impetus to future development of comprehensive action plans for the protection of regional seas and marine living resources therein through environmentally sound development.

II. The East Asian Seas

1. Background

The marine environment of the East Asian Seas and all the living organisms therein are of vital importance to the people of this region in terms of the economic, social, health, and cultural values. However, the delicate ecosystems of the oceans and the varied islands in this region have suffered from the impact of pollution resulting from human activities. The most important effect of pollution upon the marine environment is ecological disruption. There are already signs of serious damage to the marine environment in this region. The ecological and economic values are being increasingly undermined by marine pollution, poorly planned development, tourist facilities, and industries. The health of the sea and its life-sustaining systems in this region are being impaired by means of increased pollution of the sea and contamination of the ocean's food chain.

The region of the East Asian Seas is, of course, an immense one, not only in terms of the size but also in terms of the variety of problems it exhibits. Therefore, different priorities might be given to environmental problems in different parts of the region. For example, in the Bay of Bengal, the Straits of Malacca, the Gulf of Thailand, and the East and South China Seas, marine pollution, fishery resources, and mineral or natural resources would be of prime importance. The effects of organic and biological pollutants upon fish populations have appeared in the coastal waters of Japan, Singapore, Thailand, Korea, Hong Kong, Indonesia, Malaysia, the Philippines, and Australia. Thermal pollution, mainly by hot-water discharges from industrial processing and nuclear power plants, is already having significant effects in certain estuaries and inshore waters in these sub-regions. In the Seas of the Eastern Archipelago, conservation of marine ecosystems would be of prime importance. Because of their isolated evolution, distinctive fauna and flora are often found in the islands. Coral reefs are also important renewable resources, both in ecological and economic terms in these sub-regions. Coral reef communities are now suffering the impact of careless and needless human activities. And the mangrove community is almost in the same situation in these sub-regions.

2. Recent and Current Developments

It is certain that both geographical and political factors have made it difficult for the peoples of the East Asian region to cooperate in adopting the common approach to the future of the region as a whole. Expanses of the sea are vast and environmental problems diverse. Moreover, there is a great variety of environmental policies among the nations in this region. However, the common denominators and the common interests in the protection of the marine environment in the East Asian Seas as a whole are equally evident.

In the face of these situations, international scientific efforts have been successful in fostering regional actions. For example, in the field of training, participants from the East Asian region attended the Second Regional Training Course in the Marine Environment held in Japan from July to September in 1975 with the assistance of the United Nations Educational, Scientific and Cultural Organization (UNESCO). In September 1975 a regional meeting on Training, Educational and Mutual Assistance devoted to oceanographic problems of the East Asian Seas was organized in Manila by the Intergovernmental Oceanographic Commission (IOC) of UNESCO. The Food and Agricultural

Organization (FAO), in cooperation with the Swedish International Development Agency (SIDA), held, from 17 January to 27 February 1977 in Manila, a training workshop on aquatic pollution in relation to protection of living resources.

In order to identify the major environmental problems related to marine pollution and to develop a research and monitoring program for the East Asian Seas, UNEP organized a scientific workshop on marine pollution in April 1976 in Penang in cooperation with FAO and IOC. The workshop recommended a priority list of four regional and twenty sub-regional projects to be implemented in the region.[8]

The region is large and the environmental problems are varied. Therefore, protection of the sea and the living marine resources will be dealt with on a sub-regional basis, in response to the needs and priorities of the States directly concerned. The Straits of Malacca is one example of such a sub-region, where a tripartite navigation safety agreement was signed on 24 February 1977 by Indonesia, Malaysia, and Singapore, and an Association of Southeast Asian Nations (ASEAN) Contingency Plan for Oil Pollution was adopted by ASEAN member states. Another envisaged sub-region comprises the Seas of Thailand, Malaysia, Singapore, Indonesia, and the Philippines, where the regional action plan will incorporate coastal area development and management.[9]

It should be noted that in accordance with Decision 88D (V) of the Governing Council of UNEP a preliminary outline of an action plan was finally prepared after consultation with government experts and representatives of the UN organizations in the region (UNEP). The future work plan for the East Asian Seas will be implemented along the following lines:

March 1979. Mission visited the region to discuss possible elements for an action plan (governments, ASEAN, UNEP, agencies);

June 1979. Presentation of draft action plan to ASEAN Sub-Committee on Environment (governments, ASEAN, UNEP);

October–November 1979. Mission to the region to discuss revised draft action plan (governments, ASEAN, UNEP, agencies);

November 1979–March 1980. Series of training events (workshops, seminars, training courses) in the region (governments, UNEP, agencies);

March 1980. Government expert meeting to review all components of the draft action plan (governments, UNEP, all relevant organizations);

August 1980. Government expert meeting to refine the legal components of the draft action plan (governments, UNEP);

October 1980. Intergovernmental meeting to review and adopt the action plan including adoption of the regional convention (governments, UNEP, all relevant organizations);

1980–1982. Implementation of the action plan.[10]

3. Institutional and Organizational Framework: A Proposal

This section intends to give an impetus to future development of legal and institutional components of a regional action plan.

It should be recommended at first that in order to cope with existing and emerging environmental problems in the area, regional cooperation is urgently needed, especially in the fields of data collection and exchange, pollution monitoring, transfer of technology, environmental education and training, and development of contingency plans. Such cooperation may be best served by concluding a Convention for the Protection of the Marine Environment in the East Asian Seas and by establishing an East Asian Environmental Organization.[11]

With regard to the conclusion of the regional convention, we can learn from the experiences of other regions, such as the Mediterranean Sea, the Baltic Sea, and the Persian Gulf.[12] It is certain that such experiences cannot be applied without any reservation to the East Asian Seas, since economic, social, political, and environmental situations are quite different from those in the above-mentioned regions. However, in view of the importance and complexity of the problem it is advisable to make use of the Mediterranean Action Plan, for example, as a model for a comprehensive program aiming at the protection of the marine environment in the East Asian Seas.

The regional convention should deal with not only marine pollution control but also with protection of the natural state of the marine environment. In this connection, natural parks and reserves will play an important role in the future utilization of the marine environment of the East Asian region, both as reference areas for research and ocean use guidance, and as those for education, tourism, and recreation.

The combined efforts of all the states concerned are particularly needed for conservation of migratory species. These are common resources shared by all the states within their range, since they do not respect national boundaries. Therefore, migratory birds must be protected by an agreement among all the states they pass through. Similarly, marine animals such as seals and sea turtles, or purely pelagic species, such as tuna, cetaceans and some of the sirenia, require international cooperation for their protection.

For the purpose of implementing this type of convention, an East

Asian Environmental Organization should carry out the following functions:

(1) to keep the implementation of the convention and its protocols under continuous observation;

(2) to make recommendations on the regional or sub-regional rules and standards to be elaborated and on measures to be taken by the contracting parties;

(3) to determine a "specific area" in which ecological conditions, natural characteristics or the particular character of traffic render special regulations necessary and to approve regional or sub-regional rules and standards for this purpose;

(4) to designate and manage international parks and reserves;

(5) to regulate the discovery, identification, protection, and disposal of the archaeological and historical treasures of the seabed and the ocean floor beyond the limits of national jurisdiction and to draw up rules for this purpose;

(6) to examine a development program submitted by the party to the convention, and when necessary, to request it to submit an environmental impact statement and consult with a party or parties concerned;

(7) to be the center of an environmental monitoring system and to receive reports presented by the contracting parties for this purpose;

(8) to be notified of any grave and imminent danger from pollution or threat of pollution by the contracting parties;

(9) to keep under review the contents of the convention and its protocols and to recommend to the contracting parties such amendments as may be required;

(10) to promote in close cooperation with appropriate governmental bodies additional measures to protect the marine environment of the East Asian waters;

(11) to seek, when appropriate, services of competent regional and other international bodies to collaborate in scientific and technological research as well as other relevant activities pertinent to the objectives of the convention; and

(12) to perform such functions as may be appropriate under the terms of the convention.[13]

4. Conclusion

As far as the Third United Nations Conference on the Law of the Sea is concerned, its role in the development of international environmental law is restricted to the formulation of an "umbrella treaty" which can be applied universally. However, even if such a global treaty is concluded at the conference, a regional convention will be needed in order to meet different regional conditions and requirements. It goes without saying that such a regional convention will be needed if a global treaty is not concluded.

It is certain that there is some doubt whether the general climate in the East Asian region has grown ripe for the conclusion of a regional or sub-regional agreement. In fact, very complicated political and economic problems exist as the major obstacle to attaining this purpose. However, it is no exaggeration to say that the protection of the marine environment in the East Asian Seas will provide the key to man's future in the East Asian region, and the action or inaction of our generation in this region will be the key to the success of the struggle to preserve and to enhance the environment for human life on our "Only One Earth" as a whole.[14]

III. The Southwest Pacific[15]

1. Background

The Pacific region is the largest oceanic area of the world. It is said that it contains potential new sources of non-renewable resources on a large scale. At the same time the Pacific is known as the largest source of renewable resources of marine life. The interior of this oceanic hemisphere contains such island groups as Micronesia, Melanesia, and Polynesia, which constitute some of the world's most beautiful, precious, and exotic natural environments together with some of its most rich, creative, and sensitive human culture.[16]

In the islands of the Southwest Pacific, human beings achieved a harmony with the natural environment which produced and sustained cultural and social systems that proved highly stable and durable until recent times. But now, the advent of modernization to this area, bringing industry and tourism, has begun to threaten destruction of the ecosystems and genetic resources of the region on the one hand, and creative and sensitive human cultures on the other.

In addressing the Thirteenth Pacific Science Congress at Vancouver in August 1975, Maurice F. Strong, the former executive director of UNEP, said:

> Environment is, and will be, the key to the future of the region. For the natural environmental resources of water, of land and the coastal

interfaces between them, and of plant and animal life—these will remain the essential resources on which life of the people of the area depends. Modern technology and industry will modify the natural environment but cannot replace it as the basis for creating conditions of life that are both congenial and sustainable. Technology in the hands of industrial man can either enhance or destroy the natural environmental resource base; it can either support or undermine the quality of human life in the region.

UNEP has had a special interest in the Pacific region, since the region has been relatively little affected by industrial activity and urban development and offers an opportunity to promote environmentally sound forms of development from the outset. Since the Stockholm Conference, UNEP has been increasingly interested in the concept of ecodevelopment as a planning method enabling developing countries to achieve accelerated and self-sustained development, which is a part of an autonomous national strategy for integrated and environmentally sound development.[17] The Southwest Pacific, where the political climate is now ripe for taking regional actions, is a most appropriate region for pilot projects in ecodevelopment to be studied and implemented.

Because of these specific environmental situations and corresponding needs of the countries and territories of the area, regional activities for the development and protection of the marine environment have been carried out, from the beginning, as part of a broader comprehensive strategy for environmental management. It is to be noted in this connection that two regional organizations, the South Pacific Commission (SPC) and the South Pacific Bureau for Economic Cooperation (SPEC), have initiated such regional activities in cooperation with UNEP and other international organizations.

The following section will review actions taken in the Southwest Pacific for a regional program of environmental management, including the protection of nature and living marine resources, and will indicate the lessons to be learned from them.

2. Recent and Current Developments

Most countries and territories in the Southwest Pacific, except Australia, New Zealand, and Papua New Guinea, are composed of small islands, geographically dispersed and separated by vast expanses of sea. Their development has been hampered by the very fact of decentralization and isolation of their island societies. Most island countries and territories lack capital, skills, technologies, and the infrastructure necessary for economic development. In order to achieve their development and welfare, it is necessary to pool and to utilize the natural and human resources of the region by promoting regional cooperation in various fields. Two regional organizations, SPC and SPEC, were established in the region to fulfill the stated objective.[18]

In the course of development, SPC and SPEC have come either jointly or separately to launch the following regional activities or programs which are concerned with nature conservation and the protection of living marine resources.

SPC launched the Special Project on Conservation of Nature and Natural Resources in July 1974, with the appointment of Dr. Arthur L. Dahl, formerly of the Smithsonian Institution, as regional ecological advisor.[19] In close working relationship with the International Union for Conservation of Nature and Natural Resources (IUCN) and UNEP, this project resulted in producing in 1976 the Convention on Conservation of Nature in the South Pacific and the Comprehensive Environmental Management Programme.

With respect to the conservation of nature, members of SPC concluded, on 12 June 1976, the Convention on Conservation in the South Pacific,[20] in order to take harmonious action within their own countries for the conservation and protection of nature and irreplaceable resources for the benefit of present and future generations, in the face of rapid development and degradation of nature resulting therefrom. Parties agree to encourage the creation of protected areas (national parks and reserves), to safeguard representative samples of natural ecosystems, superlative scenery, striking geological formations, and regions and objects of esthetic, historic, cultural, or scientific value (Article II). Regarding indigenous fauna and flora that are threatened with extinction, parties agree to establish and maintain a list of their species in their own countries and give such species as complete protection as possible (Article V). In both cases, parties shall notify the body charged with the continuing bureau duties under the convention of the establishment of any protected areas and the list of indigenous species.

Parties agree to conduct research relating to the conservation of nature and to cooperate in the exchange of information on the results of such research, and on the management of protected areas and of protected species (Article VII). What is more important, cooperation in the interchange and training of personnel for the conservation of nature is anticipated.

The conclusion of this convention was followed by a Regional Symposium on Conservation of Nature in the South Pacific organized by SPC and IUCN, at which the regional ecological advisor, Dr. Dahl, presented the results of a regional ecosystems survey conducted earlier in 1976 with the financial support of UNEP and IUCN under their Global Conservation Project.

Apart from the 1976 Convention, there is a significant movement in the Southwest region toward establishing a World Marine Park.[21] The government of the Cook Islands offered to IUCN one of its remarkable atolls, Mauae (Harvey Islands), for the benefit of science and conservation. And the government of French Polynesia agreed that the island of Taiaro (W. A. Robinson Sanctuary) should be established as a scientific reserve to serve the cause of scientific research at an international level.

Soon after launching the Special Project on Nature and Natural Resources, SPC began discussions with UNEP on possible support for regional environmental activities, which culminated in a UNEP request in October 1975 for the development of a comprehensive program for environmental management in the region. In March 1976 SPC submitted to UNEP a preliminary proposal for a five-year program, and in response to it UNEP encouraged further development of the comprehensive program concept in December 1976. Meanwhile, the Seventh South Pacific Forum of SPEC and the Sixteenth South Pacific Conference of SPC, being held in July and October of 1976 respectively, decided to prepare jointly for a comprehensive environmental management program for the Pacific islands.

At the request of SPEC and the government of Papua New Guinea, SPC organized a Comprehensive Environmental Management Programme Planning Meeting in March 1977, which culminated in producing the following recommendations: that the regional ecological advisor draft the program documents; that after approval by SPEC and SPC he prepare a detailed program proposal; and that the South Pacific Ecodevelopment Fund be established.[22] In May 1977 the regional ecological advisor submitted the Comprehensive Environmental Management Programme (CEMP) to SPC and SPEC.[23]

CEMP provides for the sound management of the Pacific islands environment so that it will be capable of providing a present and future resource base able to support the needs and maintain the quality of life of the people of the region.[24] The basic philosophy of CEMP is termed "ecodevelopment" and is founded on the following principles:

1. Priority should be given to the basic real needs of people, such as food, pure water and shelter;

2. Development should aim for self-reliance rather than increasing dependence on outside groups or countries;

3. There must be a harmonious relationship between people and their environment that respects the requirements of human cultures and

of the ecological systems upon which natural productivity is based, and that keeps options open for future generations.[25]

CEMP helps each government to define its own environmental policy and makes resources available (expertise, information, training, and material support) to implement the policy. The funding for CEMP projects will be sought from UNEP and other sources outside the region, and a South Pacific Ecodevelopment Fund will be established to support CEMP, with the assistance of Mr. Maurice F. Strong in raising funds for that purpose.

As for the institutional arrangement, a new organization will not be set up to implement CEMP, but SPC and SPEC will be joint executing agencies for CEMP.

Priority areas for action during CEMP are defined under three broad headings: human settlement, marine ecosystems, and land-based ecosystems.[26] In terms of nature conservation and the protection of the living marine resources, the second and third categories may be subdivided into the following items, respectively:

Marine ecosystems

(1) management of fisheries in the framework of a regional fisheries agency;
(2) conservation of the genetic and biological diversity of marine environments and maintenance of their quality for the local people and as a tourist and recreational resource;
(3) management of coastal zone ecosystems and coastal resources;
(4) disaster protection from hurricanes and tidal waves;
(5) prevention of localized pollution of coastal waters and degradation of near-shore marine environment by oil, industrial or urban effluents, agricultural chemicals, dredging, soil erosion, mining drainage, and waste disposal.

Land-based ecosystems

(1) assessment of effects of shifting agricultural systems and large-scale agriculture upon soil erosion and depletion of soil fertility;
(2) environmental and technical assessment of the mining and major engineering works;
(3) environmentally sound forest management and exploitation.

Activities to be incorporated in, supported, or coordinated by CEMP include surveys and research, information services, pilot projects, education, planning, legislation, administration, and national, regional and international coordination.

Almost all countries and territories in the South Pacific are small islands with limited land resources and can only hope to expand their economy by the exploitation of the ocean resources. Therefore, it is natural that much weight be placed upon the conservation and rational utilization of marine living resources in this region. SPEC, in co-operation with SPC, has already taken steps to establish a South Pacific Fisheries Agency in order to cope with problems which will arise by creating 200-mile exclusive economic zones. Creation of 200-mile zones, once established, increases for the individual countries the necessity of control over harvesting of the living resources to promote optimum resource utilization from these zones and to conserve the living resources in such vast expanses of the sea.[27] In particular, highly migratory species, such as skipjack tuna, which is a major resource of the region, freely travel from the waters of one coastal state to those of others and cannot be conserved by fragmental measures by individual coastal states. Hence it is thought desirable that a single fishery agency for the South Pacific region should be set up to deal with specific problems which can be solved only on the basis of regional cooperation.

The South Pacific Meeting on the Law of the Sea, convened by SPEC in Suva in October 1976, decided to establish a South Pacific Fisheries Agency to promote the conservation and rational utilization of the fish stocks of the region. It also requested the director of SPEC to prepare proposals for the establishment and operation of an agency in consultation with the Secretary-General of SPC. SPEC convened a meeting of all interested coastal states within the region from 18 to 25 November 1977, and thereafter, to prepare a Draft Convention for the Establishment of the South Pacific Regional Fisheries Organization.[28]

However, the 9th South Pacific Forum meeting held at Niue in September 1978 had to postpone a time-consuming consideration of the Draft Convention, which included a disputed membership provision of the countries outside the region and decided, instead, to establish a South Pacific Forum Fisheries Agency (SPFFA) with more restricted powers, functions, and membership than the organization.[29] At that time, the Forum countries had an urgent need to harmonize their fisheries policies in the region and to adopt a coordinated approach in their negotiations with distant-water fishing countries in order to secure more than a small part of the benefits derived from their resources within their 200-mile zones. In realizing such a need as soon as practicable, they had to choose the most feasible means to establish a restricted agency.

In late 1978, the agency was established for convenience purposes under the umbrella of the SPEC agreement. In July 1979, the 10th South Pacific Forum meeting signed the Convention to Establish the South Pacific Forum Fisheries Agency, an agreement giving the agency its own independent legal status, which is now in force.[30]

According to the convention, membership of the agency is restricted to forum members and other states or territories in the region with the approval of the forum (Art. II). Article III provides that "the parties to this convention recognize that the coastal State has sovereign rights, for the purpose of exploring and exploiting, conserving and managing the living marine resources, including highly migratory species, within its exclusive economic zone or fishing zone which may extend 200 nautical miles from the baseline from which the breadth of its territorial sea is measured" (par. 1). Therefore, distant-water fishing countries outside the region, whether they recognize such sovereign rights or not, are excluded from membership in the agency.

With respect to the effective cooperation for the conservation and optimum utilization of the highly migratory species of the region, the parties recognize the necessity to establish additional international machinery which will provide for cooperation between all coastal states in the region and all states involved in the harvesting of such resources (Art. III, par. 2). It must be noted, however, that such an international machinery, once established, will be very limited in its powers and functions, since the machinery should not prejudice sovereign rights of the coastal state over the highly migratory species within the 200-mile zone, while such species migrate freely in the vast expanse of the sea of the region without respecting man-demarcated boundaries.

Regarding the function of the agency, it is restricted to collecting and disseminating to the parties relevant information on the statistical and biological data of the living marine resources in the region, on management procedures, legislation and agreements adopted by other countries both within and beyond the region, and on prices, shipping, processing, and marketing of fish and fish products. The agency also discharges such functions as providing to the parties technical advice and information, assistance in the development of fisheries policies and negotiations, and assistance in the issuing of licenses, the collection of fees, or in matters pertaining to surveillance and enforcement (Art. VII). It must be noted that a Forum Fisheries Committee to be established within the agency would promote intraregional coordination and cooperation with distant-water fishing countries and access to the 200-mile zones of other parties (Art. V, par. 2).

Since the creation of SPFFA, the political climate has grown ripe for the consideration of a more broadly based fisheries organization. At the meeting of forum government officials convened in Honiara, Solomon Islands, May 1979, officials noted that there was a need for such a fisheries organization with separate functions from SPFFA in order to provide a means of cooperation between coastal states of the region and other states whose nationals fish for highly migratory species in the region.[31] Such an organization is envisaged by Article III, paragraph 2 of the Convention to Establish the South Pacific Forum Fisheries Agency. They also noted that such an organization might be established along the lines envisaged in Article 64 of the Informal Composite Negotiating Text of the Law of the Sea Conference.[32]

The South Pacific Forum will invite the directors of SPEC and SPFFA to convene a meeting of the forum government officials at an early date to consider in detail the general principles involved in establishing such an organization and then convene a meeting of all countries and territories likely to have an interest in the establishment of such an organization.

It is true that distant-water fishing countries, such as Japan and the United States, have much interest in harvesting highly migratory species in the region and participating in a new organization to fulfill their fishing interests. It is also true that for their financial and technological reasons, the forum members have much interest in inviting distant water fishing countries to participate in such an organization. However, unless there is a change of views either in the forum members or in the distant-water fishing countries with regard to sovereign rights of the coastal state over the highly migratory species within the 200-mile zone, a new organization may not be established with the participation of distant-water fishing countries. If so, there will be no hope for "ensuring conservation and promoting the objective of optimum utilization of such species throughout the region." And even if there should be any participation of distant-water fishing countries in the organization on the premise that the organization provides a means of cooperation in the fields of conservation and management of the highly migratory species only beyond the 200-mile zone, there will be less hope for an effective conservation and management of such resources which freely travel without respecting the man-made boundary of the 200-mile zone. The membership problem of distant-water fishing countries is a very crucial factor which will decide whether or not the organization will be successfully created and whether or not the marine resources of highly migratory species in the region will be effectively conserved and managed.

3. Conclusion

The above-mentioned experiences in regional cooperation for the protection of environment in the Pacific region may be summarized as follows:

Most countries and territories in the region are in the early stage of development. They have not yet encountered such serious pollution problems as developed countries have, but there is a fear that they will in the future. In order that their distinctive natural environment of tourist, scientific, and recreational value will not deteriorate from environmentally unsound development, and that living resources will not be depleted by mismanagement, they are willing to learn lessons from the experience of developed countries and to take initiatives in formulating environmentally sound development.

International organizations, such as UNEP and IUCN, are successful in contributing to the preparation of regional programs for the protection of environment in the region. UNEP supplied financing, knowledge, and expertise in formulating the CEMP, while IUCN prepared a Convention on Conservation of Nature in the South Pacific, co-sponsored regional technical meetings on parks and conservation with SPC, and advised governments on national parks and conservation programs.

Big brothers in the region, Australia and New Zealand, are helpful in formulating and carrying out regional programs by providing the small island countries with their financing, knowledge, and expertise through the two regional organizations.

The two regional organizations, SPC and SPEC, can discharge such functions in order to conserve nature and living resources as scientific research, exchange of information and expertise, education, training, financing, and so forth.

Experiences of the Pacific region will not be automatically applied to other regions of the world, but will form a model of environmentally sound development which can be applied with appropriate adaptations.

To quote again from Mr. Maurice F. Strong's address to the Thirteenth Pacific Science Congress: "What happens to the environment of the Pacific Region will provide the key to man's future in the Pacific, and what we do, or fail to do, in the Pacific will be the key to the success of our efforts to preserve and enhance the environment for human life on the whole of our 'Only One Earth.' "

Notes

Originally the two authors of this paper made separate presentations at the 1978 Sapporo Conference, entitled respectively "Regional Co-operation for the Protection of the Marine Environment in the East Asian Waters" (by Tsutomu Fuse) and "Regional Co-operation for the Protection of Environment in the South Pacific" (by Tōru Iwama). At the time of compilation of conference papers, the two authors agreed to combine their papers with modifications and additions.

1. Recommendations 86 through 94, *Report of the United Nations Conference on the Human Environment*, A/CONF. 48/14/Rev. 1, pp. 22–24.

2. Ibid., p. 73.
3. United Nations Environment Programme, Report of the Governing Council, Second Session, Decision 8(II)A, Sec. I, par. 4(b). In United Nations General Assembly, *Official Records, Twenty-ninth Session*, Suppl. 25 (A/9625), 1974, pp. 59–60. This is the same approach being taken by the Third United Nations Conference on the Law of the Sea.
4. United Nations Environment Programme, Report of the Governing Council, Third Session, Decision 29(III), par. 1. In United Nations General Assembly, *Official Records, Thirtieth Session*, Suppl. 25 (A/10025), 1975, p. 95. See also "Guidelines and Principles concerning a Comprehensive Action Plan for the Protection of Regional Seas through Environmentally Sound Development" (UNEP/LAMRS. I/6, Annex II, June 1976), p. 3.
5. United Nations Environment Programme, Report of the Governing Council, Fourth Session, Decision 50 (IV), par. 3. In United Nations General Assembly, *Official Records, Thirty-first Session*, Suppl. 25 (A/31/25), 1976, p. 115.
6. Report of the Executive Director, UNEP/GC/90, 15 March 1977, pp. 103–4.
7. Regarding the Mediterranean, the 1976 Conference of Plenipotentiaries of the Coastal States of the Mediterranean Region for the Protection of the Mediterranean Sea succeeded in adopting the action plan and the following three documents: Convention for the Protection of the Mediterranean Sea against Pollution, Protocol for the Prevention of Pollution of the Mediterranean Sea by Dumping from Ships and Aircraft, and Protocol concerning Co-operation in Combating Pollution of the Mediterranean Sea by Oil and Other Harmful Substances in Cases of Emergency. Activity D has been completed in this region.

   Regarding the Persian Gulf, the Kuwait Regional Conference on the Protection and Development of the Marine Environment and the Coastal Areas adopted in 1978 the action plan and the Convention for Co-operation on the Protection of the Marine Environment from Pollution. One can say that Activity C is now being undertaken and Activity D will be completed soon in this region.
8. With regard to sub-regional projects, six sub-regional working groups were set up for the following regional seas: Bay of Bengal; Straits of Malacca; Gulf of Thailand; South China Sea; Sea of Japan, Yellow Sea, and East China Sea; and Seas of the Eastern Archipelago. See Intergovernmental Oceanographic Commission Workshop Report No. 8, Report of the IOC/FAO(IPFC)/UNEP International Workshop on Marine Pollution in East Asian Waters, Penang, April 1976, pp. 19–43.
9. United Nations Environment Programme, Report of the Governing Council, Fifth Session, Decision 88(V)D. In United Nations General Assembly, *Official Records, Thirty-second Session,* Suppl. 25 (A32/25), 1977, p. 124.
10. Report of the Executive Director, UNEP/GC.7/7Add. 1, 12 April 1979, pp. 6–7.
11. Japan Institute of International Environmental Law, *Protection of the Marine Environment in the East Asian Waters,* Yokohama, 1977. See the Draft Convention submitted to the UNEP by JIIEL in 1976 (pp. 82–126), and the Guideline Paper for the Drafting of a Framework Convention (pp. 58–81).
12. There were two papers presented at the 1978 Sapporo Conference in this concern: "Nordic Environmental Protection Convention" by Hiroji Isozaki, Research Fellow at Tokyo Metropolitan University, and "Role of International Organizations in the Protection of the Environment and Experiences in Europe" by Hiroshi Hashimoto, Lecturer at Nishi-Kyushu University.
13. JIIEL, *Marine Environment*, pp. 124–26.
14. Ibid., pp. 16, 56–57.
15. The geographic scope of the Southwest Pacific has been expanded to include countries and territories within the region of the South Pacific Commission and the South Pacific Forum.
16. See details in A. B. Costin and R. H. Groves, eds., *Nature Conservation in the Pacific* (Canberra: Australian National University, 1973).

17. UNEP/GC/80, 15 January 1976, pp. 1–2. UNEP has already initiated studies on pilot projects in ecodevelopment in several Latin American and African countries. Ibid., pp.7–8.
18. See the description of the basic agreements to establish SPC and SPEC, member states, and powers and functions of these two organizations in the following documents: the Agreement Establishing the South Pacific Commission (1947), Agreement Extending the Territorial Scope of the South Pacific Commission (1951), Agreement Relating to the Frequency of Sessions of the South Pacific Commission (1954), Agreement Amending the Agreement Establishing the South Pacific Commission (1964), Annex to the Agreement Establishing the South Pacific Commission (1972), and the Agreement Establishing the South Pacific Bureau for Economic Co-operation (1973).

    With regard to the geographical scope of SPC, the region includes Guam and the Trust Territory of the Pacific Islands, and all the Pacific islands south of the Equator from Papua New Guinea eastward. Australia, France, New Zealand, the United Kingdom, and the United States compose Metropolitan Governments, and territories within the Commission's region are American Samoa, Cook Islands, Fiji, French Polynesia, Gilbert Islands, Guam, Nauru, New Caledonia, New Hebrides, Niue, Norfolk Island, Papua New Guinea, Pitcairn Island, Solomon Islands, Tokelau, Tuvalu, Kingdom of Tonga, Trust Territory of the Pacific Islands, Wallis and Futuna, and Western Samoa.

    With regard to SPEC, on the other hand, it is composed of governments of Australia, Cook Islands, Fiji, Gilbert Islands, Nauru, New Zealand, Niue, Papua New Guinea, Solomon Islands, Kingdom of Tonga, Tuvalu, and Western Samoa.
19. South Pacific Commission, *Annual Report 1974/75*, p. 48.
20. South Pacific Commission, Plenipotentiary Meeting to Conclude a Convention on Conservation in the South Pacific (Apia, Western Samoa, 9–12 June 1976), Noumea, New Caledonia, 1976, pp. 28–30.
21. International Union for Conservation of Nature and Natural Resources, *Proceedings of an International Conference on Marine Parks and Reserves Held at Tokyo, Japan, 1975*, IUCN Publications New Series No. 37 (1976), pp. 126–27.
22. South Pacific Commission and South Pacific Bureau for Economic Co-operation. *Comprehensive Environmental Management Programme,* Noumea, New Caledonia, May 1977, pp. 57–58.
23. After the 1978 Sapporo Conference, co-author Iwama received a letter from Dr. Arthur L. Dahl saying that the CEMP document of May 1977 was considered by the Eighth South Pacific Forum and the Seventeenth South Pacific Conference later in 1977, and that a second technical meeting of governments held in June 1978 was requested to clarify some outstanding issues of administration and financing. Dr. Dahl also said that the Ninth South Pacific Forum and the Eighteenth South Pacific Conference approved the report of the second technical meeting which changed the name of the program from CEMP to the South Pacific Regional Environmental Programme (SPREP) and recommended the immediate start of the first phase of the program, with SPC as executing agency under a coordinating group consisting of SPEC (chairman), SPC (secretary), UNEP, and the Economic and Social Commission for Asia and the Pacific (ESCAP). The principal activity during the first phase of SPREP is said to be the preparation of country reports, national programs, and a regional action plan, leading to a Conference on the Human Environment in the South Pacific sometime in 1980, which will be jointly sponsored by UNEP, ESCAP, SPC, and SPEC. Cf. SPC and SPEC, Agreed Report of the Second Technical Meeting on the South Pacific Regional Environmental Programme, July 1978.
24. SPC and SPEC, Comprehensive Environmental Management Programme, p. 7.
25. Ibid., pp. 3–4.
26. Ibid., pp. 8–20.

27. Cf. R. E. Kearney, "The Law of the Sea and Regional Fisheries Policy: The Impact of Extended Jurisdiction on Fisheries Management in the Central and Western Tropical Pacific Ocean and the Need for a Regional Fisheries Agency," South Pacific Commission Occasional Paper No. 2, 1977, pp. 2–3, 9–14.
28. South Pacific Regional Fisheries Organization, SPFC(78) FA-CONV., 1978.
29. Summary Record and Report of the Meeting of Forum Government Officials on Regional Fisheries Policies, Honiara, Solomon Islands, 7–8 May 1978, FFA(79) H. 1, p. 1.
30. See the text of the Convention in Annex, SPEC(79) SCH. 17.
31. Summary Record and Report, p. 2.
32. Article 64 provides: "The coastal State and other States whose nationals fish in the region for the highly migratory species listed in Annex I shall co-operate directly or through appropriate international organizations with a view to ensuring conservation and promoting the objective of optimum utilization of such species throughout the region, both within and beyond the exclusive economic zone. In regions where no appropriate international organization exists, the coastal State and other States whose nationals harvest these species in the region shall co-operate to establish such an organization and participate in its work" (par. 1). U.N. Doc. A/CONF. 62/WP. 10, 15 July 1977. It must be noted, however, that this article says nothing about sovereign rights of the coastal states to explore, exploit, conserve, and manage the highly migratory species within the 200-mile zone.

Appendix 1
Basic Law for Environmental Pollution Control (Japan)

(Law No. 132, Aug. 3, 1967) (Amend. 1970, 1971, 1973, 1974)

Chapter I General Provisions

(Purpose)
Article 1

In view of the vital importance of environmental pollution control for the preservation of a healthy and civilized life for the nation, this Law is enacted for the purpose of identifying the responsibilities of the enterprise, the State and the local government bodies with regard to environmental pollution control and of determining the fundamental requirements for control measures, in order to promote comprehensive policies to combat environmental pollution thereby ensuring the protection of the people's health and the conservation of their living environment.

(Definition)
Article 2

1. The term "environmental pollution" ("kōgai" in Japanese), as used in this Law, shall mean any situation in which human health and the living environment are damaged by air pollution, water pollution (including the deterioration of the quality and other conditions of water as well as of the beds of rivers, lakes, the sea and other bodies of water. The same shall apply hereinafter, except in the case of paragraph 1, Article 9.), soil pollution, noise, vibration, ground subsidence (except for subsidence caused by drilling activities for mining. This exception shall apply hereinafter.), and offensive odors, which arise over a considerable area as a result of industrial or other human activities.

2. The term "living environment," as used in this Law, shall include property closely related to human life, and animals and plants closely related to human life and the environment in which such animals and plants live.

(Responsibility of the enterprise)

Article 3

1. The enterprise shall be responsible for taking the measures necessary for the prevention of environmental pollution, such as the treatment or disposal of smoke and soot, polluted water, wastes, etc., resulting from its industrial activities, and for cooperating with the State and local government bodies in their efforts to prevent environmental pollution.
2. The enterprise, in manufacturing and processing activities, shall endeavor to take precautionary measures to prevent environmental pollution which might otherwise be caused by the use of the products which it manufactures or processes.

(Responsibility of the State)

Article 4

The State has the responsibility to establish fundamental and comprehensive policies for environmental pollution control and to implement them, in view of the fact that it has the duty to protect the people's health and conserve the living environment.

(Responsibility of local government bodies)

Article 5

In order to protect the health of the local population and to conserve the living environment, local government bodies shall take measures in line with the policy of the State and shall also work out and implement appropriate measures for environmental pollution control which take into account the specific natural and social conditions of the area concerned.

(Responsibility of citizens)

Article 6

Citizens shall endeavor to contribute to the prevention of environmental pollution in all appropriate ways such as cooperating with the State and with local government bodies in the implementation of control measures.

(Annual report, etc.)

Article 7

1. The Government shall present to the Diet an annual report on the situation with regard to environmental pollution and on those measures taken by the Government in order to control it.
2. The Government shall present to the Diet annually a document, outlining the measures which the Government is going to take to deal with the environmental pollution situation described in the report referred to in the preceding paragraph.

(Control of air pollution, etc., caused by radioactive substances)

Article 8

With regard to measures for the control of the pollution of air, water and soil by radioactive substances, the Atomic Energy Basic Law (Law No. 186, 1955) and other related laws shall apply.

Chapter II Fundamental Policies for Environmental Pollution Control

Section I Environmental Quality Standards

Article 9

1. With regard to environmental conditions relating to air, water and soil pollution and noise, the Government shall establish environmental quality standards, the maintenance of which is desirable for the protection of human health and the conservation of the living environment.
2. In the event that one of the standards referred to in the preceding paragraph establishes more than one category and stipulates that land areas or areas of water to which those categories are to be applied should be designated, the Government may delegate to the prefectural governors concerned the authority to designate those land areas or areas of water.
3. With regard to the standards provided for in paragraph 1, due scientific consideration shall always be given and such standards shall be revised whenever necessary.
4. The Government shall make efforts to ensure the maintenance of the above-mentioned standards, by implementing environmental pollution control measures in a comprehensive, effective and appropriate manner.

Section II Measures to Be Taken by the State

(Emission control, etc.)
Article 10

1. In order to control environmental pollution, the Government shall take measures for the control of the emission of pollutants responsible for air, water and soil pollution, establishing standards to be observed by the enterprise.
2. In order to control environmental pollution, the Government shall endeavor to take measures to deal with noise, vibration, ground subsidence and offensive odors, in a manner similar to that referred to in the preceding paragraph.

(Control of land use and installation of facilities)
Article 11

In order to control environmental pollution, the Government shall take necessary measures with regard to land use and shall, in areas where environmental pollution is serious or likely to become serious, also take measures to control the installation of facilities which cause environmental pollution.

(Promotion of establishment of facilities for the prevention of environmental pollution)

Article 12

The Government shall take measures to promote necessary projects for the prevention of environmental pollution, such as the establishment of buffer zones, etc., as well as those projects to establish public facilities which will contribute to the prevention of environmental pollution, such as sewerage and public waste disposal plants.

(Establishment of surveillance and monitoring systems)

Article 13

The Government shall endeavor to establish systems for surveillance, monitoring, measurement, examination and inspection in order to ascertain what the situation with regard to environmental pollution is and to ensure adequate enforcement of measures to combat environmental pollution.

(Carrying out of surveys and investigations)

Article 14

The Government shall carry out surveys and investigations necessary for the planning of measures for environmental pollution control, such as those for predicting environmental pollution trends.

(Promotion of science and technology)

Article 15

In order to promote the development of science and technology which will contribute to the prevention of environmental pollution, the Government shall take the necessary measures such as the consolidation of survey and research systems, the promotion of research and development, the dissemination of the results of such research and development work, and the education and training of research experts.

(Dissemination of knowledge and information)

Article 16

The Government shall endeavor to disseminate knowledge and information concerning environmental pollution and also to make the nation more conscious of the need to prevent environmental pollution.

(Consideration of environmental pollution control in the planning of regional development policies, etc.)

Article 17–1

The Government shall take into consideration the need to control environmental pollution in the planning and implementation of regional development measures such as those for urban development and the construction of factories.

(Protection of the natural environment)
Article 17–2
In order to contribute to the prevention of environmental pollution, the Government shall, in conjunction with other measures prescribed in this Section, endeavor to protect the natural environment as well as to conserve green areas.

Section III Measures to Be Taken by Local Government Bodies

Article 18
The local government bodies shall, provided that the measures do not infringe laws and regulations, take measures in line with the policy of the State provided for in the preceding Section and shall also implement measures for environmental pollution control which take into account the specific natural and social conditions of the area concerned. In this case, the prefectural governments shall be responsible mainly for the implementation of measures covering wide areas and also for the coordination of measures to be taken by the municipal governments.

Section IV Environmental Pollution Control in Specified Areas

(Formulation of Environmental Pollution Control Programs)
Article 19
1. The Prime Minister shall instruct the prefectural governors concerned to formulate programs relating to the environmental pollution control measures (hereinafter called "Environmental Pollution Control Programs") to be implemented in specific areas which fall into any one of the following categories, by showing to those governors fundamental policies for such programs:

(1) areas in which environmental pollution is serious and in which it is recognized that it will be extremely difficult to achieve effective environmental pollution control unless comprehensive control measures are taken;

(2) areas in which environmental pollution is likely to become serious on account of rapidly increasing concentrations of population, industry, etc., and in which it is recognized that it will be extremely

difficult to achieve effective environmental pollution control unless comprehensive control measures are taken.

2. When the prefectural governor concerned has received the instruction referred to in the preceding paragraph, he shall draw up an Environmental Pollution Control Program in accordance with the fundamental policies referred to in the preceding paragraph and shall submit it to the Prime Minister for his approval.

3. Prior to issuing an instruction under paragraph 1 or giving the approval required under the preceding paragraph, the Prime Minister shall consult with the Conference on Environmental Pollution Control.

4. Prior to issuing an instruction under paragraph 1, the Prime Minister shall seek the opinion of the prefectural governor concerned.

(Implementation of Environmental Pollution Control Programs)
Article 20

The State and local government bodies shall endeavor to take measures necessary for the full implementation of Environmental Pollution Control Programs.

Section V Settlement of Disputes Relating to Environmental Pollution and Relief for Damage Caused Thereby

Article 21

1. The Government shall take the measures necessary to establish a system for the settlement, by such means as mediation and arbitration, of disputes which arise in connection with environmental pollution.

2. The Government shall take the measures necessary to establish a system which will make possible the efficient implementation of relief measures for damage caused by environmental pollution.

Chapter III Bearing of Costs and Financial Measures

Article 22

1. The enterprise shall bear all or part of the necessary cost of the works carried out by the State or local government bodies to control environmental pollution arising from the industrial activities of such enterprise.

2. The nature and amount of the costs which the enterprise shall bear under the preceding paragraph, the enterprises which shall bear such costs, the method of calculation of the amount to be borne by such

enterprises, and other necessary matters relating to the bearing of costs shall be laid down in other laws.

(Financial measures for local government bodies)
Article 23
The State shall endeavor to take necessary financial and other measures relating to the necessary cost of environmental pollution control measures implemented by local government bodies.

(Assistance to the enterprise)
Article 24
1. The State and local government bodies shall endeavor to take the necessary measures, such as monetary and taxation measures, to encourage the installation and improvement, by the enterprise, of facilities for the prevention of environmental pollution.
2. In taking the measures referred to in the preceding paragraph, special consideration shall be given to the small and medium enterprise.

Chapter IV The Conference on Environmental Pollution Control and the Councils on Environmental Pollution Control

Section I The Conference on Environmental Pollution Control

(Establishment and functions)
Article 25
1. There is hereby established a Conference on Environmental Pollution Control (hereinafter called "the Conference") as an Agency attached to the Prime Minister's Office.
2. The Conference shall perform the following functions. It shall:
   (1) deal with matters provided for in paragraph 3, Article 19, with respect to the Environmental Pollution Control Programs;
   (2) in addition to performing the function referred to in the preceding sub-paragraph, deliberate on basic and comprehensive measures for environmental pollution control, and promote the implementation of such measures;
   (3) in addition to performing the functions referred to in the preceding two sub-paragraphs, deal with matters which come within the jurisdiction of the Conference under laws and regulations.

(Organization, etc.)
Article 26

1. The Conference shall be composed of a Chairman and Members.
2. The Prime Minister shall hold the office of Chairman.
3. Members shall be appointed by the Prime Minister from among the heads of related Ministries and Agencies.
4. There shall be Secretaries of the Conference.
5. The Secretaries shall be appointed by the Prime Minister from among the officials of related Ministries and Agencies.
6. The Secretaries shall assist the Chairman and Members in dealing with the matters which come within the jurisdiction of the Conference.
7. The secretarial affairs of the Conference shall be handled by the Prime Minister's Secretariat.
8. Matters necessary for the organization and operation of the Conference, other than those provided for in the preceding paragraphs, shall be provided by Cabinet Orders.

Section II Councils on Environmental Pollution Control

(Organization and Functions of the Central Council on Environmental Pollution Control)

Article 27

1. There is hereby established a Central Council on Environmental Pollution Control (hereinafter called "the Central Council") as an Agency attached to the Prime Minister's Office.
2. The Central Council shall perform the following functions. It shall:
   (1) study and deliberate on basic matters related to environmental pollution control, when requested to do so by the Prime Minister;
   (2) in addition to performing the function referred to in the preceding sub-paragraph, deal with matters which come within the jurisdiction of the Central Council under laws and regulations.
3. The Central Council may express its opinion to the Prime Minister with regard to matters provided for in the preceding paragraph.

Article 28

1. The Central Council shall be composed of not more than 90 Members.
2. The Members shall be appointed by the Prime Minister from among those experts who have both knowledge and experience in environmental pollution control.
3. The Members shall serve on a part-time basis.
4. The secretarial affairs of the Central Council shall be handled by the Prime Minister's Secretariat.
5. Matters necessary for the organization and operation of the Central

Council, other than those provided for in the preceding paragraphs, shall be provided for by Cabinet Orders.

(Prefectural Councils on Environmental Pollution Control)

Articlc 29

1. The prefectural governments shall establish Prefectural Councils on Environmental Pollution Control which shall perform such functions as the study of and deliberation on basic matters relating to control measures for environmental pollution within the prefectures concerned.
2. Matters necessary for the organization and operation of the Prefectural Councils on Environmental Pollution Control shall be provided for by prefectural ordinances.

(Municipal Councils on Environmental Pollution Control)

Article 30

Municipal governments may, under the provisions of relevant municipal ordinances, establish Municipal Councils on Environmental Pollution Control which shall perform such functions as the study of and deliberation on basic matters relating to control measures for environmental pollution within the municipalities concerned.

Appendix 2
The National Environmental Policy Act of 1969 (U.S.A.)

(Pub. L., 91–190; 42 U.S.C. 4321–4347, Jan. 1, 1970)
(Amend. 1975)

An Act to establish a national policy for the environment, to provide for the establishment of a Council on Environmental Quality, and for other purposes.

Be it enacted by the Senate and House of Representatives of the United States of America in Congress assembled, That this Act may be cited as the "National Environmental Policy Act of 1969."

Purpose

Sec. 2. The purposes of this Act are: To declare a national policy which will encourage productive and enjoyable harmony between man and his environment; to promote efforts which will prevent or eliminate damage to the environment and biosphere and stimulate the health and welfare of man; to enrich the understanding of the ecological systems and natural resources important to the Nation; and to establish a Council on Environmental Quality.

Title I. Declaration of National Environmental Policy

Sec. 101. (a) The Congress, recognizing the profound impact of man's activity on the interrelations of all components of the natural environment, particularly the profound influences of population growth, high-density urbanization, industrial expansion, resource exploitation, and new and expanding technological advances and recognizing further the critical importance of restoring and maintaining environmental quality to the overall welfare and development of man, declares that it is the continuing policy of the Federal Government, in cooperation with State and local governments, and other concerned public and private organizations, to use all practicable means and measures, including financial and technical assistance, in a manner calculated to foster and promote the general welfare, to create and maintain conditions under which man and nature can exist in productive harmony, and fulfill the social, economic, and other requirements of present and future generations of Americans.

(b) In order to carry out the policy set forth in this Act, it is the continuing responsibility of the Federal Government to use all practicable means, consistent with other essential considerations of national policy, to improve and coordinate Federal plans, functions, programs, and resources to the end that the Nation may—

(1) fulfill the responsibilities of each generation as trustee of the environment for succeeding generations;

(2) assure for all Americans safe, healthful, productive, and esthetically and culturally pleasing surroundings;

(3) attain the widest range of beneficial uses of the environment without degradation, risk to health or safety, or other undesirable and unintended consequences;

(4) preserve important historic, cultural, and natural aspects of our national heritage, and maintain, wherever possible, an environment which supports diversity and variety of individual choice;

(5) achieve a balance between population and resource use which will permit high standards of living and a wide sharing of life's amenities; and

(6) enhance the quality of renewable resources and approach the maximum attainable recycling of depletable resources.

(c) The Congress recognizes that each person should enjoy a healthful environment and that each person has a responsibility to contribute to the preservation and enhancement of the environment.

Sec. 102. The Congress authorizes and directs that, to the fullest extent possible: (1) the policies, regulations, and public laws of the United States shall be interpreted and administered in accordance with the policies set forth in this Act, and (2) all agencies of the Federal Government shall—

(a) Utilize a systematic, interdisciplinary approach which will insure the integrated use of the natural and social sciences and the environmental design arts in planning and in decisionmaking which may have an impact on man's environment;

(b) Identify and develop methods and procedures, in consultation with the Council on Environmental Quality established by title II of this Act, which will insure that presently unquantified environmental amenties and values may be given appropriate consideration in decisionmaking along with economic and technical considerations;

(c) Include in every recommendation or report on proposals for legislation and other major Federal actions significantly affecting the quality of the human environment, a detailed statement by the responsible official on—

(i) The environmental impact of the proposed action,

(ii) Any adverse environmental effects which cannot be avoided should the proposal be implemented,

(iii) Alternatives to the proposed action,

(iv) The relationship between local short-term uses of man's environment and the maintenance and enhancement of long-term productivity, and

(v) Any irreversible and irretrievable commitments of resources which would be involved in the proposed action should it be implemented.

Prior to making any detailed statement, the responsible Federal official shall consult with and obtain the comments of any Federal agency which has jurisdiction by law or special expertise with respect to any environmental impact involved. Copies of such statement and the comments and views of the appropriate Federal, State, and local agencies, which are authorized to develop and enforce environmental standards, shall be made available to the President, the Council on Environmental Quality and to the public as provided by section 552 of title 5, United States Code, and shall accompany the proposal through the existing agency review processes;

(d) Any detailed statement required under subparagraph (c) after January 1, 1970, for any major Federal action funded under a program of grants to States shall not be deemed to be legally insufficient solely by reason of having been prepared by a State agency or official, if:

(i) The State agency or official has statewide jurisdiction and has the responsibility for such action,

(ii) The responsible Federal official furnishes guidance and participates in such preparation,

(iii) The responsible Federal official independently evaluates such statement prior to its approval and adoption, and

(iv) After January 1, 1976, the responsible Federal official provides early notification to, and solicits the views of, any other State or any Federal land management entity of any action or any alternative thereto which may have significant impacts upon such State or affected Federal land management entity and, if there is any disagreement on such impacts, prepares a written assessment of such impacts and views for incorporation into such detailed statement.

The procedures in this subparagraph shall not relieve the Federal official of his responsibilities for the scope, objectivity, and content of the entire statement or of any other responsibility under this Act; and further, this subparagraph does not affect the legal sufficiency of statements prepared by State agencies with less than statewide jurisdiction.

(e) Study, develop, and describe appropriate alternatives to recommended courses of action in any proposal which involves unresolved conflicts concerning alternative uses of available resources;

(f) Recognize the worldwide and long-range character of environmental problems and, where consistent with the foreign policy of the United States, lend appropriate support to initiatives, resolutions, and programs designed to maximize international cooperation in anticipating and preventing a decline in the quality of mankind's world environment;

(g) Make available to States, counties, municipalities, institutions, and individuals, advice and information useful in restoring, maintaining, and enhancing the quality of the environment;

(h) Initiate and utilize ecological information in the planning and development of resource-oriented projects; and

(i) Assist the Council on Environmental Quality established by title II of this Act.

Sec. 103. All agencies of the Federal Government shall review their present statutory authority, administrative regulations, and current policies and procedures for the purpose of determining whether there are any deficiencies or inconsistencies therein which prohibit full compliance with the purposes and provisions of this Act and shall propose to the President not later than July 1, 1971, such measures as may be necessary to bring their authority and policies into conformity with the intent, purposes, and procedures set forth in this Act.

Sec. 104. Nothing in Section 102 or 103 shall in any way affect the specific statutory obligations of any Federal agency (1) to comply with criteria or standards of environmental quality, (2) to coordinate or consult with any other Federal or State agency, or (3) to act, or refrain from acting contingent upon thè recommendations or certification of any other Federal or State agency.

Sec. 105. The policies and goals set forth in this Act are supplementary to those set forth in existing authorizations of Federal agencies.

Title II. Council on Environmental Quality

Sec. 201. The President shall transmit to the Congress annually beginning July 1, 1970, an Environmental Quality Report (hereinafter referred to as the "report") which shall set forth (1) the status and condition of the major natural, manmade, or altered environmental classes of the Nation, including, but not limited to, the air, the aquatic, including marine, estuarine, and fresh water, and the terrestrial environment, including, but not limited to the forest dryland, wetland, range, urban, suburban, and rural environment; (2) current and forseeable trends in the quality, management and utilization of such environments and the effects of those trends on the social, economic, and other requirements of the Nation; (3) the adequacy of available natural resources for fulfilling human and economic requirements of the Nation in the light of expected population pressures; (4) a review of the programs and activities (including regulatory activities) of the Federal Government, the State and local governments, and nongovernmental entities or individuals, with particular reference to their effect on the environment and on the conservation, development and utilization of natural resources; and (5) a program for remedying the deficiencies of existing programs and activities, together with recommendations for legislation.

Sec. 202. There is created in the Executive Office of the President a Council on Environmental Quality (hereinafter referred to as the "Council"). The Council shall be composed of three members who shall be appointed by the President to serve at his pleasure, by and with the advice and consent of the Senate. The President shall designate one of the members of the Council to serve as Chairman. Each member shall be a person who, as a result of his training, experience, and attainments, is exceptionally well qualified to analyze and interpret environmental trends and information of all kinds; to appraise programs and activities of the Federal Government in the light of the policy set forth in title I of this Act; to be conscious of and responsive to the scientific, economic, social, esthetic, and cultural needs and interests of the Nation; and to formulate and recommend national policies to promote the improvement of the quality of the environment.

Sec. 203. The Council may employ such officers and employees as may be necessary to carry out its functions under this Act. In addition, the Council may employ and fix the compensation of such experts and consultants as may be necessary for the carrying out of its functions under this Act, in accordance with section 3109 of title 5, United States Code (but without regard to the last sentence thereof).

Sec. 204. It shall be the duty and function of the Council—

(1) to assist and advise the President in the preparation of the Environmental Quality Report required by section 201 of this title;

(2) to gather timely and authoritative information concerning the conditions and trends in the quality of the environment both current and prospective, to analyze and interpret such information for the purpose of determining whether such conditions and trends are interfering, or are likely to interfere, with the achievement of the policy set forth in title I of this Act, and to compile and submit to the President studies relating to such conditions and trends;

(3) to review and appraise the various programs and activities of the Federal Government in the light of the policy set forth in title I of this Act for the purpose of determining the extent to which such programs and activities are contributing to the achievement of such policy, and to make recommendations to the President with respect thereto;

(4) to develop and recommend to the President national policies to foster and promote the improvement of environmental quality to meet the conservation, social, economic, health, and other requirements and goals of the Nation;

(5) to conduct investigations, studies, surveys, research, and analyses relating to ecological systems and environmental quality;

(6) to document and define changes in the natural environment, including the plant and animal systems, and to accumulate necessary data and other information for a continuing analysis of these changes or trends and an interpretation of their underlying causes;

(7) to report at least once each year to the President on the state and condition of the environment; and

(8) to make and furnish such studies, reports thereon, and recommendations with respect to matters of policy and legislation as the President may request.

Sec. 205. In exercising its powers, functions, and duties under this Act, the Council shall—

(1) Consult with the Citizens' Advisory Committee on Environmental Quality established by Executive Order No. 11472, dated May 29, 1969, and with such representatives of science, industry, agriculture, labor, conservation organizations, State and local governments and other groups, as it deems advisable; and

(2) Utilize, to the fullest extent possible, the services, facilities, and information (including statistical information) of public and private agencies and organizations, and individuals, in order that duplication of effort and expense may be avoided, thus assuring that the Coun-

cil's activities will not unnecessarily overlap or conflict with similar activities authorized by law and performed by established agencies.

Sec. 206. Members of the Council shall serve full time and the Chairman of the Council shall be compensated at the rate provided for Level II of the Executive Schedule Pay Rates (5 U.S.C. 5313). The other members of the Council shall be compensated at the rate provided for Level IV of the Executive Schedule Pay Rates (5 U.S.C. 5315).

Sec. 207. The Council may accept reimbursements from any private nonprofit organization or from any department, agency, or instrumentality of the Federal Government, any State, or local government, for the reasonable travel expenses incurred by an officer or employee of the Council in connection with his attendance at any conference, seminar, or similar meeting conducted for the benefit of the Council.

Sec. 208. The Council may make expenditures in support of its international activities, including expenditures for: (1) international travel; (2) activities in implementation of international agreements; and (3) the support of international exchange programs in the United States and in foreign countries.

Sec. 209. There are authorized to be appropriated to carry out the provisions of this chapter not to exceed $300,000 for fiscal year 1970, $700,000 for fiscal year 1971, and $1,000,000 for each fiscal year thereafter.

Information on Contributors

Yasutaka Abe has been professor of administrative law, Kobe University since 1977. He was born in 1942 and received his LL.B. (1964) and LL.D. (1972) from the University of Tokyo. He was visiting scholar at Hamburg and Tübingen universities (1972–75). Dr. Abe is the author of *Furansu gyōsei soshōron* [French Administrative Litigation] (Yūhikaku, 1971) and *Eine Skizze über die Entwicklung des Umweltschutz rechts in Japan* (Law in Japan, vol. 2, 1977). He is member of the Expert Committee of the Central Council for Environmental Pollution Control.

Fred P. Bosselman has been partner of Ross, Hardies, O'Keefe, Babcock and Parsons in Chicago since 1965. He was born in 1934 and received his B.A. (University of Colorado, 1956) and J.D. (Harvard University, 1959). He has served as reporter for the American Law Institute's Model Land Development Code. He is director of the American Planning Association and the Metropolitan Housing and Planning Council of Chicago. Mr. Bosselman is the author of *The Taking Issue* (United States Government Printing Office, 1974), *The Quiet Revolution in Land Use Control* (United States Government Printing Office, 1972), *In the Wake of the Tourist* (The Conservation Foundation, 1978).

Richard A. Carpenter is research associate at the Environment and Policy Institute, East-West Center, Hawaii. He was born in 1926 and received his B.S. (1948) and M.S. (1949) from the University of Missouri. Mr. Carpenter has written "Using Ecological Knowledge for Development Planning," 4 *Environmental Management* 13 (1980). He was visiting professor at Dartmouth College in 1976, and Executive Director of the Commission on Natural Resources, National Research Council/National Academy of Sciences, Washington, D.C.

Peter S. J. Chen is professor at the Department of Sociology, University of Singapore. Dr. Chen was born in 1938, received his M.A. (1966) and Ph.D. (1970) from Washington University. He is the author of *Development Complexity: East and Southeast Asia* (University Education Press, 1971), *Studies in ASEAN Sociology: Urban Society and Social Change* (Chopmen, 1978), *Public Policy and Population Change in Singapore* (The Population Council, 1979), and *Culture and Industrialization* (McGraw-Hill, 1980).

Perfecto V. Fernandez is professor of law at the University of the Philippines. He was born in 1931 and received his A.B. (1954) and LL. B. (1957) from that University. Professor Fernandez is the author of *Philippine Constitutional Law* (1977) and *Philippine Political Law* I. II. (1975).

Tsutomu Fuse is lecturer at Meisei University. Mr. Fuse was born in 1941 and received his LL.B. (1965) and LL.M. (1970) from Chūō University. He is the co-author of *Shinkaikaitei shigen to kokusaihō* [Deep Sea-Bed Resources and International Law] (Meisei University Press, 1979).

Tōru Iwama is research fellow at Hitotsubashi University. He was born in 1945 and received his B.A. (International Christian University, 1969), M.A. (University of Hawaii, 1974), and LL.M. (Hitotsubashi University, 1976). Mr. Iwama is the co-author of *Shinkaikaitei shigen to kokusaihō* [Deep Sea-Bed Resources and International Law] (Meisei University Press, 1979).

Mattaya Jarupan is assistant professor of law, Chulalongkorn University, Thailand. Professor Jarupan was born in 1948 and received her LL.B. (Thammasat University, 1972) and LL.A. (Chulalongkorn University, 1957). She is the author of *"Kodmai kuabkoom sapawa waedlom sumrub rong-ngarn utsahagam"* [Environmental Control Law for Industrial Factories] (1979).

Ichirō Katō is professor of civil law at the University of Tokyo. He was born in 1921, graduated from the University of Tokyo (1943) and received his LL.D. from that University. He was visiting scholar at Harvard (1962–63) and Berkeley (1967–68). He was president of the University of Tokyo (1969–73) and vice-rector of United Nations University (1975–76). Dr. Katō is the author of *Fuhō kōi no kenkyū* [Study of Tort Law] (Yūhikaku, 1961), and the editor of *Kōgai hō no seisei to tenkai*

[Formation and Development of Environmental Law] (Yūhikaku, 1968) and *Gaikoku no kōgai hō* [Environmental Law in Foreign Countries] (Yūhikaku, 1978).

Shōzō Kondō has been professor of administrative law, Kyūshū University, since 1970. He was born in 1928 and received his Bachelor of Laws from Kyushu University in 1954. He was a *boursier* of the French government at the Law Faculty of Paris University (1958–60). Professor Kondō is the co-author of *Gendai gyōseihō* [Modern Administrative Law] (Yūhikaku, 1968). He is member of Fukuoka Municipal Council for Environmental Pollution Control.

Nobuo Kumamoto has been professor of administrative law at Hokkaigakuen University since 1974. Dr. Kumamoto was born in 1935 and received his LL.B. (1961), LL.M.(1964), Hokkaido University, LL.M. (1974) University of California (Berkeley), and LL.D.(1973) Hokkaido University. He was Fulbright visiting scholar at the University of Michigan Law School (1968–70). He is the author of *Amerika ni okeru seikyō bunri no gensoku* [Separation of Church and State in the United States] (Hokkaido University Press, 1975). He has been member of the Labor Commission (Hokkaido Prefecture) since 1978.

Sunee Mallikamarl is assistant professor of law, Chulalongkorn University. She was born in 1946 and received her LL.B. from Thammasat University (1969) and her LL.M. from Chulalongkorn University (1976). She is the author of "Kodmai kuabkoom sapawa waedlom kiewkab rong-ngarn utsahagam" [Environmental Control Law for Industrial Factories] (Institute of Environmental Research, Chulalongkorn University, 1979) and "Kong toon tod tan sing waedlom" [Environmental Compensation, 1978] (Chulalongkorn Law Journal, 1978).

William H. Matthews is Director of the Environment and Policy Institute, East-West Center, Hawaii. Dr. Mattews was born in 1942 and received his S.M. Electrical Engineering (1968), Professional E.E. (1968), S.M. Political Science (1970), and Ph.D. Socio-Technology Engineering (1970) from Massachusetts Institute of Technology. He is the author of *Resource Materials for Environmental Management and Education* (MIT Press, 1975) and the co-editor of *Renewable Energy Prospects* (Pergamon Press, 1979).

Akio Morishima is professor of civil law at Nagoya University. He was born in 1934 and graduated from the University of Tokyo in 1958 and

Harvard University Graduate School of Law (LL.M. 1968). He was visiting professor at Harvard Law School (1976–77) and University of British Columbia (1980). He is co-author of *Environmental Law in Japan* (MIT Press, 1981). Professor Morishima is member of the Advisory Committee for Environmental Problems (Aichi Prefecture).

Yoshihiro Nomura has been professor of civil law, Tokyo Metropolitan University, since 1978. He was born in 1941 and graduated from the University of Tokyo in 1963. Professor Nomura is member of the editorial board of *Law School* and *Environmental Journal*. He is co-author of *Kōgai hanrei no kenkyū* [Studies on Environmental Cases] (Gyōsei, 1971), and author of *Kōgai to hō no chishiki* [Information on Environmental Problems and Law] (Gyōsei, 1971), and *Kōgai no hanrei* [Environmental Cases] (Yūhikaku, 1971).

Twesukdi Piyakarnchana has been professor and Head of the Department of Marine Science, Chulalongkorn University, since 1979. He was born in 1930 and received his B.S. (Chulalongkorn University, 1953), M.S. (University of California, 1960), and Ph.D. (University of Hawaii, 1965). He was Director of the Institute of Environmental Research, Chulalongkorn University (1975–79). He is the co-author of "Species Diversity Indices in Marine Benthic Communities as a Pollution Indicator in the Upper Gulf of Thailand," 5 *Jour. of Science Society of Thailand* 97 (1979).

Nik Abdul Rashid was appointed Director of Mara Institute of Technology, Selangor, Malaysia, in 1980. He was previously Deputy Dean and professor at the Law Faculty, University of Malaya. Mr. Rashid was born in 1936 and received his LL.B. (University of Singapore, 1967) and M.P.A. (University of Pittsburgh, 1969).

R. Tjang Mushadji Sutamihardja is lecturer in biochemistry and Water Quality Manager, Center for Studies of Natural Resources and Environment, Bogor Agricultural University. He was born in 1939, graduated from Bogor Agricultural University in 1963, received his Master of Agriculture from Gifu University, Japan, in 1968 and Doctorate of Pharmacy from Gifu College of Pharmacy, Japan, in 1972. Dr. Sutamihardja was Deputy Director for Research and Development, Bogor Agricultural University (1975–77).

Fukashi Utsunomiya is assistant professor of political science and economics at Tōkai University. He was born in 1936 and received his

B.A. (Waseda University, 1960), M.P.A. (International Christian University, 1968), and Ph.D. (University of Southern California, 1975). Dr. Utsunomiya is the author of *Politics of Development and Environment: Toward a New Civilization* (Tōkai University Press, 1980), *Kaihatsu to kankyō no seijigaku* [Politics of Development and Environment] (Tōkai University Press, 1976).

Index